Coco is fifty-three years old and lives in Scotland. She grew up in a working-class background and has always wanted much better in life than what she had. She chased that dream at a cost, so now she has decided it is time to tell her stories her way. She lives on her own, with her dogs, and her house décor is like the inside of a witch's cottage or a cabin in the mountains.

Her little dogs are her world, her real heroes, and each one owns a part of her heart. She is a proud mother of two children, a son and a daughter, whom she taught to chase their dreams and that is exactly what they do.

I dedicate this book to anyone who has ever loved someone who didn't belong to them.

Coco Houston

UNDER PURPLE SHEETS

AUSTIN MACAULEY PUBLISHERS™

LONDON · CAMBRIDGE · NEW YORK · SHARJAH

A CIP catalogue record for this title is available from the British Library.   .

ISBN 9781528902212 (Paperback)
ISBN 9781528902205 (Hardback)
ISBN 9781528956680 (ePub e-book)

www.austinmacauley.com

First Published (2019)
Austin Macauley Publishers Ltd
25 Canada Square
Canary Wharf
London
E14 5LQ

Table of Contents

Chapter I
Wisdom Begins with Wonder

Monday, 22nd October 2012

Lying in my lounge along a huge chocolate wool carpet, I started to yawn, stretching out my aching body like a cat. My legs were beginning to get stiff, causing them to cramp due to the fact I had been lying in the same position for far too long. The rug lay on top of Canadian redwood flooring, which had some sheepskins scattered around to offset the wood, giving it a rustic feel. This is my favourite room in the house; it's my own personal space, offering me a presence of being at home with nature, humbled by simpler times.

The walls are decorated in wood panelling stained in a deep red mahogany, with Indian knives hung throughout; the room is also full of taxidermied animals, creating the ambience of being in a hunting lodge. There is a log burner embedded into a huge stone fireplace, with a railway sleeper across the top to form a mantle, on which sits a stuffed fox with squirrel in its mouth. Above that owning pride of place is a huge stag's head. Covering leather sofas are all kinds of animal fur cushions with wolf fur throws. On a table nearby, made with old rough railway sleepers, stands a candle, its burning wick made of wood, which makes a crackling noise that resembles the effect of a bonfire and its pumpkin scent reminds me of the delicious smell of my grandmother baking cookies.

Rolling over onto my back, trying to distribute some more of the pain, I notice on staring up at the traditional old-style wooden beams that run along the ceiling, from one of them hangs a delicate, very intricate cobweb (which wasn't there yesterday). Forcing myself up to go for my feather duster to remove it, I felt something underfoot. On looking down, there lay my notebook and pen, which I'd been scribbling with for hours now. That wasn't my intention, it just happened that way instead of me doing housework which needed to be done, as the unknown spider had just established. Passing by the window, it was beginning to get dark out. Glancing over to where sat a magnificent stag ornament, there stood beside it a beautiful antique clock ticking the time, informing me that it was already four p.m. The afternoon had gone so quickly but I had been busy I suppose, so I hadn't realised just how much time had passed by.

It had got chilly, so on the fire which still smouldered, I flung some logs before lighting more candles. Wandering over to the corner of the room, I switched on the fairy lights that covered a tree sitting in a stone flowerpot; it was most unusual, built in cream bricks with large cream rocks either side of it matching the stonework on the hearth and smokestack, which altogether added more character, enhancing the primitive yet cosy atmosphere. On an old whiskey casket nearby sat a milk jug filled with wild thistles; their appearance made my place look like it belonged to or was something you would find hidden away in a log cabin amongst the Nevis mountain range.

On leaving my hillbilly hideaway, I pass through the dimly lit hallway; on heading upstairs I flick a switch to activate the heating system providing warmth to the rest of the house. On reaching my bedroom, I toss the book and pen, which lands on the bed. I feel a draft blowing in through from an open window somewhere, making the already cool air in here colder still. I go in search of it, whereupon I realise I'm still wearing my vest top, a little thong under soft cotton pyjama trousers with Ugg boots. *Shit! Coco, get your arse in gear!*

On entering the bedroom once more, it was beginning to feel a little warmer in here now. I put on more fairy lights, which sparkle like little diamonds in the dark (I prefer the subtle lights and also enjoy the kind of magical imprint they create). Taking a fleeting look in the mirror, my long wild, knotted hair is reflected back at me so halting in my tracks, I shake my head upside down whilst running my fingers through it, thinking I should go for a coffee now. Besides, I had to arrange dinner for my Chihuahuas – Versace, Rio de Janeiro and Solo Dancer, ignoring the fact that I haven't spring-cleaned my kitchen, so this straw-like mess had to wait until later to be shampooed, and then deep conditioned. I was already behind with my chores as on a whim I started to write the manuscript for a book while waiting for my married man to phone me back. On leaving my bedroom I stop again, this time at my dressing table, where I lift a bottle of Coco Chanel perfume, spraying a mist of its rich fragrance onto my skin; it evokes the feeling of pure luxury whilst arousing a sexual desire within.

Just at that moment I hear a noise, which sounded like a key turning the lock on the front door, followed by footsteps coming upstairs. There, in the doorway of the bedroom stands the married man I am having an affair with. Bradford Riley Blake. "Hello, darling," he smirks, looking at me, obviously wondering why I'm still in bed wear (which I don't wear in bed), taking in my boots, wild hair, whilst smelling the just sprayed Chanel scent, he seems kind of amused. Walking forward he kisses me, more desire awakened by his touch. He tastes as good as I smell. "What is this, Coco?" he asks, holding my notebook as he sits down on edge of the bed.

"I'm writing a book," I reply. He curiously looks at the closed diary as he lays it down with the pen beside my perfume.

"Am I in it?" he asks, questioning me.

"Oh yes, Blake. Oh yes, you definitely are!" I say, smiling. I get by the expression on his face he doesn't believe me for one minute. "I will write a bestseller," I smile, continuing to tease him; he looks more interested now but I can see him calculating what I just said, but he is still slightly bewildered as he is not sure how to take me.

"Okay, write a bestseller!" he instructs me in a firm tone, smiling. I smile back as he sprawls out along my bed, within a minute he is back up, stripping off his trousers with his pants before lying back down on top of my duvet in only his t-shirt. Only wearing my pale pink thong, I get on the bed, and then up on to him, crawling, slithering in a snake-like motion, moving slowly upwards over the length of his body as I draw my hard nipples over every inch of him. On reaching his mouth, I gently kiss him before flickering my tongue over his lips.

"What do you want, Blake? I thought you were just going to call me back?" I whisper huskily.

"No, I got the chance to get out, so I sneaked down to see you instead, darling," he replies, proud that he managed to achieve this. I lean over touching his hair, smirking wickedly to myself, delighted his wife had been had; yet again. Moving back down his body, the full firmness of his hard cock is irresistible, so I take my lips to it. I feel its warmth on them, noticing the pure white sperm leaking from his tip is being illuminated by the fairy lights. Taking him into my mouth and using the end of my tongue, I flick it over his penis time after time. He tastes like sugar candy slightly infused with salt, like warm salted caramel. Taking him further down my throat, I moan as he releases more of his milky syrup. Holding him in my hand, he grows harder still as I move up and down on his long hard shaft until he can take no more. Brad is now responding by lifting his hips, shoving himself deeper into my mouth, his breathing shallow as he moans, and coming to a climax. The hot liquid shoots out pumping, squirting as I swallow every single last bit of the sticky sperm down my throat. He lies contentedly as I greedily suck on him, ultimately taking the final droplets.

I cuddle him thinking that the feeling of belonging is surreal due to the fact I now have part of him inside me and the amount of love felt between us in this relationship is phenomenal, regardless of the circumstances. I stay for a while in his arms, and then cover his chest with feather-light kisses, moving down to his thighs, leaving behind a trail of kisses leading right to his testicles (I love how the hairs tickle my lips as I press my mouth into them). Oh! In the name of God, how I loved the smell of him, the way he feels against my skin. Just the thought of him makes my clitoris tingle, so suddenly my tiny pink panties are wet. *He is so sexually attractive!* I get up from the bed, debating whether to command him to lick me, giving me oral sex in return or simply just ask him to make me a cappuccino. Smiling, I go for the coffee, deciding instead, for just this once, pleasuring him for a change and asking only for coffee in return would be different, I guess.

Downstairs as Brad prepares dinner for my little dogs and makes my cappuccino, he talks away as I cut some of my witches' recipe homemade gingerbread for us. Brad turns around handing me the coffee, telling me to make sure I have my bags packed for this Wednesday as we are going on a trip whilst informing me that we would treat it as a little romantic holiday. I am putting the gingerbread to my mouth when instantly I stop in shock with it halfway there as I think he must have decided it was time to leave his wife. The little romantic holiday, which is, if I am right, going to be a getaway of some kind, where we would be hiding out for a few days away from her. He was planning on leaving her, so I supposed this address would be the first place she would come looking for him; therefore, we would be officially on the run. Informing Brad of this, we both agree, with both of us finding it very funny not just about who we were running away from but hiding away at our age being even worse.

Just as well River was here to look after my little dogs. River is my son who lives with me, and he is twenty-one years old. He has my colouring of dark Italian looks and my sense of humour. He was very much aware of the fact that I'd been having this affair with this married man for some years now. He neither approved nor disapproved; he just accepted it without questioning anything. Brad says he will instruct River that under no circumstances is he to answer the door to her, if caught out, and then he is to just run like we did. *Fucking run, River!* We laugh even more at this thought. I am excited plus curious about where we might be going, whether it would be to his sister's place down south or up north to a hotel on our own… then I start to wonder if realistically he would have the bottle to go through with this after all…

"Brad, Brad, when do you intend to tell her?" I ask him shakily, more than apprehensive of his answer, with me being frightened of both results at the same time, terrified that he would leave her, also that he wouldn't.

"Coco, I'm leaving my wife. I am telling her tomorrow that I don't love her and I never did. I shall explain I am still in love with you, that we share a sexual relationship; besides, I need you," he replies nervously, yet determined. I can't do anything but stare at him woefully. "Coco," he informed, "it will be done," he reinforces the seriousness of his statement. I look at him anxiously, *Coco, it will be done!*

Really, will it? I wonder, picking up my coffee cup, trying to hold back the tears. I guess right now I just feel insecure, no matter the outcome. If he leaves her, my freedom will be restricted as I am used to living as an independent woman. There is some pressure on me that it won't work out long-term because of knowing that everything changes, including the relationship, as it becomes entirely different when you start living with someone. To be honest, whether we would lose the rush of euphoria or not on seeing each other every day is the least of my worries right now. Having to commit to somebody financially – I am not very keen on that idea at all. *No, mam!* Maybe I'm worried that if he doesn't come, then it confirms he had no intentions of leaving her, because he truly does want us both, keeping me well as, just as a mistress… Perhaps. No. My biggest fear is that if he does come to stay with me, then he realises he has made a mistake, so he then leaves me again to go running back to her.

As Brad leaves, I am filled with conflicting thoughts on the situation, which combined can be summed up as miserable. I am so lost in past times feeling very cold, tired and unsure, with no motivation. I should relax, just forget about it all for tonight; this was what I had wanted for so long, was it not? I shall just have to wait in anticipation to find out what the rest of the week holds. Continuously going through my head though is an old saying reminding me to *always be careful for what it is that you wish for!*

Later that night whilst lying in bed, I find it impossible to sleep. I feel a sense of hopelessness… an emptiness as I think of him, I'm stuck on thoughts that he is back in that house with her. I was never jealous of Brad's wife, but there was a wishful envy of the time she shared with him in their so-called marital home. An annoyance that she believed he was her husband, so he belonged with her when he had specifically told me that he belonged to me, he was mine. In the dark I come to the realisation that today's date was once my wedding day, many moons ago. Finding myself reminiscing over the past three years of the affair, I wonder if he will he go through with this tomorrow for surely by now the time must have come when I shall find out… I hope to fuck I'm ready.

Tuesday, 23rd October 2012

On wakening up to the morning light, I find that despite my comfy mattress, last night's sleep was insufficient. On getting out of bed, I fondly remember the day that, while his wife was in

Canada, Brad bought this bed for me, which came with a cheap mattress. A few months or so later, while I was doing my nails, I heard a commotion outside so I got up and went to the window to investigate. I saw Brad coming up the garden path humping a huge mattress awkwardly. I could do nothing but laugh in amusement. Brad brought it here for us from the house he had shared with her; it was from the bed in the back room where he sometimes slept. She had replaced the mattress and quilt on his bed with new ones, so he brought the old ones here. She had just assumed Brad had taken them to a work colleague, obviously with no idea it really was for him and me. The quality of the mattress was so much better than the one we had on our bed before. That first night I was sinking into the thick bouncy mattress, delighted at the feeling of the luxurious duck down feather quilt fluffed up on top of me. I lay wrapped in its extraordinary soft feeling, pretending that I was once again in bed in a Hilton Hotel or the Ritz rather than my own bedroom.

The following morning Brad phones again to confirm to me that he is telling his wife today that their marriage is finally over as they are finished as a couple. He further instructed me to have my bags packed, ready to leave early the following morning. Once I get off the phone, I smile softly as I tremble with trepidation cum tolerance of the situation in hand. Is this happening? Will Brad leave his wife to be with me? This is what I question myself on the lull of hindsight of the phone call.

Later in the evening I am unable to concentrate on anything as all kinds of thoughts are going through my head. I keep wondering what is going on in that house, playing out in my head every possible scenario with the curiosity as to how his wife would be feeling right at this moment in time. *Why the fuck should I be concerned about her?* I then repeat this statement out loud to inform my witches' broom as I walk into my kitchen. As if in answer my phone rings, Brad calls warning me that he is on his way to my home. I can't sit still; I am like a cat on a hot tin roof. I am up and down the stairs plus pacing anxiously about through the house and garden. Coming in from the outside once more, I glimpse around my witchy kitchen, then propositioning my broom on the wall, I start chanting out loud, "Broom, come just fly me away, bring me back another day." The fucking broom just stays put. (As it always does but just for this once it would be great if it didn't, because I would get on the thing and fuck off to Noo Noo land, wherever the hell that is!) While I am waiting for him, I grab the broom off the wall, and then start dancing along the kitchen with it to a song playing on the radio. I then go upstairs to bring down my grandmother's music box. I wind it up whilst the soft tinkling music plays, I dance with my broom, I twirl round and round like a spinning top, then I stop on holding the broom shaft, I go up onto the point of my toes like a ballet dancer, *ouch!* then repeat the same. In my head, the tune of the music notes are the silent words of, *"He loves me? He loves me not? Oh! He does love me!" Does he honestly, Coco!*

Brad stops in his tracks, as coming in through the back door he catches me now dancing on the table, playing air guitar with the broom; I have my back to him so I have no idea he is standing behind me as I pretend to have gone from Swan Lake to being a rock star. As soon as I notice something out of the corner of my eye, I drop the broom to find him standing with a look on his face of non-description. I jump down off the table, running over to kiss him. He is stunned by my behaviour. Once we have both stopped laughing at my performance, Brad tells me that he had gone through with it, he had told his wife that he still loves me, that he isn't happy with her and they both already know their marriage is over, it has been for a long time; therefore, he has decided to leave in the morning. She asked if he was going to his girlfriend, to which he had replied he wasn't sure. He hasn't told her yet, not quite in black and white, that he is leaving her to be with me, which plays on my mind but at least he has finally told her he is still in love with me, so I suppose it's a start, right?

He informs me that we are going to go down south to his sister's for a few days plus I had a few more hours to get organised as he would now be picking me up a little later at midday, as first thing in the morning he had some important financial stuff to sort out with her. He holds me tightly to him, reassuring me he would show up tomorrow for sure. He kisses me tenderly, gently wiping my tears, before he leaves me once more. He returns to the house he shared with his wife, he would stay there with her for one last night, besides having to sort out the finances, there were his clothes to pack up.

After he leaves, I know I would suffer hell all night long on knowing where he was. I hate that yet again he is back in their marital home… but I just keep myself occupied with the knowledge that it would be the very last night ever he would spend in the place, then we can be together. Or would we really?

24th of October and the Week That Follows

Brad arrives on time, so we quickly put my luggage into the car. Brad has brought only a certain amount of clothing with him; he has still left most of his belongings in the house. Deciding to pick them up when we returned. Inside the car, the atmosphere feels tense and uneasy as I look over at Brad… I am hurting inside unsure of our plight as I try to figure out what his status quo is on the state of our affairs; how ironic is my choice of word on describing the situation. Judging from his appearance on the outside, he doesn't appear to be upset or regretful but perhaps on the inside he sits on different footing. Sizing him up in my opinion though, I don't think he is that bothered about leaving her at all. I smile as he catches me watching him.

"I love you, Coco," he softly reassures me. "Forget about her, I have; she's in the past, Coco. I don't love her and have no regrets on leaving her. I should have done this a long time ago. I owed you that much, not just for you but I owed it to myself too. I am now with the woman that I love more than anybody who has ever been in my life. The first time I ever felt what I know now is real love was when I saw you." He says truthfully in an adamant tone as smiling at me he reaches over rubbing my leg seductively as he drives on.

Inside I do know that he loves me, deep down I don't doubt that, not a single bit. I take my black boots off to rest my legs up on the dashboard. I have on a crisp white cotton shirt worn to compliment a long black layered gypsy skirt, which underneath hides silk stockings with delicate suspenders, no panties. "Nice legs, Coco, you're making me hard!" Brad says, checking the black lace showing on the top of the stockings. The serious tone of his voice on the factual statement has me laughing as I decide to play some of my music in the car to further lighten the mood. On the radio somebody is singing about somebody leaving them with a packed up suitcase and they want to know what is happening. Fuck, wrong song to come on in this situation; it is making me feel kind of awkward again, so I just start singing along anyway.

"Coco, you're a brilliant singer," Brad chimes in, taking the piss, seemingly oblivious to the relevance of the song lyrics; if he is aware of them it doesn't show, and then he winks at me laughing, so then again perhaps he is.

Hours into the car journey, we are not far from Megan's. It's starting to get dark out so we stop for a drink and to buy some chocolate at a service station. We are by now almost on the outskirts of York. On the cold October evening, rain is falling through a thick mist as we hurry across the car park. I am glad to get indoors, desperate for a pee and some hot coffee.

As we walk inside, I notice the place is mostly full of guys in work clothes, who all seemed to be staring at me. *What the fuck are they all looking at?* A strong aroma of filtered costa coffee fills the air. There are parallel black shiny tables and uncomfortable-looking fake black leather chairs, much like a school cafeteria. The walls are covered in white tiles, portraying the room to be very huge, wide and bright.

What were they all looking at me like that for? I wonder to myself for the second time as I head into the ladies' toilet. Speculating in bathroom mirror, I find myself utterly surprised at my reflection, not a dark chocolate colour with fake tan as I thought, just a more very appealing naturally deep tanned look with wild sexy hair and perfect eyeliner, all complimented by my pure white shirt. I spray on some more perfume, adding a slick of lip gloss to my lips before leaving the toilet. Brad is waiting for me by the coffee shop area holding our drinks. I notice that the guys are again watching us, so I hold my head high, do a little sassy catwalk up to Brad, saying out loud enough for them to hear as it is so obvious they're all listening, "Let's go, babe, and I'll give you a blow job in the car!" I glance around this time to see all the astonished faces as I walk on by with Brad in tow. In my own opinion, I know that he really is proud of me with what had just happened as it shows on his face. Back in the car we find the look on the faces of those workmen hilarious, now there was a story for the lot of them to tell.

It is dusk when we finally arrive. The atmosphere in the car is yet again very strange; I'm disturbed by its caliginous undertones. Everything feels distant, like something is horribly wrong. I'm not entirely sure what Brad is thinking. I'm nervous, even scared of him. I'm frightened of what has taken place today;

it's carrying a cloud of gloom over us, wrapping itself around as if enveloping us in a murky blanket. Worse still, I'm mortified at the thought of having sex with him tonight. Not exactly a virgin with him; no, not at all. Yet I sense I'm very much out of my depth tonight for some unknown reason. Now that is even stranger than the awkwardness between us on the way down the road. We are supposed to be ecstatic, so how come I am hurting over her, even caring, because deep down I know she is another human being. I am part of the reason has been badly hurt yet again as I got what I wanted. He parks the car.

"Right, darling, we're here," he announces to me smiling; he's steadily watching me as he undoes his seat belt.

"Well, let's go in," I suggest shakily, leaning over to kiss him. We get out of the car. Going up the path I have butterflies in my stomach, noting my legs are hardly capable of holding me up; coincidentally, I struggle to keep in step behind Brad, feeling nauseated. He enters the front door leading into the hall; unsteadily, I follow him slamming the door closed behind me. Brad's sister is standing in the doorway of the just done up brightly lit kitchen. Barging in after the obscurity of the hall, I retract a little backwards, lifting my hand to shield my eyes from the glaring white light, which is making me feel even more uncomfortable. She looks up at me standing in the doorway.

"You've a fucking neck on you to come here, Coco, after ignoring all my calls and texts for months, not bothering your arse with me until now because suddenly it fucking suits you," she sarcastically accosted me. Fuck, I sure was expecting this.

"Yeah, I know I'm sorry. It's complicated," I profess.

"Always fucking is – complicated. Fucking complicated," she huffs. "I've made soup." She motions towards a large pot on the cooker. "Bowls in there," she informs us, pointing over towards a cupboard. She heads out the kitchen, going through to the dining room. She goes on her way, shaking her head with a cigarette in her hand, talking out loud to herself about fucking affairs, then stating in more mumbled tones how her days for sex were long gone.

"Not for us!" I mouth silently at Brad, smiling, *bold me.*

"Not for us, Megan," he addresses her, shouting as he winks at me.

I giggle, saying, "SSHH!"

"I fucking know that. You see that's the reason why all this trouble started in the first place. Coco or you Brad, for that matter, couldn't keep her fucking knickers up," she establishes. I laughed even more since I wore none. I was standing in her newly embellished illuminated kitchen in my bare arse.

Brad comes over to where I'm standing, holding me close he holds up my skirt; his penis feels hard against my stockings, he gently takes his finger over my clitoris, making me wet; his hand on my flesh results in my skin tingling at his touch, *God, I want him*. I push him away mortified, forgetting about the broth for now, both of us laughing at being sexually aroused; we wander through to the lounge where Megan is now seated. I cuddle up beside her on the sofa while we talk, the earlier animosity now laid to rest. Together we girls share a bottle of wine, albeit with none of the soup. Brad has some port just before we head to bed. Now the wine is making me feel relaxed, I feel tired; it has been a long eventful day for everybody, I guess.

24th October, 11 p.m.

We bid Megan goodnight, she is now left alone as her husband has also gone to bed. I am walking backwards up the stairs with Brad, giving me a kiss for every single step. Meanwhile, it is extremely dark and under my feet I feel the soft, rich and thick wool through the sheer silk of the stockings. *God he can just take me right now, laying me down on this luxury carpet.* Brad kisses are demanding me to climax as he runs his fingers through my hair. All the time I feel like a teenager in love who is desperate to have her first boyfriend inside her, but shaking, almost terrified at the thought, while at the same time talking rapturously to her friends about wanting to have her virginity taken and her first orgasm with him. I smile at my own stupidity as knicker-less I head into our given room. *Coco, get a grip! You tease him by wearing no underwear, and then get all virginal, eh! I don't think so. No!*

Lying on the bed, Brad pulls me on top of him; he gently slides the material of my skirt up over my legs once more, I feel his hard-on pulsing against my flesh, just then he pushes his fingers deep into me. I moan in ecstasy as he rolls me over, laying me down on my back. I raise my leg up to his waist so I can have his fingers further up me. I feel the cold quilt cooling the hot skin of my bare buttocks. Brad goes down on me, pressing his mouth against my clitoris, taking his tongue over it, touching me ever so ethereally, as light as if it was 'The Angels Share' of the alcohol evaporating from the barrels of whiskey, so much so it's barely noticed in the air. His touch even softer than a feather tickling my little button hidden behind secret lips, he makes me climax as my whole body begins shuddering with the sensation.

Brad stands up, taking his trousers off. I lean forward, taking him into my mouth, loving the familiar salty caramel taste of him. I can't handle the tension any longer; I remove my skirt and bra, now I dominatingly push Brad down on the bed. He's naked with me only wearing my suspenders and stockings. I move myself up the bed, kissing him on the mouth, before placing my secret lips just above his cock, then sliding down the moist warmth of my little tight pussy, which encases every inch of him deep inside me. All nervousness long gone. Now I have him under my control, picking up speed; he does likewise, moving his hips in rhythm with me, faster and faster. I fling my head back, his hands playing with my nipples, my long dark hair hits his legs behind my little firm bottom as my love juices cover him, enhancing the wet slushy sex noise he loves as he slides in and out of my little pink treasure.

"Coco, I'm cumming. Fuck, I'm cumming!" he calls in a deep sexy tone, his warm sperm squirts time and again, shooting it way up into me. In his ejaculation he causes me to spray more of my womanly milk with him.

Afterwards we lay in the arms of each other, he holds me tight, massaging my head, playing with my hair, he makes me feel so loved, so special.

"I've made a mess, darling," Brad announces, looking down.

"No, no you haven't, Brad, it's all in me," I respond, gazing into his eyes I smiled.

Wishful thinking, Blake, but next time you will, because when you're wanking yourself all over me, you drive me crazy as I think it's so sexy and I just want you to do it endlessly, which by the way, Blake, you will be doing very soon, so next time yes, there will be a mess, believe me! We continue cuddling each other, I feel that I am safe in his arms, that nothing can hurt me now as I wish we could stay like this forever. *Just the two of us, cast a spell to claim him mine, to keep him lying here beside me until the end of time.*

Sexually satisfied for now, we remain snuggled up together. The last thing I remember before drifting off to sleep is hearing Brad's voice as he breathed in hushed tones, "Marry me, Coco!" It was more of a statement than asking me a question.

25th October 2012

I wake up this morning to the sound of a hoover (a fucking noisy old machine burring away inside), outside birds chirping. As I open my eyes, Brad is already up calling out to me: "Good morning, Coco, are you getting up now? It is quarter past nine." *Why is everyone so happy in the mornings? I hate the fucking mornings!* I hate them, I think to myself as I struggle to wake up. I have always been nocturnal (a night owl myself). Way back in the days when I worked as a high-class exotic dancer (I danced on a stage and by the end of the very famous song, I was completely naked in a shower of water of that colour – standing in the nude in purple rain. I was totally an exclusive performer but in other people's view, at the end of the day a stripper is a stripper) so it was in the night time that I thrived. I was awake all night, then slept all day, which suited me perfectly unlike Brad, who worked down the mines from a young age and was always up at the crack of dawn with little sleep at night, so you see his old habits die hard. Now he works nights in a forensic cum mental health unit yet he hardly sleeps at the end of shift, still functioning on very little sleep, although his night has been turned into day also. Fuck, I've no idea how he manages it. I hate the fucking daylight hours more so in the summertime. Brad calls me his 'Princess of the Darkness', which little does he know I am very much so and in more ways than one. He is not aware of the fact I am a Queen Witch. Seriously.

I get up, having to drag myself out of bed sighing and making faces. I can't be bothered with this up in the morning before ten o' clock, pish. This was a regular thing here, where hoovers were your alarm call, that with those awful squawking birds. I grab a shower, pulling on a white robe with wet hair, I head downstairs for breakfast. I can't stomach eating a fried breakfast presently, so I have some fresh fruit with yogurt instead. Being naked under my robe, I stand in the kitchen again in my bare bum, so on

22

making coffee I flash my tits at Brad; he laughs, shaking his head at me. A little later, while Brad is talking away taking his breakfast out the range, I am dancing to the radio holding my robe up in the air this time, showing off my fanny. We both go into hysterics as I just manage to get my robe down in time on hearing Megan coming towards the kitchen.

"I've landed myself with a nutcase," Brad asserts to his sister on entering the kitchen, to which Megan replies, "I could have fucking told you that, Brad!" oblivious to the fact that Brad was referring to the nonsense of my stupid dancing.

I now style my hair then apply face moisturiser before applying some light cosmetics. During the daytime I normally just wear a little foundation with mascara, going for a natural look; when night falls and the evening appears, I wear heavier and darker products when going out with Brad, kind of like stage make-up but keeping it classy.

Brad does appreciate the time and effort I take on looking after myself, he comments on how proud he is of the way I look after my image, which is costly, however he views it as money well spent. He is always buying me expensive gifts, including perfumes, clothes and stunning exclusive underwear (perks of being a mistress!). He never buys shoes though, I used to love owning loads of pairs, but I was put off them as when working I had to dance in high stiletto heels for hours, sometimes horrendous purple glitter ones. He buys me boots instead, I prefer that the ones I have wear a price tag that screams a fortune, but he don't mind and now I have a rather verifiable collection of them.

Brad's wife is fifteen years older than him. He is very embarrassed in going anywhere with her as rather than a couple going out together, many people mistake him for being out with his mother; it certainly doesn't help matters that she's so very old-fashioned in her way and dress sense. He told me she never takes care of her image and that she never ever has, also that never in all the years together has he ever heard her sing, besides that she has no personality and very rarely smiles. Brad admits to all that she was never ever anything to look at. Brad likes to think of her, in fact constantly refers to her, as an old crow (The Craw), with me in comparison being a beautiful black swan, both in my stunning elegant looks and with my wild dangerous nature.

Just as we're about to leave the house to go to town, Megan gets a phone call. It's Brad's wife asking if he is there plus informing Megan to advise Brad that she has packed the rest of his clothes for him. "Aw, well!" Brad states, we all laugh, saves him doing the job; he sarcastically smirks, not given a shit either way. I'm slightly annoyed, however, as she thinks Brad is there on his own as nobody has told her yet I'm with him. Not even Brad. Then again deep down she knows, she is not that stupid surely, woman's instinct and all that, she must know.

"Coco, who is making a cunt of who?" He broke into my thoughts, winking at me. "Who cares what she thinks or what she knows, just as long as we both know that I couldn't get to be with you quick enough (eh! Understatement took him years) and that, Coco, you're my world. Fuck her and her sour face, she thinks packing my clothes upsets me; I don't give a toss, I am delighted it gives me more time to spend with you and less time spent in that jail she calls home. I fucking hate being there," he says with so much passion. I lean over kissing him, smirking with satisfaction, knowing that he was correct.

We set out for town together to share a special day, which Brad had arranged just for me. We spent a magical time together, which consisted of completing a list of going to all my favourite places and doing what I wanted to do. As a white witch practising a form of magic, I always need different things, like unusual herbs that are sometimes hard to come by. I very much like to go into all the little dark time-gone-by aged curiosity shops that sell magic stones with antiquated enchanting witchcraft spell books which I cannot find in my own home town; therefore, I often therefore have to wait until I am away visiting towns elsewhere that stock what I need, so I can buy all my uncommon ingredients with other stuff to make my special potions and lotions. Besides, they also sell all the colours of the candles that I require for use in all the different kinds of bewitchment sorcery, in which the candles are properly colour-coded for use depending on the spell being made. I also adore cute little old-fashioned coffee shops there that you find sometimes off the beaten path as you go down the town's ancient cobbled streets. The atmosphere there can be amazing. With shafts of the light from the sunshine hitting the crystal ornaments and sparkling jewels in the shop windows spreading warm glows, casting shadows, with soft multi-colours of the rainbow across the old stonework creating a magical aura as if hidden away in another secret land. Sitting drinking cappuccino with great views into gardens or across little rivers with the scent of coffee and vanilla from the home baking in the air is a sacred place of contentment for me to be.

Before we go back to the car, Brad stops in at an old bookshop that sells stuffed animals plus distinctive candles, which he buys for me. The stuffed foxes with the candles are for my lounge at home. I adore the smell of the scented candles drifting through the house while the animals complete my décor, making my place even more beautiful, and the wild flowers which I pick in the woods add to creating an earthly haven resembling a witch's cottage.

Afterwards we pass through a graveyard. This is a whereabouts I like to visit often on my own, wandering about looking at the inscriptions on tombstones. I find a lot of peace here imagining all the complex lives these people had, the good times with the bad, the failures and the successes, questioning if these people here had lives just as intricate as my own, wondering to if they ever had immoral love affairs with secret illicit sex. I am fascinated, wondering about the drama and history of these people now gone from this life, leaving behind a legacy of themselves with just a name on an expensive stone in the graveyard. It reminds me that whilst I am still alive, I continue to create my own story. As Heidegger once said, "People should spend more time in graveyards."

I imagine changing the words on an inscription in a poem that Rabbie (Robert) Burns wrote; I smile, considering this to be the epitaph on my head stone.

"Here Lies Coco, Blake's Banes
Oh! Satan when you tak them
Gie her the skulling o' yer weans
Clever strippers, she'll mack them."

Or maybe perhaps it could say, 'Coco, always The Mistress but never The Wife'. Now that would make whoever read it talk. Or 'The Coco, The Dancer, The Stripper', and 'May Heaven have chocolate and rain the colour of purple. *Or I am not going there.*

I sit there on a bench for a while as Brad heads off to the shop to pick up some goods for Megan. Alone in the graveyard enjoying some time by myself, I reminisce about the time in my life spent around Father Peter. Father Peter was a monk who took me in when I needed somewhere to go. Father Peter and I became very close, and I was very appreciative of him always being there for me. My first religion is witchcraft although I am a Protestant, I prefer the Catholic ideals of worship. I became a member of the Catholic Church, taking the vows that were required of me to join; it changed my life not only in the way I perceived the world but because I feel I became a better person towards me and others in this life in a different way from witchcraft. I feel I was less solitary but on practising my craft a lot of the time, I chose to work alone despite the fact I was personally in charge of five covens. This was similar again with the kind of same basic rituals. I used all three of religions to my advantage, it worked for me, albeit it was definitely not the proper thing to do.

One time, after praying with Father Peter, I asked him, "What do you wear under your robes, Father, is it just your bare arse?" to which he had responded mortified at the very thought, "No Coco, indeed not, I wear black trousers."

"Unfortunate then that was for all of us as we (as in the female congregation) have been on our knees for months trying to peek up the gown for nothing!" I declared. We both started to laugh, after that he would cross himself, smiling when he saw me coming. One day I asked him if Satan really did exist. His answer was of course, so I questioned him on how he knew that. "Well, how do you know that, Father?" I persisted. To which he answered that he did know because his daughter was sitting in front of him. We both found it extremely funny as he was horrified with my behaviour most of the time. Secretly and in fun, he called me The Devil's Daughter from there on in.

Father Peter understood my personality and he once said, "I have never met anyone quite like you, Coco, and I don't suppose I ever will again. You are so full of life filled with mischief, but you know what, God knows of your past; he knows your present status as a stripper, but he forgave Mary Magdalene, so I know you are forgiven too, my child, you think with your heart more than you do your head." Perhaps Father Peter was right on that count. I speculate as to what he would say today about me in this affair. Committing adultery is not acceptable neither was witchcraft and I was always in serious trouble and at confession for that, Father Peter would probably go fucking nuts at me. Or would he even be surprised?

That is what I loved about Father Peter, he was a priest but he had a strange sense of humour that I just got; he was never judgemental of me, no matter what I said or had done in my past, so he would be the same now I supposed after all, perhaps he would just say 'you can't help who you fall in love with, my child. Nothing startles or leaves me dumfounded with you anymore, Coco'. Yes, Father Peter would probably say exactly that, then some. I remember Father Peter with fondness, smiling at our time together. One day Father Peter said to me, "Coco would you help with my dinner party tonight?"

I replied, laughing, "I suppose so, but tell me Father, how does a stripper like me fold the napkins?"

Affronted, he crossed himself, "Coco, my child, I shall teach you. We shall make the Pope's hat."

And so we did. Just before everybody was due to arrive, I filled the napkins, in shape of the tall hat, with fruit sweets and thongs, chocolates and popcorn. I also had homemade witch wine for them. The priests all sat to dinner, drinking the wine, which was strong liquor, so they all got drunk very quickly. So funny. Perhaps not! They were pulling all the stuff out the napkins, laughing and holding the thongs up in the air as in trying to work out what they were. The looks that were worn on the church elders' faces was a fucking picture at this, I was once again in serious trouble. The next day Father Peter sent for me. "Why did you put underwear in the napkins, Coco?" he sternly demanded.

I hung my head. Then I lifted it up, looked straight into his eyes and said, "Because when I asked you about the vow of celibacy and not having sex, you said that you had not even seen a woman in underwear in the flesh. So at least now you can all say that you held a pair of knickers!" For me. Confession to ask for forgiveness for leading the priests astray. Plus 3 Hail Marys', including having to write out three chapters from the bible and set up the altar for four Sundays in a row. Now that suited me just fine, because I drank the wine while doing it. I walked towards the door of the church very much reprimanded. As I looked back behind me, Father Peter was bent over the pews, holding his side and I heard him ending himself laughing, just at that the older priest came out the door of their changing room, holding his head, declaring loudly which echoed through the silence that he was ill with the amount of wine drunk last night, which caused Father Peter to laugh even more. That was me and that was us I surmised, oil and water.

Brad arrives back, kissing me he tasted of chocolate; much to my delight, he hands me a huge box of chocolates plus half the bar he was eating. So now it is time for us to make our way back up to Brad's sister's house. While Brad is driving the jeep, I pull back the little pants I am wearing and start playing with myself, and then I put my fingers in Brad's mouth, enticing him to taste me. Brad shows restraint laughing as he tries to focus on the traffic in the middle of the road; he orders me to behave for once. I shout out: "No!" Then I continue to play with myself, flinging my head back moaning as Brad loses concentration and goes straight through a red light, causing a commotion with him swearing and swerving his car to safety as all the other drivers blast their horns in fright and anger. I just smile angelically, putting my finger back to Brad's lips as he starts to laugh, shaking his head. "You're wild, Coco, fucking wild man!" is all he says.

When we get back to Megan 's, we immediately go running upstairs to our room, leaving her wondering what the hell the rush was as we come in through the front door. "What the fuck you two running for?" she shouts behind us, getting no answer. "Fucking tornado hits York rushing in through my hall today," she says, talking out loud to herself as she once again walks away with her cigarette in hand as we laugh quietly behind the bedroom door.

Still playful from the car, I push Brad down on the bed; taking his cock out from his jeans, I begin to suck it. Brad lay back enjoying it as I sit on top of him, fulfilling my desire to have his cum inside me my way. As I am about to climax, I sexually demand my only request from Brad, "Cum inside me." Brad obliges on hearing these words, he fills me with the hot sperm that I have been wanting since we got in the jeep. When still perched on top of Brad, I make a gesture with my arms up in the air like a fountain. "Pshpshpshpsh, that's your sperm spraying way up me, Brad, on sucking you I need a golf umbrella for me to stay dry, it covers my hair and sometimes hits the wall," I say to him cutely. Now satisfied that I got what I wanted, I climb off the top of him. Lying down beside Brad I cuddle into him, noticing that in my haste to take Brad, I had left the bedroom door wide open. Oops, fuck me, a good job no one came upstairs.

We take some time out to be alone together in the room for a while. The rest of the night we spend downstairs drinking wine, rudely whispering, sharing our secrets and dreams with each other. Planning our future, I still couldn't believe he had left his wife as it had not actually really dawned on me yet. On realisation that it certainly was the case, I was at first astonished, then ecstatic. It felt amazing, I felt so privileged that he had chosen me over her.

The rest of the holiday continued much the same – with us going out for most of the day, and then spending time in evening with Brad's family. But we had made definite plans for the final night of our holiday to go out together to York's old town.

31st October

Samhain or All Hallows Eve to us witches, but commonly known as Halloween. I won't be celebrating the Sabbat tonight in the way I usually do as I am here on holiday. I feel kind of out of sorts, this is one of our major celebrations; however, I decide to do something when I get back home so I don't feel so bad about missing out on my celebration tonight. Father Peter would lay an egg if he knew as he certainly doesn't approve of my witchcraft. At all.

Brad and I are going out as agreed earlier in the week as this our last night of our romantic rendezvous. I wanted to have my nails done for this evening, so Megan booked me an appointment for that afternoon. Later that day in the salon, Brad is sitting on a sofa near the window waiting for me. I can see the workers in the nail salon looking over at Brad, then back to me again. I get it in my head that they are comparing his weight to mine and laughing to themselves, so the little voice in my head starts to think how Brad is like Humpty Dumpty sitting over on the sofa (having lost his wall) while the Noodle is getting her nails done.

My nails are perfect, "That's it done, Humpty Dumpty time to pay for Noodle's nails," I yell over at Brad. He gets up to pay laughing, attracting more strange looks from all in the nail bar. As we left I was still giggling.

Brad asks, "What are you fucking talking about, Coco?"

"Oh! Just the stories, you know, the voices in my head, Noodles with Humpty Dumpty," I reply… Brad just shakes his head, he was speechless. Given Brad's confusion, I decide to wind Brad up even more. Showing him the colour of my nails, which are dark forest green, I clarify, "Brad darling, what do you think of my lovely red nails?" No answer, he just looks blankly. He must be baffled as he doesn't answer me, he just stares vacantly right through me. Then he looks back down at my nails without saying a word about the colour, not a fucking word.

"Brad, where did you park the jeep? We need to get out of this fucking rain, I am getting soaking wet!" I assert, continuing to tease him. Brad, looking more bewildered, mystified glances up at the sky before holding his arms to check for rain drops to clarify it before contributing, "Coco, it isn't raining."

"Brad, please not today; don't start being stupid, it is raining, it is raining rainbow rain, look at all the lovely colours," I counter him, keeping my face poker-straight the entire time. Hurrying on towards the jeep, I pretend to shield the rain from me; as he follows he's still watching me, who knows what the fuck he is thinking as at this point his face is blank like it was set in stone. I just get amusement out of playing these little games then watching his reaction. He must think that I'm psychotic. (He often comments this, mostly in an argument – "You're fucking daft!") I may be older now but I'm still childish and full of mischief at heart. Brad falls for it every single time; he seriously thinks I am borderline mentally ill, but are we not all?

On the way to my favourite coffee bar we stop by a dress shop; Brad picks out then pays for a stunning very exclusive dress in the same shade of dark forest green of my nails, it matches them perfectly. The colour is very alluring on me, it suits my dark skin. The dress also sparkles, complementing the Swarovski crystals on my nails. I thank Brad profusely, telling him I now have a beautiful new red dress that glitters to match my nails. He looks at me, then at the dress, then at my nails; still he says nothing. He just nods and smiles at me; I think he is not sure what to do.

Now that I have my outfit sorted for tonight, we head for Megan's house. Brad and I get ready, and then William (Megan's son) gets changed to come out with us for a drink. William has no intention of staying long with us as he has planned later that night to meet up with his own friends, staying with us only for a while at the beginning of the evening. William and I get on very well. Brad's nephew accepted me into the family with open arms; his nature is not one of many. As we entered in the doors of old worldly bar, we immediately notice that everyone else in the establishment is dressed up in Halloween costumes.

"I'm the Green Goddess," I turn, gesturing to Brad and William, curtseying in my dark green dress with the matching fingertips, wearing black leather shoes sprinkled with green crystals, holding a bag of the same.

"No, Coco, you're more like the Wicked Witch of the West," Brad replies, laughing. William is also buckled at this remark.

Needing a cheeky comeback, I notice William has gelled and spiked up his hair. "Oh yeah, well I am the witch from the West and you're the lion with that big round face topped with a mane of spikey hair, so that leaves you Brad to be the wardrobe, since you're as wide as you are fucking tall." Everyone bursts out laughing, so it's sorted then, this year we are all out as The Fat Lion, The West Witch and the fucking Wardrobe.

Sometimes in my thoughts I start to wonder how many times I had longed to go through my wardrobe into a new magical world. How amazing it would've been to get away from boring day-to-day life, exploring a mysterious new land. I'd love for it to be a land of snow with me as The Snow Queen Witch of The Coco Kingdom, except in my Kingdom all the snow would be made of real cocaine (to hell with Turkish delight sweets) and in that land where all would hail the Snow Queen Witch wrapped in a huge pure white fur cloak, may all my servants live crazy, magical lives far away from the monotony and the hypocritical governing bodies of the real world.

On leaving the bar, as our time was coming to an end here, we decide to go for a meal at the best Chinese restaurant in town. After our dinner was finished and we were on our coffee liquors, an argument fuelled by alcohol starts when we discuss his wife. In all the euphoria of the holiday, I had forgotten that at the end of the day I was just Brad's mistress, we were still having an affair. As I get more upset, I just get up from the table, marching into the toilets. I sit crying in the stall. It just suddenly hits me that although I have had a sex and fun-filled romantic runaway jaunt with Brad, legally he belongs to someone else. I am still not his wife, even if we refer to us being each other's spouse.

I must have been in the toilets longer than I thought, because Brad got worried about me so he sent a woman in to find his WIFE Coco to please ask her to come out. As the woman who came in to help said the word wife, I burst out, "I'm not his wife okay that is the problem! He's married but not to me!" This makes me feel even worse now; I feel bad for shouting at the messenger on top of everything, I also felt that the entire pub had heard me and was by now judging me behind my back. What a terrible way to end a perfect holiday… Then it dawns on me – legally, he is my common-law husband if we stay together, so he is mine now. Besides, what about our secret wedding vows made to each other? So even when he did stay with her, I was his wife in his head and his heart, with him being my husband likewise. He did call her his landlady because believe it or not, that was just exactly what she was.

Brad smiles at me as I approach him, we kiss, making up and apologising to each other. Then laughing we go hand in hand back to the table with glasses of wine, forgetting about the stupid row. Brad informs me that I know I am his wife and he is my husband in our world, so fuck everything else. I agree. His marriage to her was one of convenience, as everyone told me and Brad acknowledged himself. On returning to Megan's, we find that she didn't know we had eaten so has cooked food for us coming back from the pub. I struggle to eat the steak, having to keep slyly putting my food on Brad's plate. I have no idea how he manages to eat it all, it is so funny. After our second dinner of the night, we have to go and lie down on top of the quilt on the bed; I am feeling so ill with the over indulgence of food. No Kama Sutra tonight. I was spread out like America while Brad was lying there like Moby Dick beached out of the water. Adding to the fact we both drank a lot of alcohol; my tummy feels even yuckier. Brad falls soundly asleep, as I struggle to do my face with cleansers and night creams before finally toppling into bed in my underwear, then passing out beside him.

1st November 2012

This morning as we're getting ready to leave York to head back home to Ayr, unfortunately, we receive a phone call bearing bad news about Brad's mother. Doctors have found her to be very ill. It is quickly agreed that Megan will come back up to Scotland with us given her mother's condition In the jeep on our way back up the road home, the news has hit Brad and Megan hard, they're so close to her, lost in thought, so the journey is mostly silent. Although I am only having an affair with Brad, I also have a very close relationship with his mother. She has always been kind, very accepting of me. It depresses me that she has fallen so ill so quickly, because selfishly I would've liked more time with her. I'm so worried about her, very much actually and angry at the illness inside her, it feels like I've been robbed, losing her now; I wish I'd met Brad earlier in life. I can't accept 'whatever will be will be' – I just don't want to.

Once we arrive back home, I get dropped off at my house. I nervously make coffee while Brad and Megan go to visit their mother at her house to find out how she is doing. I understand the situation, knowing the circumstances why I can't go; however, it doesn't make it any easier as once I'm alone at home, things just start to begin playing on my mind. I wonder if his wife is there. I also stupidly question why Brad and I couldn't have been together earlier; I am so different in nature from his wife, with him telling me that I am completely the opposite of her in every single way, besides his mother knew that I made him so happy. I often apply that statement to me and Brad though, that of the bird and the fish. They fall in love, but where do they stay? It was like that for a long time as Brad stayed with her up there and I stayed down here. Well, that was then as both of us are supposed to be living here now. But with Brad circumstances may change again, he may want to go back to her now his mother is so ill as the house he shared with his wife is just across the road from his mother. He still has most of his belongings there, and she doesn't know I was with him in York, so him leaving her can be easily sorted. Brad can go home if he wants. Guess what? I won't stop him but I also won't be waiting for him to come back to me again. Not anymore. But just for now all I want more than anything is to be able to go and visit his mother… to offer her my condolences, to be able to spend some time with her, treating her like the mother-in-law I have felt (I know) she has been to me in the short space of time I have had with her.

Brad returns from his mother's sad, and I question him as to his whereabouts all the time he was out of the house, then all my stupid thoughts result in an explosive argument with Brad at a time he needs me most. I start going on at him about his wife, how he didn't love her so the time spent there with her had ruined the chance I had to be a real part of his family; therefore, it short-changed the time I could've had with his mother. How right now because he hasn't got the guts to tell the Crow (Craw as he calls her) I still can't properly see his mother as her daughter-in-law to be able tell her how I feel, tell her to fight, tell her I want her to get well again. The arguing stops as Brad understands how I feel; besides he still hasn't brought the rest of his belongings from his house yet. But mostly I don't give a fuck about his wife or where his clothes are, the most important thing right now is his mother. He tells me he is staying with me as that is what he wants to do and that is what his mother wants. I don't get the chance to ask if he is going back, he has told me quite clearly that he isn't going to her as his home is now with me.

In total confusion, thinking stupid thoughts plus making problems in my head, I was now in a foul temper as on top of all of that I had a bad headache. I had taken all my anger out, emotionally burdening him with more shit when all he really needed was my support. It was selfish, me being me, because I don't like what is happening, how can Brad stop it? Yet I expect him to. I try to cheer myself up by thinking about all the things I shared with Brad (basically everything except a child). I start to wonder if maybe we would've had a child if we had met sooner in life... he would have made a brilliant father, and I know he has regrets big time of not having a child of his own. Fate had decided that it wasn't to be with me, I guess. As for her, well he tells me he certainly hadn't wanted one with the crow, it would have been an ugly child, he says, and the thought of it makes him feel physically sick. I just look at him, saying nothing; my thoughts are that it is strange of him to refer to an unborn child as perceived to be ugly.

Brad makes us supper downstairs, as I go upstairs for a bath, then my phone bleeps as a text comes in, it is from Brad.

"You're my life, you're my wife. I need you so much, please don't ever leave me. xxx"

Feeling even worse now about everything, I text back,

34

"You're my world, Brad, I love you infinitely. xxxxx"

3ʳᵈ November

Brad goes to his hometown to visit his mother. She is so frail now Brad told me; at this point I just walk away from him crying, feeling very sad and empty, just so hopeless with the situation, and worse was still to come.

Later that evening, Brad ventures out to the shops to buy bubble bath salts with some bottles of wine. Chocolate, also cake, all that make you feel good, shit we eat when we're feeling down. When he comes back, he tells me that he wanted us to share a bath.

We have a romantic bath together, lighting candles, drinking the red wine in the bubble bath. It is a very nice atmosphere, besides it kind of feels good to see him unwind, relaxing even just a little bit, given how he has been since he heard about his mother. I don't like to see him so upset. At least it is me he has come to for comfort; it's me he wants rather than his wife.

We get out of the bath, dry each other laughing and snuggle into bed. We reach over to kiss each other at the same time. My clitoris is tingling for him as our romantic evening has set the mood for me; I want him inside me, but I refrain from acting upon it, given that I understand the last thing he needs is sex.

I was wrong as Brad cuddles into me; his hand wanders down between my legs. I lie there, breathing heavily as he slips his fingers into me. He rubs my clitoris in soft circles, and then pushes his fingers deep up me. He plays with me for ages, the movement of his fingers getting faster and faster still, I raise my ripe swollen lips up to him as my legs start to tremble with excitement before I cum all over his hand. Then he slides down my body, placing his head between my legs before licking my clitoris with his tongue, followed by gently kissing it. Opening my legs wider as Brad gets up on his knees, he asks me to play with myself as he watches while he is wanking himself. I play with myself then cum again. Brad is groaning as he looks on, masturbating hard and fast, ending in his hot white sperm shooting out of his tip, landing all over my tummy, finally dripping on my glistening pussy.

Afterwards, we clean up, get back in bed to try to get some sleep. I lie awake awhile thinking, Brad spent so much time pleasuring me despite the pressure he's under but I guess it was just his way of showing me he still loves me very much. He doesn't need to do that, so I'm unsure why he perhaps thinks he does, especially at a time like this; maybe he just wanted too, I guess.

4th November 2012

This is D-Day… or should I say THH-Day (To his hometown day). Brad is going to his wife's house today to get the rest of his belongings that she'd packed for him. This makes me feel physically sick, and I end up throwing up multiple times, once I vomit straight onto my bedroom carpet.

I am sitting in the kitchen with my head in my hands when Brad goes to leave; he comes in to give me a kiss.

"Just go," I mumble, refusing to look up.

Brad attempts to say something to me but then thinks better of it, instead he just lifts his car keys, deciding simply to shout from the doorway: "I love you, Coco, I'll be back very soon," those were his last words before leaving to go there.

The back door opens then shuts, he is gone. While Brad is away, I don't know what to do or think; I sit on the table with the mug of coffee, talking to my broom, convinced I'm going insane!

Brad is soon back with all his gear. We quickly sort it out before making some dinner. He has to be on his way to work the night shift soon, he starts back tonight. I still have another week off. After he leaves I'm alone in the stillness of the house. I'm left to think over everything that's happened recently, Brad leaving her as we go on holiday in York, then the strange emotional journey since discovering Brad's mum was ill. Next Brad has moved in with me for real, bringing all he owns in the world with him. It's a lot to observe when I'm still not sure if this is for the best, attentively asking myself if this is what I truly want.

A text comes in from Brad whilst he is at work:

"Coco ur my life ur my wife, need you so much please don't ever leave me"

Class, Brad, just fucking class. Given the thoughts I have been having alone, those words cut through me like a carving knife. He is the one who had been constantly leaving me to go back to her, it is only now that he has apparently left her for good that he now claims he has no regrets; if he has this time left her for good, I wonder for how long? He is the one now who is terrified I will walk as he is the one now who is always constantly begging me to stay.

Looking down at my hand, I admire the gold wedding band Brad gave me. It reminds me of the day he put it on my finger. Brad took the signet wedding ring his wife gave him and one of my gold rings, then taking them both to be melted down in the goldsmiths creating two plain heavy gold wedding bands. We wore one each as a commitment to each other, sealing our love with our hearts. He says he wants me to never take it off, that it protects me, keeps me belonging to him, and tells the world that I am not available (Fucking suiting Brad). Despite his reasons, I love the fact he calls me Coco Blake. Mr Bradford Riley Blake and Mrs Coco Blake. I think it suits us nicely.

In a happier mood now with his wedding ring on my finger, I text back before bed;

"You are my world, Brad. I swear I love you infinitely. Always have done, always will. Goodnight. xxxx"

Do you really, Coco, or do you just say that? Perhaps, sometimes I do; others I don't.

5th November 2012

Brad is in from work now sound asleep as I lie awake beside him. I get up, tiptoe downstairs so that I don't wake him. This morning my mood has changed once more, I'm so happy that we live together now. I decide to make a special treat for Brad. He usually doesn't sleep much; therefore, he always makes dinner soon after getting up, so today for once I will.

I prepare him roast chicken with spices using Jamaican Jerk sauce (one of his favourite dishes). I leave the doors slightly ajar so that the scent travels through the house. As the chicken is browning, I sprinkle a little brown sugar over it, and then add the Jamaican Jerk sauce while chilling some Chardonnay, and for our dessert, I finish the dinner off with my homemade Eton mess with Channel Island cream, before making my own homemade raspberry coulis to compliment it.

When I want to be, I am brilliant cook, although most of the time I pretend I can't just to get out of doing it, which Brad finds cute, and other people who know my culinary capabilities find it rather amusing that I do this, just lazy maybe or just because I can get away with it. Well, mostly.

Brad wakes up; he comes stumbling downstairs half asleep to see what is cooking. As he enters the kitchen, I kiss him as he tells me the smell of the roast is amazing and it's drifting through the house right up to the bedroom. He sniggers at me cooking, making fun of me, but the laugh is on him when he is presented with the meal, which he eats enthusiastically, along with his earlier words.

We both enjoy the dinner with wine. Brad only has one glass as he is working later but I have a couple of glasses. I finish the whole bottle.

"You excel in your cooking of chicken, darling, it's delicious," he says, handing me an empty plate.

"Aww thank you, Brad," I respond, pretending to blush with a little smirk showing on my face.

After our dinner is finished, I take on the chore of cleaning up, which consists mostly of piling dirty dishes into the dishwasher. *Every woman's best friend!* We have a few hours before Brad has to leave for work so I climb up on his knee as he cuddles me in his arms, holding me tight while we chitter chatter away about the usual pish as well as everything in life. At one point though he started rocking me back and forth, singing love songs with the wrong lyrics and out of tune. It was so funny, cute and fucking awful at the same time. I start to wish he didn't have to go to work tonight after all. Sometimes, no, perhaps most time, I can't wait for him to get out the door. I love my own space, enjoying my own company very much.

I stare over at my broom on the wall, urging it to stop time with a witchcraft spell; this would suit me to make this moment last longer but not forever. No response, broom just sits there. As it gets close to the time for Brad to leave, I try propositioning the broom once again... nope, still nothing. *I will deal with this disobedience later!* I think to myself before realising I do really need to move my ass as time is running out, and I want Brad to make me coffee before he gets organised for work.

After Brad's car disappears out the street, I change my mind again. Now pleased with the broom for not obeying me, I thank it by dancing with it around the kitchen. I pour more wine before going to the fridge for some chocolate cake and cream. *Now this is my kind of heaven!* I go to the lounge, light more candles, and then cuddle up on the sofa with my little dogs. I consider my situation with Brad, thinking sometimes I worshipped him in some higher form as if he was a love god, putting him so high up on a pedestal, seeing him that way blinded by love, instead he was just an ordinary bastard of a man. Other times, more so since he moved in, I can't be fucked with him. Honestly. To hell with analysing this shit, tonight I'm going to enjoy my evening, just forgetting about it all, I will finish making my decision about us and where we stand tomorrow; after all, it is only a day away. Later after watching a film along with emptying the wine bottle, the clock reads time for bed, so I let my dogs out to pee. Standing in the garden looking up at the full moon shining in the dark sky, I start to think about the legends of werewolves, of vampires, including all the glamour that surrounds them due to the recent movies. Apparently because of all this, the definite general impression now is it would be pretty cool to be a vampire actually, well especially if you really lived forever; apart from that, they are considered to be very beautiful people. I am a white witch, perhaps I can make a spell to live for eternity. I should make use of the full moon for casting a spell but decide not to because I am very tired. I just go back indoors with my little dogs, smiling to myself at the thought of vampires visiting me tonight, I would love that. I put my wand, crystals and pentagram from my altar to charge in the moonlight though. Brad phones from work and I tell him I saw vampires in the garden. He laughs asking me if they ran like fuck on meeting me, I say no, but they weren't looking for me, they were out searching for you, wolf boy. I hang up on him laughing, leaving him on the other side of the phone wondering, as I talk to myself about Edward and Jacob from the Twilight movie. Now Edward in my opinion is definitely something else!

6th November 2012

Brad comes in from work earlier than usual this morning so on waking up; I find he has already prepared breakfast for me to have in bed. He hands me a tray which has scrambled eggs made with fresh cream, hot buttered toast, coconut cookies lightly warmed in the oven, with a milky cappuccino coffee. There is a little wild flower on the tray with a tiny box of champagne truffles, now this is my kind of breakfast, now he's my hero, besides what a lovely way to start the day on a cold and frosty morning!

Afterwards Brad doesn't go to bed; he decides just to stay up as he is off tonight anyway. We relax in my lounge under sheepskin rugs in front of the log fire with my little Chihuahuas. Brad mentions possibly going out tonight to a bonfire display. I complain that it is freezing outside, but it sounds like a plan. I love fireworks but wee Rio, my Chihuahua, is not so keen; the rest don't bother. Later at eventide it is so romantic when Brad seduces me in front of the log-burning stove. Sprawling naked on my rug, I promise to get dressed after he makes me a cup of hot milky coffee. I want something warm other than sperm inside me before I go out into the cold night but lying all cosy in the heat from the flames of the fire, I am fast changing my mind about that scenario.

After a bit of convincing while moaning, I eventually shift myself. I have a quick shower, put on my perfume with the warmest clothes I have got, before heading out grumbling about it being as cold as Siberia.

The bonfire display is amazing, so much more romantic than I could have imagined. Brad holds me close with his hands under my heavy winter jacket, both to keep his hands warm whilst and to play with my nipples in public, but no one notices as it is hidden under the thick material. The sky is shimmering and glittering with all the stunning colours of the rainbow. The bonfire is roaring in front of us, yet still doesn't take the chill out of the air.

As the fireworks show comes to end, I turn to Brad whispering, "Let's go for a walk, Brad. Look at the stars, the sky is gorgeous tonight." Brad looks up agreeing with me as we go along the shore. The crowd starts to disperse, so it is quiet now but just as cold still it felt so romantic holding hands in the crisp night air.

Walking along the beach, we arrive at Greenan Castle, which we pretend belongs to us. Brad is the prince, with me his princess. The setting is idyllic, a once elegant old castle sitting on the coastline. We go into the castle ruin as Brad takes me firmly in his arms, undoes his jeans, bends me over, takes down my pants, entering me from behind, moaning aloud, he pushes every inch of him up into me as he wraps his arms around my body. Pushing up my clothes he firmly grips my breasts, playing with them once again. I am so excited, with my nipples hard as he thrusts faster still; looking up through the open roof, I can see the stars twinkling above me in the dusky, navy-blue sky. I can hear the waves bashing the rocks beneath us, in the air I can smell the salt from the sea and seaweed; it is an alluring, enchanting magical place to make love. As he cums, I feel his legs shuddering with mine, me gently cat calling in pleasure responding in the same way. I love his sperm being put right up inside me. "COW!" I say to myself out loud. Brad laughs.

We kiss each other, sorting our clothes back together, kissing again just before we leave; we hear voices coming from dog walkers who take the path right by us. Risky business this fucking outdoors, we almost got caught; laughing about it, Brad feels that is part of the excitement, I just think of it as a charming thing to do in my castle. If I'm being very truthful, the ruined castle is perfect because in a lot of ways it's as fucked as me. It was in bad need of repair, taking thousands of pounds to restore it to the once grand magnificent self; well, I smile thinking to myself, *I could also do with some of that.*

On the way back home we stop off at a take-away to pick up a Chinese meal, and then we go to buy some red wine. On entering the house the warmth of it envelopes me like a hot blanket, making me realise just how icy the night air outside has become. I light candles, and then there on my rug in the candlelight with the glow from the hearth, we eat our food, drinking wine just as fireworks bang in the distance. Rio bolts, landing on me, toppling us all including the wine onto the floor. Rio is flat out beside me covered in my drink as Brad is screaming with laughter. Later in our bed, I am so content inside as we have just shared two of the most amazingly resplendent days, being so happy together. I look over at him sleeping, kiss the curls on his head, whispering to him, "Goodnight you," before pulling the quilt over my head.

The following weeks pass by with Brad's mother's condition worsening. There is lots of tension between us leading to loads of arguments. Sometimes we are great together and I do try to be very supportive, whilst other times we are just in days of continuous fighting, which condemns the relationship to being extremely rocky. It is like Christmas day every day when it's great, he is all my presents on legs, but mostly recently, it is like most evenings having the devil to dinner. Brad hides how he is feeling, but I know how much he's hurting. The pressure of Brad's mother being so ill as well as trying to adjust to living full-time with me, plus the fact that doing so he is much further away from his mother now, not just across the road anymore, everything taking into consideration is beginning to take its toll on the relationship. Both of us are losing hope, knowing however much I scream at Him to stop it and make her well and as much as I pray, God is going to take her home anyway.

As Christmas approaches, it is a dire time for us all. I did not even celebrate Winter Solstice, also known as Yule. A similar celebration to the twelve days of Christmas, that Christians celebrate at this time of year. Although, Christians celebrate the birth of Christ, and Yule is connected to the birth of the Sun God, child of the goddess. I just make a spell, casting some serenity and peace in the home. I re-energise myself and my crystals, cleansing negativity away. It helps me, but Brad is beyond himself as it becomes clear that his mother is dying. I take the situation very badly, screaming, refusing to believe she is leaving me. I find myself being quite selfish without meaning to be. I don't want her to die, not now. Not ever. I want more time. There is so much I want us to do together. She had to see me in my wedding dress… she can't die, especially not now, please God, not at the time of year. She wanted to see Christmas, she told me so. I get so focused on how much I just want the illness gone from her body, giving me more time with her, that I don't even notice what Brad is going through… I am so out of it all that I'm not there for him at all really. Our relationship even gets to the position of hopelessness, where we fight almost every day; we hurt each other deeply, using words we don't mean. In my frustration I tell Brad just to fuck off back to his wife in his hometown. Brad is losing his mother; he is losing me as I lose faith in everything else.

22ⁿᵈ December 2012

Today Brad's mother takes a turn for the worse and Brad takes me up to the hospital to visit her. What I am faced with is so devastating… she is no longer the woman I remember. Her beautiful doll-like face has become so pale – a horrible shade of grey, she is hallucinating, adding to the fact that the morphine drip doesn't even begin to touch the constant pain she is suffering. When I say, "Hello, Mum," she smiles but I have no idea if she even recognises me as she struggles to stay awake.

I go to her, holding her hand, talking to her for a while, calling her mum because that is what she feels like to me. She loved me calling her that, getting me to say it over and over when she came to my house with Brad. I remember back to last week when late at night I visited her at home. She told me she was happy to have met me, thanking me for making her son happy. She then said that no matter how many people disapprove of us, I am to attend her funeral with my head held high. She also asked me to keep my promise to her that I would marry Brad. Then she stated quite clearly with vengeance, I was not to let Brad go back to stay over the road in that house ever with HER (his wife), not ever again. On saying that, she then instructed me that I was not to let anybody take any more of Brad's money, under no bloody circumstances, as she felt that the household took more than enough from him as the Craw spent most of Brad's pay on her family for years upon years. She was very bitter and very defiant that I would follow this request. One of Brad's sisters witnessed this conversation that night and was very much in agreement on both counts.

Just before I leave the hospital, I promise her with tears streaming down my face to honour my word to her. Before I leave the hospital room, I go over to her bedside, leaning down to kiss her forehead, whispering "Goodbye and goodnight, Mum" softly into her ear. That night when I get home, I light candles that symbolise health and wishing she has a longer life, I make spells asking for a miracle for her to live, then I pray and pray to the Lord not to take her away. Deep down I knew no matter what spells I made to the high priestess or even to the Lord, they weren't going to listen to me, they were going to take her anyway.

Christmas Eve 2012

The spells of course would not work this time as it was time for her to go. I cast a spell asking for help to save her from suffering, I did my best and my prayers to the lord went unanswered, but I tried to keep her no matter what. Brad's mum died tonight on Christmas Eve; she went to sleep forever. God went ahead and took his angel back home, as her work down here on earth was now finally done. When I kissed her saying goodbye, I knew that would be the last time I would ever see her. Brad had spent the final days going in and out the hospital to visit her. I can't imagine what he must be going through right now, I was just numb with shock and the pain I felt inside was unbelievable. On hearing the sad news that she was gone, I couldn't believe it and fucking wouldn't accept it. I went straight and phoned her house; it rang out she wasn't home; as the phone rang and rang still I waited and waited for her to answer my call. She never did.

Christmas Day 2012

Christmas morning is a nightmare for us. Just fucking awful. Brad is lying in bed staring into space when I come in from working night shift. We don't work together anymore in the forensic unit, I now work nightshift elsewhere. I go to Brad, he holds me tight, kissing me. It's like a desperate need to fill the emptiness he feels inside. He is so lost and for me he's trying to make our first Christmas together special, as normal as possible under the horrific circumstances. Brad gets up, trying to continue the day in the best way he knows how; he wants us to be happy together, knowing that it is what his mother would have wished for us. He gave me a beautiful wife card with lots of expensive gifts as in; leather boots at £300 with a bottle of Moet & Chandon Champagne including Christian Dior foundation and J'Adore perfume plus COCO Mademoisselle Chanel perfume both large bottles. I am completely spoiled. After giving me my presents, we have some breakfast, and then decide to go to lie down for a little while as we are both completely shattered.

Brad also bought me some different things from Ann Summers, which hadn't yet been used as there has been so much going on. Some very pretty, sexy underwear, strawberry lubricant, with a glitter pink vibrator. Brad asks me to go and get all the stuff. I look at him, thinking this was a strange request at a time like this. He orders me to put the underwear on. I just sit staring at him. "Go Coco, now," ardently he repeats himself, so I go.

Into my bathroom I wander to put on these beautiful silk garments whilst still half asleep. When I return to the bedroom, I find Brad is now lying naked on top of the covers with his hard cock standing straight up in the air. I walk up to the bed slowly, gently touch his hard-on by running my nails down it, looking at him sadly. I feel it is inappropriate to have sex just now but I drop the robe off my shoulders anyway to reveal the white silk delicate lace bra beneath. With my sad eyes searching his face, I notice that in his excitement the expression he is wearing is showing me a look of passion. I lower myself down next to him, he touches me on top of the material of the silk knickers, commenting that he loves the fact that my vagina is as always as smooth as ice (I don't allow any hair to grow there) for him. My little tattoos are peeping out the sides of my little pants. I have a four-leaf clover on the right side and four little hearts on the left side (One heart for each letter of his name, so secretly the hearts spell B.R.A.D.). It feels like it has been so long since he touched me there, I have missed him so much.

He grabs me in his arms, holding me close while running his fingers through my hair, seductively putting his tongue in my mouth. His breathing becomes laboured as he whispers to me, "God you are so beautiful, Coco. I have missed being with you like this so much." I French kiss him, flickering my tongue back in and out of his mouth; he groans, pulling me into him by the hair, kissing more hungrily.

"Fuck me, Coco, please, Coco," he gasps between breaths, unable to hold back any longer. Brad then rolls me over, putting his hands between my legs, opening them wide. He removes my tiny panties, sliding his fingers into my little secret place. He picks up the glitter vibrator, covering it in lubricant, turning it on as he touches me so lightly with it, playing with me, allowing its buzzing tip to almost hit my clitoris, sending pleasurable little sensations through me time after time. He is teasing me so much, putting it inside me a little farther each time, changing the settings to see the effect it is having on me. He is driving me crazy using it, then as he switches it on to a pumping mode, making it produce the feeling in me of him ejaculating in me over and over.

"Oh God, Brad, that feels like you are filling me with your sperm. I'm going to cum, oh! Brad, please don't stop!" I scream as my legs tremble while the warmth rushes through me and all over the vibrator; I feel I can hardly move my legs, they are numb with being in the same position so long. He leans over me, kissing my mouth, moving down to suck my cute hard rocks of nipples. I glance down; his hard-on is pulsing with excitement. I can't take this teasing anymore, I need him inside me. Taking him in my hand, I place the throbbing cock right at my little secluded lips. He puts his hardness deeply into me, I don't think I want him ever to stop, not ever. I am so ecstatic as he lies on top of me, holding me so tight while he says my name each time he penetrates me time and time again, then, getting faster still, when he is approaching his climax, my body shudders. I can feel my vagina tighten around him, causing him to squirt his entire load up me, completely emptying him for now. This causes me to have another orgasm, putting my sweet juice on his still hard penis. Afterwards as we cuddle up together, both of us in agreement that was some of the best sex we have ever had.

"You're some ride, Brad Blake," I blurt out, causing us both to buckle in hysterics. I am teasing him in fun, but this is not an appropriate time. He smiles all the same though saying that I do have a way with my words. Deep down inside me, way behind all this sex lay a dark emptiness, what were we doing trying to do bury an unbearable pain? Pretending everything was normal as Brad's mother lay asleep forever on this Christmas morning. Fuck knows, but I do know this was not the answer by far.

We decided that we better get up, moreover, go to prepare the Christmas dinner. Just at that, someone is furiously knocking on the front door. I quickly throw on my robe, running down the stairs in a panic. The desperation of the person who is banging it off its hinges for an answer on a Christmas morning, is making me worried that something awful has happened or is seriously wrong as the glass on the front door get desperately rattled even harder. I pass by front door at the bottom of my hall, I saw through the frosted window, a shadow which looked like the young boy from up the road, he brings me a Christmas card and one chocolate every single Christmas morning. I go out of the back door, then hurry around the side of the house; to my surprise, I see an old lady standing on my doorstep. She turns on hearing me approach. I recognised her instantly from the photographs I had seen in their marital home, it was Brad's wife. *What the fuck was she doing at my house on Christmas morning?*

She stays put, gaping over at me for a moment as if considering her next move, suddenly flinging her arms way up in the air while holding her handbag; she comes marching down the steps wearing a look of madness. In a very high-pitched shrill voice she comes towards me, waving the bag and screaming, "Who invited you to Meg Blake's funeral?" She yells so loud that the whole fucking street can hear her. "Well, who invited you, what right have you got going to her funeral?" I just walk away but she follows me; she pushes me with the bag into a bush, then the bag attacks me, knocking me onto the wet grass in my bare feet, it isn't even worth a response. I should have just got my wand though and landed her on her fucking old arse!

Stupid, squealing banshee of a decrepit woman with this dangerous bag, wearing bright blue eyeliner, which is just as horrendous as her! She obviously has no idea of the close relationship that I had with Brad's mother, besides it was her wish that I be there, because that is what Brad's mother had told me she wanted. The other reason was that Brad's mother always claimed she considered me to be her daughter-in-law now and not this fucking squawking crow doing karate with a clutch bag. Brad's mother was a wonderful woman with an extraordinary personality; she loved all the secrecy of the affair. She had been on holiday to Megan's with me and Brad and she wore my coats. I loved her like she was my own, but there was no point in explaining this to Brad's wife because she had clearly arrived at the door early on Christmas morning hell-bent on causing trouble despite everything else that has been going on. I thought this was shocking behaviour, especially as Brad's mother had just died. I am horrified at her performance, Brad even more so, he is totally mortified, his face bright red with embarrassment at this nonsense. Megan is getting the blame of it all, as usual. I said it has nothing to do with Megan but she continues insisting that it is and her fault. Her carry on is deplorable, demanding information, asking personal questions about Brad and me, which if I had answered truthfully, would have destroyed her illusions very much, so for her sake they went ignored.

I just go round the back again into the house, closing the door behind me on her face, *so rude* I thought. She now bangs at that door blaring to be let in in a voice similar to the singer Kate Bush, when at the top of her range. *Fuck me; the whole town will hear her.* I am about to open it and invite her in when Brad appears behind me in his robe. Brad answers it and she barges into the kitchen. Brad talks to her a while but regardless of that, she is still demanding blatantly to speak with me.

"Who invited you to Meg Blake's funeral?" piercingly her voice shrieks he question s again as I enter my kitchen.

"My mother-in-law did," I say sternly, taking a step forward; Brad comes to stand beside me.

"I already told you my mum invited her to the funeral," Brad adds, backing me up. Glancing at me and then Brad, she scowls.

"Is he sleeping in your spare room?" she squeals. *"Are you kidding me?"* Apparently not, as she is very serious asking me this question too, clearly looking for an honest answer. I glare at Brad, *"Is she having a fucking laugh?!"* wondering if this is what he has told her or told somebody else, who has then forwarded this information on to her. I am speechless, I don't know what to say and I certainly don't want to hurt her on Christmas day if this is her belief, "This is like, like a script for a soap opera, you, you are like a character out of *EastEnders*!" I acknowledge in referral to her. This statement adds further fuel to her fire, as she screams even more mortified at the comparison, still demanding to know if I am sleeping with him. I am confused, looking at Brad and back to her again. I can feel his sperm running down my leg. Is she fucking asking me this for real?

"Don't even answer that, your face says it all!" she yells hysterically before storming out, slamming my door behind her.

After ensuring she was gone, I discuss with Brad whether or not I should go to the funeral if his wife and family were going to create issues. Brad reassures me that I am going to the funeral with him and that they can all go and fuck themselves because we were honouring one of his mother's last wishes in doing so.

I really did not expect this on Christmas day, when we were trying to make it as normal as possible. *What the fuck is normal about a time like this?* Despite everything, I tell Brad to go after her to see if she is all right. He takes the presents from us to the house of the horrid, deplorable step-grandchildren informing me they are as ugly as her as is their mother. Brad expects that the Craw will also be there. She isn't. Brad assumes she has gone to her first husband's grave as apparently she had always done this at Christmastime. This is surreal, I look at him in disbelief, this script should be written for television drama right enough. We have Christmas dinner with my son, River, accompanied by a very expensive Chardonnay he bought for us. It is lovely meal, unusual but nice. We have all the trimmings but no turkey; it got put in the freezer as we were unsure of what was going to happen under the circumstances. Still I just have extra of the luxury Christmas pudding with homemade sherry cream. *With chocolates and more wine, to the Lord I be thankful for a frozen turkey.*

Afterwards I sit thinking about how much Christmas had changed. Not so long ago on Christmas mornings my children Jet and River would be up at the crack of dawn opening all their presents in front of the log fire. Fairy lights and candles would glow everywhere in the house. All the rooms would smell of cinnamon from the warmed mincemeat pies. We would all sit around the table for a fancy dinner, served in the best china crockery. Then I would quickly tumble everything into the dishwasher to sit down with some of the leftover wine and truffles to watch the old movie 'Gone with the Wind'. When as a child I always wanted a dress like Scarlett O' Hara's, my daddy used to say I was enough trouble without wearing that. It wasn't like that anymore with the kids all grown up now and my daughter far away from home. I just wish for one minute I could turn back time, just for this one day, as it has been the most terrible of Christmases for us all, I guess. Would have been even worse for the Christmas morning squawking eejit of a crow Brad announced, if she'd been taken into my lounge as she would have noticed the wife Christmas card Brad gave me, with all the expensive romantic gifts which she never at all got from him, not once. Then there is sitting beside the fox a beautiful loving photograph of Brad and me and the pictures of his mum and dad, all in old-fashioned expensive dark wood frames; she would've freaked and her answer to her questions would have truly been answered.

Brad and I share a relaxing bath together before he had to get ready for his night shift. Given everything that has happened today, I just want to spend the night cuddled into Brad. Our relationship, well that's another story, anyway tonight we both should be at work. The mental health unit needs Brad and I feel I need the mental health unit, so it is our first Christmas night together spent apart, with Brad in a forensic ward and me not going in to work to the most horrible job I ever had in my life. The staff rota was changed to suit me. So I stay home drinking my Christmas bottle of Champagne, eating chocolates whilst watching a movie, happily relaxing under the fairy lights of the Christmas tree.

Boxing Day to Hogmanay 2012

Boxing Day comes and goes; we have our turkey for dinner with an amazing sherry trifle with bramble cream for dessert. Trying to get through the week, we have a lot on our minds. It certainly isn't the rosy festive period we had wished for, spending our first Christmas living together as husband and wife. It didn't really matter that much to me as we had other years to play Mr and Mrs Blake in a romantic Christmas fantasy. Brad's mother just wanted this Christmas, which she didn't get and now all her Christmases were gone forever just as she was. Gone forever.

I spend a lot of time making sure Brad is okay, being supportive, making sure not to slip into pointless arguments, which just made matters worse for everybody concerned.

As the New Year approaches, I realise that a few people apart from attacking crow, also disapproved of me attending the funeral, another one person in particular, a member of his family, definitely did not want me to attend on January 4th, but there was no way Brad was denying his mother her final wish, so he tells me we are going and that is final. "We will stand at the very back of the crematorium with River, so we are the last people to go in and the very first out as we will leave through the back exit. Fuck them all, Coco." He meant every single word he said.

The New Year Bells, 2012–2013

We decided not to go out partying, so we would just watch the Edinburgh ceremony bringing in the New Year on TV instead. Sharing a couple of glasses from an exclusive bottle of Pommery Cuvee Louise Rose champagne (a little luxury I became acquired too that I first tasted in Dorchester Hotel in

London many years ago) that Brad had bought for us. At midnight the bells rang as we say goodbye to the old year holding our crystal flute glasses in a toast to all we have loved and lost. May God bless all of us left behind on earth, until in Heaven we meet again. So the New Year came in bringing with it hopes, dreams and promises to change our lives but most of all, reminding us never to forget we only have each other on borrowed time. Champagne finished as hand in hand we climb the stairs, sadly wishing to find happiness amongst all the hurt, as we go to bed.

Lying in bed staring out the window, I can't sleep. As fireworks from the celebrations explode loudly wakening up the night, sprinkling the dark sky in a rainbow of glittery colours, my mind wanders back over the past few years. Remembering in such clear detail everything that has happened, from making the decision to have an affair with a married man, leading up to Brad next to me sound asleep. Then on to him leaving his wife for me. What a whirlwind this relationship is, wrong description. My feelings have been up and down as much as my knickers have been. Being a mistress was amazing sometimes, no, not really as it came with a lot of emotional turmoil, with the correct description of this affair being that wisdom begins with wonder…

Chapter II
The Beginning of the Affair

October 2008

The Mediterranean air is hot and humid. Even with the air con on, inside the apartment it still feels all clammy, causing these chocolate coloured silk sheets to cling to my body, the expensive body lotion is melting leaving me all covered in a sticky slime. Thunder is booming outside with rain battering hard against the patio doors. In the tropical storm large shadows are waving in front of the window in the dark, making it a very ghostly picture outside tonight. I realise it's just the palm trees swaying in the wind. Fuck, I came to Portugal for the good weather! Unable to sleep, I decide to get up and go out onto the balcony. The lightening is streaking across the sky, which lights up the bay in a beautiful pale purple hue. The raindrops are warm as they land on my naked body, yet still it is a refreshing change from the suffocating heat indoors. Going back inside, I notice the floor is wet where the rain has marched in through the open doors.

This is my luxury timeshare apartment in Praia D' Oura; it costs a lot of money but is very much worth it. Football players with other high-flyers stay here. Who would have thought Coco from the council estate could afford all this fancy shit... yet I feel so comfortable here in this amazing very expensive space. I feel that I do belong and could stay forever in this exotic place. I feel very comfortable in the world of the rich. Sometimes however, just at certain times, but not always, I just wish I had a husband to share it all with. Perhaps I should attempt to find one soon these are my final thoughts before heading back to bed to sleep. I finish a glass of pink champagne, the Dom Perignon Rose was taken from a complementary wicker basket containing two bottles, the other was a Brut, and they were left with Rose

Champagne chocolates along with a crate type box filled with other luxury foods which I received on arrival.

I wake up the next morning to sun shining brightly high in the sky. I can hear drunken singing outside, likely guys just getting back from their night out, Welsh boys I presume, because it sounds like they are singing the Welsh national anthem I am out here with my son, River, who accompanies me to the restaurant downstairs. Mother and son, out for another champagne breakfast together, with nobody bothering about River being under age though, besides he looks over eighteen that's for sure. I hope everyone thinks brother and older sister. *Wishful thinking!* The food is always delicious and so fresh, there's such a lot of variety to choose from.

River and I then proceed to have a wonderful two weeks living in this luxury lifestyle. We explore modern places as well as go into the old town with its old-fashioned cobbled streets, where little unusual shops had found a hideaway. I enjoy being with River, he is having a fucking ball! Champagne breakfasts, lunch on little tables outside on the pavements of exclusive little restaurants, where they served some the best wines in Portugal with their expensive food. More wine with dinner in the evenings, the way of life here is so laid back and is a world away from back home. The wicker baskets in the apartment are filled with different expensive champagnes each day, not inclusive in the price of course, you pay for what you drink. Anyway River had to be limited in the amount of alcohol he had, I was floating never mind him. Still as much as I loved my son, I can't help thinking again I'd like to be here with a husband. This place is so romantic. I'm very independent though, so perhaps I could find myself a married man to share it with instead, one who would spoil me by whisking me away to other luxurious places like this, someone to love and share things with but without the constant rules and tediousness of a full-time partner. Yes, that is what I decided to do. That night as I paddled along in the warm sea, on the beach at sunset, I smirked wickedly thinking, *I will have an affair. Cast spells asking for an illicit lover who will spoil me. What about love? What's that?*

Soon it was time for River and me to pack up to head back home to my everyday life in Scotland, but by then I had declared my decision that I no longer wanted a husband, instead I desired to experience the glamorous life of being a mistress... with glamorous being the thought. I will approach it like a business contract, the terms and conditions designed to suit both of us, and with self-discipline will most definitely not fall in love with him. Now I just have to find the right married man to negotiate my proposal with. *If Coco sets her mind to do something, then she will do it, as she always does exactly what she wants.*

Upon returning home, I find a letter offering me an interview at a forensic mental health unit. I guess that now I will attend as the plan I had of being able to set up my own business of opening a strip club in Portugal was at present no longer an option. The club was not available for sale anymore, so this job would be great in the meantime, until I find more suitable premises. I attend donning my new expensive suit, whereupon I'm delighted to learn that I got the position applied for. I start work almost immediately. A few days into the new job, I'm informed that from the 16th of the month I will be working with a Bradford Riley Blake, who will be returning from his holiday in Canada back to work soon.

16th October

Well, tonight I head to work as normal and on entering the ward, I notice a new face sitting on the chair by the window staring at me. I subtly lean over to a colleague, asking if the person is a new patient.

"No, Coco that is Brad Blake, your new night shift partner," my co-worker replies, giggling.

Glancing back over at Brad, he is still watching me intensely, our eyes lock. It is slightly uncomfortable, so I look away. After or during the report, due to the ignorance of the staff, nobody introduced us, so everybody then left, leaving me and Brad alone in the room.

"Hi, you must be Brad. I'm Coco, I'm your new night shift partner or so I'm told," I say confidently, introducing myself whilst presenting my hand to Brad.

"Yes, I'm Brad, pleased to meet you. Yes, it looks like we will be working together for a while anyway, according to the staff rota. I thought the guys were winding me up when they'd told me your name was Coco, apparently not," he responds smiling, shaking my hand.

"No, it's different," I reply.

"Yes, you are!" he answered, turning his back then walking out the duty room door.

17th October

The nurse in charge this evening suggests that Brad show me the role of security nurse with the responsibilities it involved. Once we get upstairs, Brad attempts to inform me about all the different types of security keys. Whilst he is doing this, I just keep on staring up at him. Thinking that me looking at him indicates that I don't understand what each key is used for, he starts the explanation all over again. I understood perfectly, I was paying attention; however, I was seriously thinking that I just wanted to kiss him – like there and then. I watch how his dark green gypsy eyes sparkle in the low lights of the hallway; I feel his full lips are just waiting to be kissed as he stares back at me. Although we have just met, the connection in the atmosphere is intense, my feelings for him are so dangerous... well maybe, but was this not what I wanted after all, as in Portugal I'd decided I wanted to be a mistress, so Brad Blake, being already married, was perfect a candidate for my plan, was he not?

I go to Adam's place (he's my gay best friend) first thing the next morning to tell him all about Brad Blake. Adam is shocked at my behaviour. Adam and I go way back, he is one of the wealthy people who befriended me in my younger days. He taught me how to dance way up at a different level as he was qualified as a male ballet dancer. Adam's opinion is that I should have an affair with Brad Blake if he is willing, as after all, what have I got to lose?

31st October

One of the witches' 8 Sabbats, as well as, being one of the major ones. We call it Samhain, also known as Halloween. It is the night when spirits of our dead friends and of our loved ones return briefly to celebrate with us in the living world. It is a very old custom of the ancient Druids to carve out eerie faces on pumpkins, as this was believed to scare away the bad witches and the malevolent who would return to haunt the living on Samhain night.

It however, is also the Druids' New Year, and the most important of all to the Sabbats, as it is a sacred festival marking the end of a goddess-ruled summer and welcoming the beginning of the god-ruled winter. Tonight, I celebrate in style, eating wild berry bread I baked earlier and drinking homemade Samhain cider until I can hardly see my fucking broom. Bad witch. Me. Besides, I am certainly not scared of the evil spirits. I am drunk and shouting out to Satan asking him to come and join my party. I can dance to him playing his fiddle. *Fuck off Coco, this is not what you are supposed to do, you are a white witch, but you are so moving more and more to the dark side!*

6th November

Brad and I continue to work together constantly on the night shift. Tonight, the ward is very quiet at mid shift as everyone is in bed, so we just sit talking about various areas of our personal lives. We speak about how we grew up, where we came from… then eventually, that I was single and that although Brad was married, he was very unhappy in the marriage, with him and his wife living separate lives. He tells me that he hasn't had sex with her for years or with anyone else for that matter. Well, well, well! This is a perfect situation for me. We both know that night we'd end up in bed together. It was only a matter of time. "Just time, Coco!" he says to me as he goes off to make us coffee. I know exactly what he is talking about without further explanation.

November–December 2008

Over the next two months, we become extremely close. There are a few times when Brad asks to kiss me when taking me home in the jeep after our shift, but I'm still unsure, so I always change the subject to deflect the situation. Brad becomes jealous of the other guys at work spending time with me, it is clear he wants me for himself.

Brad becomes quite obsessive with me and for some reason he questions what I did and who I was with on my nights off, which were very few because we worked most nights together. When Brad put his name in to do overtime at the clinic, he put my name down on the off duty along with him to cover all of the spare shifts. I request the 21st of December off, to celebrate Winter solstice which we also call Yule. It is another celebration on the witches' calendar. We celebrate the birth of the Sun God, this being the shortest day and the longest night of the year. From this point on, the days become longer. We have yule logs and mistletoe, just like at Christmastime. I get no peace, Brad constantly phones me demanding to know where I am, what I am doing? I switch my phone off, completely ignoring him. The following night when I am on the ward and he is off, I don't answer my phone to him, so he phones the ward and I instruct the nurse in charge to tell him I am busy. He knows that is a lie and comes into work at ten o'clock at night looking for me. Staff are now very much aware of the relationship forming between us as at work people are starting to say that Brad is totally besotted with Coco. My thoughts are exactly that, though I prefer to think of him as bewitched by me, and I wonder at what he has told his wife to get out of the house so late, probably something like he had to return to work with keys or a similar story, whatever it was, the lies he told her just to get to see me… Hmm!

Christmas Day 2008

Today Brad and I have made plans to have sex tonight in my lounge, on my rug in front of the log fire, with the twinkle of the Christmas tree fairy lights glowing in the dark. We haven't even kissed yet, so at this point I have no idea at all why I agreed to do this with him. Maybe because I thought it would be such romantic thing to do, making love with him for the very first time on Christmas Day. Brad comes down as agreed but on seeing him arrive at my house, I rush out to the jeep, so Brad doesn't get the chance to come in. I don't go through with it, so we ended up at work over an hour early instead. Later that evening Brad tells me a sad story pretending to be upset, hoping that I would comfort him. I don't. Instead, I tell him an old tale of how when the geese were in a pond outside my childhood home, a very long time ago, one Winter it snowed so heavily so that the pond, well it very quickly, froze over, so the geese, they flew away taking the pond with them, now that pond lies today somewhere over in Mississippi. It keeps the mood light-hearted. Brad is disappointed we never made love, but then again in a sad kind of way, so am I.

Christmas–New Year 2008

The week following Christmas the air is electric between Brad and me, and it must have been obvious as multiple members of staff and patients now began to pass comments about us. One night I have to work a night shift on my own as Brad is off. Having coffee with Bobby, we get talking about my situation, he was our charge nurse. We laugh about how I would cope on shift tonight without Brad as he'd become my wingman, which led to us getting the nicknames of Maverick and Goose (from Top Gun), little did I know then that he would go from being my wingman to becoming my fucking wings.

Even though we aren't in a sexual relationship yet, it is round about this time that Brad starts to buy me little presents like strawberry milkshakes from McDonald's and randomly brings gifts of bars of chocolate and cheesecake. I love the way he spoils me, calling me his Princess Coco. *The spell I cast has worked this time for sure.*

Hogmanay 2008

Hogmanay arrives with another year almost over. I am at Adam's house today, waiting for the limo to pick us up as I am performing in Edinburgh tonight, I'm dancing there to celebrate the bringing in of the New Year. I'm excited, so I'm looking forward to the evening, but I really do wish Brad could be with me for the bells. As I sit in my old ripped jeans, Ugg boots and white T-shirt (with no bra) – this is my trademark outfit when travelling to do a show – my mind wanders off and I'm thinking about Brad, wondering what he will be doing tonight, whilst Adam is frantically double-checking times, PA systems and stage arrangements before it's time to leave.

Glancing down at my T-shirt, clearly seeing my nipples, I remember how one cold night at the clinic Brad had commented that he was impressed because he could see them showing through my underwear and my shirt. I've always been proud of how big and dark they are, so often I don't bother to wear a bra.

I snap back to reality as Jamie and Michael arrive with the purple limousine edging its way up the driveway. I love the huge letters along the side that read 'COCO'; it seriously gives me a high each time I see it, every single time. But I still feel disappointed that Brad can't be in my limo or share this night with me.

"Coco, no bra, as per," Michael says smiling, he greets me, with a kiss.

I hug him back. "Nope, no bra and no Brad," I say in a monotone response.

"Who the fuck is Brad?" Michael asks, playfully rubbing my hair which is already in a mess, but before I get a chance to answer him, we both turn around at the sound of a door opening behind us.

"Well! Well! Well! Look what the fucking wind blew in!" Adam bellows as he comes outside to greet Michael, whom he hasn't seen for some time now.

"You're the fucking fairy man, you're the one that flies with the wind," Michael laughs, shouting back at Adam. They walk up to each other, high-fiving with their hands.

"Right, Tinkerbell, you and fucking Peter Pan here hurry up and get in the limo. We're working to a tight schedule and now we're late as it is with Jamie fucking things up, giving me the wrong time to pick up the car," Michael says as he gestures us to get our stuff into the limo as time is really running out.

Next Ward turns up in his car to join us. He is wearing a very expensive designer suit in a dark purple. The suit is as always immaculate (and probably full of snow). He's a bit of a Mr Know-all but a great guy, besides we are very close and he is special to me in his own way. With everyone now here, we all depart for Edinburgh later than we had initially planned (This was the usual for us – always late, never early or even on time, for that matter). Looking around the limo at us all sat there, I think we must look an odd lot to outsiders. Ward has lightly tanned skin, extremely slim, very tall with blonde hair falling over in a side shed always flopping over his eyes. He is very handsome in an old-fashioned sort of way, with his shirt and tie and the tweed jackets he wore at times (a gentleman due to his upbringing and education, I suppose. He had old-school mannerisms as in times gone by). Michael is half his height, with Italian looks, dark hair, dark eyes and deep olive-toned skin; he is also very good looking. Women throw themselves at him (well actually they also throw themselves at Ward and so openly even more when they know or become aware of his fortune). Michael grew up in a deprived area in Glasgow. Looking at him now with the way he conducts himself and speaks, you can never tell, plus he also wears very expensive suits with handmade shoes, which screamed money to all who pass by. He had educated himself so well that you would never have guessed in a million years where he originally came from.

Then there is our Jamie, he is a big guy but a little smaller in height than Ward. He is very overweight and he carries it well. Deep down he's a kind nature with a big soft heart but his appearance makes him out to be different. He is bald-headed with tattoos, lacking education, which you noticed the minute he opened his mouth, he is also well known as the hard man from Glasgow. He is the total opposite of Michael, although from the same neck of the woods.

Then there is Adam, who is of average height, his physique is very toned with clear definition of six packs due to the ballet dancing. He is tanned (fake) very good looking, blonde hair, soft eyes. Adam has the same effect on women as Michael but he, as we all know, is only interested in men. I am extremely close each one of them, I have been for a long time now. They are what I call my shadow dance team as every time I move, one of them is there. Michael and Jamie are my personal security (Michael specialises in all the different forms of self-defence arts, whereas big Jamie just fucking fights). Ward deals with all the financial stuff. Adam sorts out the stage arrangements as well as playing the roles of personal trainer/choreographer, including being my dance partner on many occasions, depending on what is required of him at the time. I smile to myself, thinking I love them all very much.

Sitting in the limo I'm hungry as I don't eat before I dance. I forget about the hunger as my mind goes over the dance routines in my head, Brad constantly creeping into my thoughts, with me questioning whether he is going to be thinking of me tonight or not. Adam is mostly preoccupied, wearing headphones, looking for property to buy as an investment on the internet.

We arrive at the venue around six p.m. I head into the dressing room to start getting prepared for going on stage. First, my hair is shampooed again as it needs to be soaking wet so ice cubes can run down the strands to create a shine, once my hair is blow-dried and has a massive amount of volume due to all the products they use, my tan is then done (three layers) and left to dry. Next, all the body art is painted on, followed by all the individual jewels stuck on by hand one by one, and are all prepared accordingly. Now I may have a coffee. *Fuck! Thank you.*

Food is forbidden before I go on stage, so I am not allowed anything to eat. Ironically, however, I can take a line of snow, which Ward puts out for me as they start working on my hair. As I snort the white powder up my nostrils, I am hit with the sensation of the dry powder tickling the inside of my nose. Shaking my head as I look in the mirror, with a tissue I wipe my face, cleaning away any tell-tale traces of the powder. I don't take a lot of the so-called snow but I usually have a couple of lines on special occasions or sometimes on dance nights, it depends on my mood or perhaps if it is available for free, of course.

Even snow can't keep my mind off Brad though, so I decide to excuse myself, asking to leave the dressing room on the pretence I need to go to the bathroom (so I could go and try to call him), much to the annoyance of the hairdressers, who are half-way through doing my hair. It is awkward out in the hall trying to get signal with security watching me; also I'm shivering terribly with the cold from the ice being used on my head. Eventually, I get through on his house phone. His wife answers, so I just ask her if Brad is available to speak to please. Brad is in bed she tells me, but then his wife informs me that she'd take the phone through to his bedroom to let me talk to him. Brad says that he couldn't stop thinking about me and I had been in his thoughts all afternoon. He continues, saying he'd been out drinking all day with Jim and he'd told him how he felt about me so for now he is just resting a while as he intends going back out again later at night to avoid being with his wife at the bells ringing in the New Year as he wants only to be with me. He listens as I speak away a lot of pish before telling him what I really wanted to say, which is that I was missing him too, I just wanted to be in his arms naked. I hang up at that, hurrying back to the dressing room, thinking about what I had just said. Boldly I think *I am what I am!* I hold no regrets, I make no excuses. Well maybe a little but not much.

Speaking to Brad does not help me at all though, as after hearing his voice, I just want to be with him even more; however, secretly I am delighted he wouldn't be with her either at this special time of year. But the show must go on regardless, so I have to have my hair finished off like it or not

Standing in the wings of the stage waiting to perform my dance, the atmosphere is incredible. Coming out on to the stage makes me feel amazing. The crowd is endless, as far back as the eye can see, and they are so welcoming of me. The smell of hot dogs with the sweet scent of burnt sugar from the candyfloss is wafting in the breeze from nearby stalls. I don't even feel the chill in the night air as the adrenaline pumping through me keeps me from being cold in the tiny dance costume. Dancing in the streets of Edinburgh with the castle standing so tall and proud behind me is an honour. The dance on stage is one of the best I'd ever performed, the crowd sings along whilst dancing with me to the music, holding sparkling light sticks. As they sway back and forth, it looks like a sea of candles blowing in the wind. I am sorry when it is over. My favourite song of the night is being played, it reminds me of Brad. The lyrics are about having an affair with a married man and about the sweet deceit that comes with it. Heartbreakingly true are those words.

Back in the dressing room afterwards, I'm still on a bit of a high from knowing everything went brilliantly on stage, so after drinking some milky coffee, I indulge myself in another line of snow. The night has been extraordinary so far, but I can't fully enjoy myself, still wishing Brad was here with me. Sitting looking around at my friends, make-up off, snow on my face, I can't shake the feeling of being disappointed because he isn't. He'd have loved my performance. I guess I kind of hoped that Brad would have turned up at the concert as a surprise, but of course, he never did. How could he? Even if he could've driven with all that alcohol in him, then how would've he found me? Michael refuses to go back to collect him and bring him to me, besides it is very stupid of me to ask him, I suppose. Rather than dwelling on it too long, I enjoy the music I can hear from the other performers singing. I'm passionate about music and my dancing, so *forget about passion with Brad Blake*, I order myself for now. Fuck it. My friends, now all excited, are taking coke and drinking the hospitality champagne, which I choose not to do, when I take snow I prefer not to take alcohol. I just drink chilled water besides I'm dehydrated from all the dancing. Behind me I hear them all laughing, catching up with each other, gossiping about their lives. Smiling I join in, thinking this year I'm going to have a new life too. I add to the gossiping by informing them that I'm going to go to bed with a married man. *Seriously, Coco, so childish!*

I enjoy some time with everyone celebrating bringing in the New Year. As I hold my glass to the stars, I whisper in the darkness, "Happy New Year to Jet and River and Happy New Year to you Blake." I'm not up for an after-party, besides I can't stay anyway as my management team won't allow it, so we all just head for the limo to get on our way now. On the road back home, I decide I want to go to his hometown to see Brad first before going to my house. Considering it a good plan, I decide to ask the limo driver to take me. He says nothing. In the dark, Michael pulls out his guitar, playing old songs whilst singing of times gone by, the deep melody of his voice echoes through the car in the night. Big Jamie joins in the singing. Well, he can hold a tune, I guess. Soon the whole limo does the same, as everybody makes requests to Michael, he plays song after song as they all sing along. Me, I just stare at the darkness flashing by, the tinted windows make the night look very cold and the moon look eerie, besides I wonder if Blake sees the same moon I do. Or is he sleeping now?

In the end though, I do not get my way I am not allowed to go to his hometown, no way am I allowed to do this, neither am I allowed to get dropped at Adam's place. I am taken fucking straight home. You would think I was ten years old the way I got ordered around. On saying goodnight then wishing them all a good New Year, I get out of the limo, not pleased but exhausted going into my empty house. Lying in bed, I cuddle into my covers, pretending Brad is with me before eventually drifting off to sleep.

Waking up a while later, there are texts from Brad wishing me a New Year, followed by – to my surprise – some very angry voicemails from him ranting that I should've called by now to wish him a happy New Year. I am stunned by his reaction but call, which calms him a little. His actions make me wonder about our relationship, which is at present none existent. Yet.

It was last night that for the first time I realised just how much I really felt for Brad Blake. Wanting only him there with me, feeling lonely without him. I wished he could've brought in the bells with me, and then we could've gone to bed together, naked, with his body touching mine. Now I am beginning to think he feels as much for me, if not even more than I feel for him.

Later he phones me back apologising for his earlier behaviour, stating that he loves me so much and last night was hell, like the worst New Year ever as he had to bring it in without me. After that, he goes off the phone. It was then that I decided for certain I wasn't going to shy away anymore, I was going to start being intimate with Brad Blake. In 2009 for sure, I would become Brad Blake's mistress.

New Year Dance Is Over – 2009 Begins

I start my New Year with a tidy house, and then prepare a nice New Year Day's dinner. Homemade soup to start, followed by traditional steak pie with all the trimmings. To follow is hot chocolate fudge cake with cream. Later in the bathroom I lay out what little snow I have left over. Changing my mind about taking it, instead I rinse it down the drain, watching the white powder wash away. I don't like taking snow every day, besides now I have a new addiction in a whole different league… Brad Blake. As I look at my reflection in the bathroom mirror, I say out loud, laughing, "Oh! Mirror! Mirror! I'm sure to fall; he's going to be the biggest addiction of them all." The voices in my head reply for the mirror as it talks back, *"Oh Coco, how the truth you do talk, he will become your oxygen and without him you won't be able to breathe or walk."* Damn, fuck damn it with an answer like that, maybe I would be better off with the snow. Looking back into the mirror, I acknowledge with deep thought that no maybe about it, I know I would. Perhaps I knew this from the beginning of the affair.

Chapter III
January to March – Valentines, Spellbound and Bewitched

January brought snow (the weather kind) along with crisp cold mornings which I love. I always wanted to get married in the snow, but it never happened.

This month Brad and I continued to grow even closer. Brad would leave his house for work an hour and a half earlier each day, picking me up sooner so that we could spend more time together. We would often go down to the beach, sitting in the jeep, kissing each other, watching the ocean waves lapping against the sand with the Isle of Arran in the distance as he held me to him. It is a beautiful view and I felt so happy inside. We were perfect for each other. He constantly told me how much he loved me, saying I made him feel so young again, whereas his wife had made him feel he had been put out to grass. We laughed so much; he said her face would turn the milk sour.

Although we never had sex, all through January we would continue to kiss and cuddle at the beach whilst touching each other in the car. I could see his erection sticking out in his black work trousers. We would often arrive at work with him hard and my knickers soaking wet. The sexual chemistry is so intense now that we had started to become sexually intimate with each other, it was apparent to all our colleagues that we have become an item. Every so often Brad would just come out and say, "Time Coco, just time. You will be mine; I will have you as mine. You will belong to me."

We share a lot of brilliant fun at times as we work away together. One night on the ward we spent hours laughing, making up a football team with all the staff members in it and what positions they would play. When we finished the teams, we pinned the lists up on the duty room noticeboard for all to see, but the staff were far less amused by it all than we were. They went berserk when they saw it, with them not knowing who was responsible. When we were asked, we just denied that it was us; after all we were in the teams too, as the managers. This made us laugh especially more so as all the staff could not work out who done it, blaming each other.

February with Brad
2nd February

Today I look forward to celebrating Candlemas: The Feast of Lights. It is also known as Imbolc, a fire festival celebrating the Goddess of Fertility, us witches say "sweeping out of the old" is symbolised by the sweeping of the magic circle with a witches' broom or besom as it is often called. Either the Priestess of the coven wears a brilliant crown of 13 candles on top of her head or I do, The Queen Witch, me, a crown of lights is prepared and left by the altar to be lit during the ritual. Another important Sabbat we celebrate is with traditional feasts of gypsy tea, fertility bread, poppy seed cake and homemade sage wine. I celebrate this, while Brad is at work. Brad has some time off work soon too though, he has also booked holidays as the 11th of February was his 50th birthday

3rd February

Brad turns up today in the jeep unexpectedly at the house, announcing that he'd been missing me with him, and then asking me to go out with him on our first official date. He's told his wife that he is required to attend fire training courses at the clinic that night, so we could spend quite a lot of time together without being uninterrupted by her. I agree to go with him so he comes back at six p.m. to pick me up, with him kissing me as soon as I get into the jeep.

We drive out to Dunure harbour, where there is an old-fashioned little pub he wants to take me too. It is romantic and out of the way. But when we arrive, it is all shut up so we headed to Croy Bay beach as an alternative. As we reach the shore, the stars above the ocean are so clear in the night sky. In the jeep, we play love songs as we talk some more, then in between that we are constantly kissing each other.

After a while we decide to go to a Chinese restaurant for dinner. We drive back to Ayr and go into a little quaint one at the bottom of the harbour. Brad has duck curry with fried rice and I chose sweet and sour pork. The food is excellent. At a little table hidden in the corner we share wine, and then have liquor coffees, making secret plans for spending the summer together and promises of always loving each other. Childish in a world of broken dreams, but it gave me hope. The candles flickering on the table along with his sweet forbidden kisses are so romantic in comparison to the storm in my heart from fear of the unknown.

After a lovely dinner, we leave the restaurant and we drive along Ayr beach in the darkness, you can hear the waves hitting the sand. We start kissing again, touching each other, we both become sexually aroused; the passion felt between us is unbelievable. Brad's tongue is going in and out of my mouth, his hands on my breasts; it is so erotic the way he whispers that he wants me. I have my hand on his jeans on top of his penis, which is solid in my grasp; I now want him inside me so much. Holding him, I whisper for the very first time, "Fuck me."

He moans, kissing me harder. "I can't, Coco, you're bleeding," he says hoarsely. He knows this because Brad was security nurse at the clinic a few nights back (which meant he was responsible for and held all the keys on him) so he had to go to the store cupboard to collect Tampax for me, that was the type of relationship we had, he knew everything about me including private things like when I had my period.

Brad continues to kiss me, holding me tightly, he teases my nipples. I continue to rub him hard on the material of his black jeans. The two of us are so excited, causing Brad to come in his pants. "Fuck, Coco, you make me feel like a teenager," he says, shaking his head. We laugh at knowing his pants are soaked, all sticky and wonder at how he would explain that to his wife after fire training. Well, after years of him having no sex, I just thought, what do you expect?

"Coco, stay out with me tonight. I will book us into a hotel, then phone her to tell her I'm stuck at work, having to do a night shift as the ward is short. Baby please, I need to be with you, I want you," Brad says to me, his voice pleading; in fact, he is begging me.

"Brad, look, I want you to okay but you know I'm bleeding, I can't make love with you tonight," I reply, annoyed at myself, thinking this stupid period, as always, had come at the wrong time.

"I don't give a fuck about that, I don't need sex but I really do need to be with you. Just us lying together naked, holding each other, spending the night with you is enough for me," Brad replies as he continues to kiss me ardently. I unbutton his jeans this time, with my hands on his penis I gently massage it, making him come again, now all over the jeans. Laughing, we clean up as best we can as now both pants and jeans were in a mess. Deciding to take me home as I refused to stay out all night, we leave the beach.

I look over at Brad. "I want you in my mouth, Brad," I say to him. Why would I do that? Why did I feel that way? I don't know; I just did. His face is expressionless as he just keeps driving, concentrating on the road as the car came onto a roundabout outside the police station.

"Brad, did you hear what I said?" I ask as I never got a response.

"Yes, Coco, you said you wanted me in your mouth," he answers, not looking at me. "I haven't had that in years, God the things you do to me," he informs me. I say nothing. All too soon we've reached our destination; he kisses me good night then goes back to his hometown a little despondent.

In my bedroom that night I wonder why I hadn't spent the night with him before… What was I thinking? I guess I just wanted our first time to be special but surprisingly, I really did want him in my mouth.

9th February

Brad's wife has left to go to England, so Brad is taking me to his house for the very first time. As soon as I get into the jeep, he compliments me for looking 'stunning'. I am wearing a soft brown and cream fur fleece, fawn jodhpurs and high wedge heel sheepskin boots with cream fur tops, which make the outfit exceptionally classy, also suited to the snowy weather. The snow lay thick on the ground as Brad drove the jeep up some hill called after his hometown which sat behind his house. An eerie feeling of emptiness hits you up there; apparently, houses stood at the top of that hill once upon a time. Highland cows are walking about, one of them being rather bold, comes right up to the window of the jeep, curiously looking in at us. "Look, Brad! Look at the cow, look at its beautiful face with its huge eyes and long eyelashes."

"Roll down the window, Coco; see if it's still there," he replies as we both laugh. From that moment on I became known between us as Brad's cow. Eh! Highland cow! I was classier than your normal one. Then he decides to take me to his house. I am kind of unsure of this but I go along with the idea anyway as he heads the car in that direction. On entering in the door leading to a dimly lit hall, I can see as I squint in the shadows after the brightness of outside that the house is aged looking, very old-fashioned inside, with plain décor and a stale smell of cigarette smoke not very welcoming at all; a cold and empty damp atmosphere hung in the air; no feeling of good karma in between these walls, were in fact my thoughts, as it is far from welcoming. This house knew no love. So, then this is where Brad stays with her, I clarify to myself. No wonder he finds it depressing, it is very dated. Brad makes me a coffee then we sit in the lounge on a large light fawn suite. In here is a little more modern than the rest of the vintage place, it has a large flat screen television; however, despite that it is still obvious to me that the décor taste spoke of an old woman. Out of the blue, Brad makes a comment about her, which totally shocks me, saying he wishes she was dead and I could live there with him. *Eh. No thank you.*

He talks about where we stand in the relationship, which eventually leads to some awkward discussions about his wife. Brad goes on about how he isn't in love with her and how he never ever had been, not ever. The marriage was one of convenience from the beginning; sex over the years was almost non-existent, besides it had been a chore to her, which suited him as he didn't find her sexually attractive anyway. He also states that she is a lot older than him, which he finds disgusting. He can't be bothered with her old-fogyish ways with her constant nagging. He says the thought of kissing her makes him feel physically sick as she repulses him. I say nothing.

I see an old photograph of her (Brad has taken it from where it sat displayed on a unit in the lounge then hid it in a drawer, knowing I was coming to the house. On talking about her, he then brings it out to show me for myself what she is like, then he quickly shoves it back in). I can clearly see he is very embarrassed by her. I remember how someone at the clinic thought he was out shopping with his mother (Brad had been mortified). The image that had been in front of me portrayed a quite ugly woman, even back then when young she looked older beyond her years. Dressed in tasteless clothes, which were very much considered to be passé but complimented the antiquated style of the surroundings of this house. Therefore, coincidentally, I find myself agreeing with Brad's opinion on everything. Brad being spot on in his description of her, I find zero competition as a mistress; Brad is in hysterics at the thought. I can't believe someone still so young is with this pensioner. I am not that interested in her, I never had been really, so the subject of her is dropped abruptly as we start kissing again on her sofa.

After a while Brad lies along the sofa, pulling me on top of him, as he kisses me more intensely, he lifts my top, feeling my breasts through my bra. We are both so aroused that once again he is hard under his jeans with me being left moist beneath my jodhpurs. I resist the urge to sleep with him today though… it wasn't planned to happen like this as his birthday would be special, and we'd make love for the first time in the bedroom of this house. His wife's house. That was what he wanted so much and I agreed, she meant nothing to me, so why should I care? It just showed me all the more now that she meant nothing to him either – which suited me just fine. I sure liked that.

Brad is taking me out later that night, so I go home to get changed. I have a shower, then did my hair all wild before sorting out my clothes, choosing tiny black silk underwear, which I think Brad is going to love. I put on ripped jeans with a peach silk nightie (as my top), worn with high leather boots.

Brad picks me up on time, and then we make our way to a little pub in the nearby village of Straiton. Brad drinks there often and it would go on to become our wee haven from the world. It is a nice homely place with a log burning fire, complete with a huge, stuffed, bull-head ornament hanging above it.

After a few more drinks in the bar, we go back to Brad's house once more. We have to sneak in through the patio doors at the back of the house as we are supposed to be doing this quietly so the neighbours don't hear us. The snow still carpeted the ground so I gather up snowballs, flinging them at him as he unlocks the doors. Just as he opens them, all the snow comes through the air, some hitting Brad, with the rest going straight through the door, hitting the kitchen table and landing on the floor inside. Brad then throws snowballs back at me. I am freezing cold with snow in my hair, the thawed water running down my nightie, made my nipples hard in the damp silk. We are squealing with laughter, running around like teenagers so much in love, the noise we make is awful, considering we were meant to be stealing quietly in the night into the house. We are all covered in snow; we tumble, falling together into the house, landing on the wet furniture. Hell, you should've seen the mess all over her floor. "Fuck it! The crow can clean her nest when she returns," Brad shouts outside the door into the night air of the garden, at this we just giggle even more. The neighbours by now have their outside lights on; a man is in his garden in the snow trying to see over the fence what the fuck is going on. Brad bangs the patio doors shut deliberately quite hard, shutting the neighbour and his nosiness out, along with the snow, which had started to fall again.

We have an amazing few hours there. I have a hot shower as Brad dries my nightie while making us supper. Afterwards, I just sit in my underwear on the sofa. Brad keeps kissing me as I try to watch the music channel drinking the wine he bought especially for me. Brad hands me a box of my favourite chocolates, which is very sweet of him. We relax together very happily in the lounge without Brad giving a toss about his wife. As I pulled on my jeans with my nightie to go home, Brad begs me to stay. NO! I smile. He starts us laughing all over again as he pretends to be her: "Bradford, get that cow home now, right now!" he mimics her voice, then smirks as he tells me he can picture the look on her face if only she'd known. Pushing me out the door still laughing as we go sliding in the snow holding onto each other tightly as we reach the jeep,

"Stay the night, Coco," making a statement more than asking me the question.

"No!" I shout as I get in the car then Brad drives me home.

11th February

Brad comes to pick me up on his birthday; we go over to my parents' house as they are eager to wish him a happy 50th. We visit regularly, going in for coffee on our way to work some nights. They've been talking non-stop about me and Brad. My dad is so happy that finally he met a man he very much approves of, finding him a perfect husband for me; ignoring his marriage and all the stories it entailed. After we have coffee, we go to the jeep, it's then I give Brad his birthday presents from me (A bottle of Boss aftershave and a 50th card). It is a beautiful day for February, so Brad decided to take me to a lovely little port village called Port Patrick, which is about 60 miles away.

On the way to Port Patrick, Brad decides to stop in at Girvan to have a Chinese meal for lunch. While we wait for our food to arrive in this enchanting little restaurant, Brad suddenly gets up from the table, then goes down on one knee.

"Marry me, Coco; please say you will marry me?" Brad speaks in serious tone, gazing into my eyes intently. *Surely, this cannot be happening*, I think to myself. This is only our third date together on his 50th birthday. How can he be so serious as he is still a married man? Yet I could tell by the way he is staring at me he means it all right. He meant every word of it; by now everyone in the place was paying attention to us.

"Get up," I whisper sternly, still shaken from the event I just look at him (now back on his feet, he stands waiting in anticipation) for what seemed like several minutes. "Yes, Brad Blake, I will," I eventually retort, not sure what to think or do, at least he has no ring. Brad is ecstatic at my approval, kissing me before ordering a bottle of champagne for the table and a drink for everyone in the place. Everyone stares as I sit quietly stunned by his behaviour. He takes my hand, saying how much he loves me, more than anyone in this world. He loves me more than anyone ever in this whole world. He tells me I have become his life.

As we arrive at Port Patrick, we parked up the jeep. We go into a hotel that sits on top of a hill overlooking the bay. I am so proud to be here with Brad. As Brad is up ordering drinks, I peer out the window, admiring the amazing view of the harbour below. I imagine going down to the boats bobbing about in the water, wishing I could sail away forever in one of them with

Brad. We have a few drinks with me cuddled in his arms. It is so nice that he doesn't care who saw us together, kissing me in public. Afterwards, we go around the village hand in hand, looking through the gift shops; one of them sells some unusual items. Brad buys me an old book, which is leather bound with a bronze clasp. It has blank pages inside, and Brad tells me to write my secrets in it, now that I've plenty. He writes the date inside the book; under it how much he loves me.

Before heading back to Brad's house, we decide to grab some dinner from a seafront hotel. I have scampi while Brad has fresh fish; romantically, we shared hot chocolate fudge cake with cream. I drink wine followed with coffee liquors while Brad can't, he is driving.

After a wonderful day out with Brad and luckily with the weather being good, we arrive back in his hometown. Back in his house in the lounge, we are kissing each other when Brad lays me down on the sofa once more. His tongue is going in and out of my mouth as his hand roams down my legs, caressing the skin through the ripped sections of my jeans. He slides his hand into a rip near my bum as his finger eases its way to my underwear, which he gently slides aside, now touching me for the very first time, he feels me silky smooth (as I have no hair at all), he whispers sexily "Oh God Coco!" before pushing his finger deep inside me.

"Can I make love to you now, Coco, because I don't think I can wait two more months?" he says desperately.

"Brad, take me to bed!" I reply, wanting him so much but terrified at the same time. The two-month time limit of us waiting before we have sex is dismissed.

Brad scoops me up instantly, carrying me to his room. As he kicks open the door, the cold air hits me; I can see the dim light of the moon shining through the window onto the bed. He puts me back down on my feet, he sat on the edge of the bed in front of me as he undoes my belt and slips off my jeans, then proceeds to unbutton my shirt, playing with my nipples through the silk lace before removing my bra, leaving me now standing wearing only my expensive silk tiny G-string.

"God, Coco, you're so beautiful!" he sighs, removing my tiny pants to reveal my fully naked body. He places his hands firmly on my bare buttocks, pulling me towards him, then flickers his tongue on my clitoris for the first time. He gets up then lays me on the bed, using his tongue on me over and over, causing me to whimper on the soft quilt. He spends ages pleasuring me as I orgasm multiple times.

"Brad, oh Brad," I half-whisper, half-scream as my body trembles at his every whim. "Fuck me," I whisper in the shadows.

He removes his clothes, laying his naked body on top of me, his chest pressing against my nipples as he enters me for the first time. His gorgeous cock pushes deep into me. We make love in the moonlight as the snow continues to fall. Brad moans as he pushes his hardness inside me, holding my hair. I respond raising my lips to his, scratching my nails down his back. Brad then kisses down my throat to my chest, sucking my erect dark nipples. We come together as his throbbing member penetrates me, filling me full of his sperm. I have wanted this for so long; it was as special as I wished it be, because it feels like I gave myself to him as a final birthday gift.

Afterwards, we lie in each other's arms. He tells me I am the best sex he's ever had plus now he knows what love really is like and he also informs me he'd never given any woman oral sex before (not even her), he just couldn't resist me.

As I look down, I can see he is hard again. I slide between his legs now, taking him into my mouth for the first time. He tastes so sweet as I suck, licking every inch of him. He comes quickly from the excitement.

Afterwards, he keeps my tiny G-string. He hides it in the inner pocket of his navy wool jacket. I smile watching him as I stand naked under his playboy robe. We laugh about how a playboy robe could only be got from the mansion. It is even funnier that Brad thought it was a Guinness one, it is brand new, never been worn and was a gift to him one Christmas some time back. I can hear water running as the bath fills. I go through to see what he's doing, only to find he'd run me a lovely bubble bath. Sitting there I look around this woman's bathroom, it feels a little strange to be in her home. I won't stay the night here, I decide, not tonight anyway (plus that will keep Brad keen). I go back through and I sit in her kitchen in my bare just laid ass, wearing Brad's robe, drinking her coffee, looking out at the snow in her garden, thinking I'm the happiest mistress in the world tonight.

As Brad takes me home in the jeep, I am drinking wine from the bottle, singing along to the CD playing. I feel so rich sitting beside him with his sperm inside me. Brad thanks me for giving him the best birthday he has ever had. Brad also tells me he loves me more than ever and sex with me is so much better than ever he could imagine. Which he did, as he had masturbated many times thinking about me. To this confession from him, I am both shocked and absolutely delighted.

"No problem, Blake, walk in the park, Blake, walk in the park," I smile. As Brad drives through a white world of snow, I know for sure I have no regrets. Neither does he.

Valentine's Day

As Brad and I are about to share our first Valentine's Day together, I can honestly declare that this is the first time so far that I have felt the downside of being a mistress… you reap what you sow, I guess. This was sure to come eventually, I knew that. Now that it has arrived, I know the feeling would be back with a vengeance, no doubt at times bringing with it a lot more emotional baggage along the way.

Holding this thought as I go to get ready for Brad coming, as he suggested we go out for lunch rather than dinner this evening as we both have to work tonight. So he is picking me up shortly and taking me to a little old-fashioned restaurant tucked out of the way, it sits across from Robert Burns' (Famous Scottish poet) cottage. It's a special place to us as it is the first place we ever went for coffee together. He hands me a Valentine's gift. It is a bottle of expensive perfume (Coco Channel, Mademoiselle) with a lovely card. Inside it reads, 'You are special, I have never bought perfume for anyone before (not even her) or ever given a Valentine's card. I love you, Coco'. I adore the fact he makes me sui generis as compared to her, delighted I kiss him, saying thank you for his unique gesture of choosing this scent especially just for me.

Brad takes my hand as he explains that he wants us to have sex exclusively with each other. Saying that he doesn't do mistresses, that in his heart he considers me to be his real wife. He repeats that he doesn't want me to sleep with anyone else, so he won't either. I agree to his proposition... I will be completely faithful to him, so he better be to me. Doesn't a mistress accept though that the man she sleeps with also has sex with his wife? Brad wasn't having sex with her though, so his proposition wasn't about whether he had sex with her or not, he was making sure I had sex with no one else, full stop. Brad was looking after Brad.

Later that night in the ward, one of the male patients gave me and another nurse a cake each with little plastic love heart rings on it.

"Didn't you get me one?" Brad jokes with the patient. The patient questions a ring or a cake or both. To which Brad answers laughing, a ring, of course.

All of us in the ward tonight have already received Valentine's Day cards, other than the other nurse who likes Brad, she is raging Brad didn't get her one. She tried putting on the plastic ring from the cake but it broke on doing so, which only added fuel to her fire. When she got a moment alone with Brad, she asked him out on a date... absolutely no competition here either, Brad told her very clearly where to go and that he was not interested whatsoever... This made matters even worse as on the shift opposite to Bobby, she was our charge nurse. She made it quite clear on many occasions that she was obsessed with him, and she arranged a party on the ward for his 50th birthday, complete with a cake and candles, her motive being just so she could kiss him. She was telling me all of this with no inkling I was sleeping with Brad but then again even if she did, she was in complete denial because she told me she was determined to lay him. I could do or say nothing as she was more than capable of phoning his wife because he chose me and not her.

The following few weeks pass by with Brad and I on same shifts but different wards. Now I'm working permanent shifts in the female-only unit. We spend our breaks together, but I miss working with him a lot, we made a great team, even the patients agreed on wanting me back on the ward. He takes me back and forward to work still, then when we spend the night together in little exclusive hotels (Brad tells her he's working overtime). It is great being with him; we share so many romantic moments, having amazing regular sex. He spoils me so much now. I love being his mistress. Everything seems to have turned out so well for me. We belong together, Brad and me.

As I go about my life, I now look at the world in a different light, I wonder how many couples I see are in affairs, how many women are mistresses that I assume are out with their husbands, just like people take for granted that Brad and I are married. Husband and wife. Not a gentleman with his mistress. Wives are for cooking and cleaning, then moaning. Mistresses are for special occasions, I clarify in my stupid head, who grant naughty sex; mistresses, for a price, had you fucked on Valentines, spellbound and bewitched.

Chapter IV
April Brings Canada

Towards the end of March, my rose-tinted view of the love affair begins to fall apart. On the 21st of March, when I celebrate Ostara, also known as Spring or Vernal Equinox, I don't feel right. As I honour Ostara, who is the Goddess of Spring that we witches' worship at this time of year as the season changes from dark winter to the brightening of spring, I feel deeply sad inside instead of looking forward to the new beginnings. I plant seeds in my garden to represent new life and paint some eggs to represent fertility. I hide some of these painted eggs, go for a walk in the woods to clear my mind. I come home make some coffee, eat some chocolates eggs. I clear my sadness with positive thinking but still I am constantly concerned about how I can't invite Brad to spend the night with me at my house as I still have to consider my son, yet in other ways I suppose it suits me very well as we stay over in different high-class hotels as that was exactly what I had wanted was it not? Knowing how much he spoils me is great but despite that fact, it hurts too, because he stills goes back home to his wife every single fucking morning. Now in the forensic unit we barely get to see each other as although we are working the same night shift pattern, it's in different wards, which have become unsettled so we can't spend our breaks together anymore. Brad, however, still takes me back and forth to work when possible. Yet regardless of this and the fact of him being married, shit, I still can't bear to lose him. Although sometimes if I'm to be honest to myself, I wish I'd never started this affair in the first place.

April arrives, bringing with it warmer weather. The warm breeze blows the cherry blossoms off the trees in my garden; all the pink petals cascaded downwards in the wind. You would think the grass had just been married! It looks like pale pink confetti everywhere, *it's beautiful.* I smile, thinking this is a very peaceful place to have my coffee; I love the smell of the rich beans first thing in the morning. I also enjoy eating them, first you feel the hard texture of the bean crunching, tasting the coffee dust in your mouth, next a feeling of smoothness follows as you taste the chocolate they're dipped in melting. They're expensive but worth it, not quite a suitable breakfast to have sitting amongst my trees but I do it anyway. I'm fascinated with trees, I always have been. As a little girl I would wander through the woods, wishing I had a huge tree house to stay in, so I'd able to hide amongst the trees, , all in a secret garden just for me. I smile sadly, reminiscing upon those days, with a fondness I can still imagine the soft scent of the pine conifers, especially when the smell of them is enhanced just after the rain. I do have my own trees now but not quite that forest. Robin Hood's way of life very much appeals to me, even until this day. To stay in a den in the forest, taking money from the rich to give to the poor, I think wistfully is very much my style. Brad calls me 'Coco of the Hood'. He torments me saying I steal all of his money now; yes perhaps, well maybe I do, but it's not my fault he spends so much money on me, I don't take it or ask him, he just gives it to me, so surely that guarantees that he can afford it! I tease him back.

The fallen petals remind me of confetti being flung all over me many years ago. The weather on my wedding day was terrible, wasting it all, the delicate tiny pieces of coloured paper in shapes of hearts and horseshoes all got broken by the heavy rain melting them into the ground, leaving behind a mess of wet mush in colours of the rainbow. Perhaps a sign I should've never taken those wedding vows, they meant nothing to me then or now. The broken omens of that day spoke clearly, how could there've been a Cinderella fairy-tale ending when I married him for money? So no happily ever after that expensive scenario turned out to be. No wishing it was different either, I never loved him anyway, I confirm to myself in honesty.

Looking around all about me it suddenly dawns to me how big the trees have grown. Since then how much my life has changed, it seems like yesterday I planted them one by one. The dreams I had back then of how my world would be when the trees grew were all broken. I think of Brad, our affair and how his marriage is also broken. I'm going to get broken next, I think. No, I know I am. *China, I feel made of china, china in his hands, with only time before I'm dropped.* I also know given time or not this love affair is going to be very destructive, turning it into something very ugly that it is not. My instincts are warning me and they aren't being subtle. As I sit here ironically thinking, *if the trees could talk, fuck knows what they would tell the wind? If the petals could too, what would they whisper to the grass?* I wondered as they continued to dance over it. Trees don't talk in our world, they just stand silently watching over everything, sometimes out-living us in our adult lives, but they too tell their own stories by their appearance.

I sat under one of them many moons ago, an ancient oak tree which was so tall, weather-beaten and known to be at least a hundred years of age or more and it showed. I sat down for a while in the shade under its old branches, whereupon a decrepit gypsy woman dressed in dirty rags approached me, offering to read my Tarot cards. I was very curious at the time and not so sure about going through with it. Father Peter would class both practising white witchcraft and Tarot cards to be considered to be dealing with the occult. Not the case in witchcraft though as I have three sets of Tarot cards now, I had my first set of Tarot cards at fourteen years of age, I never used them, I did not know how to but I wanted them anyway and kind of got the just of it. She gave me a piece of lucky heather, which I took, agreeing to the reading, that I was scared to refuse in case she put a curse on me. I was terrified even more so at how accurate the old gypsy so clearly read my past, trembling as she was so correct in my present day but delighted yet surprised of how she'd predicted my future. The cards clarified that I would someday have everything I ever dreamed of and everything that I ever wanted, but I'd need to wait a while for it until some time had passed but in the end, eventually, all my wishes would be granted... The cards must have been referring to Brad as my situation promised that the person who would become the love of my life was an older gentleman, the relationship would be formed in an unusual, far from suitable situation, wrong time, wrong place, but he would be the one. My position now was just this; he being married to someone else must have been what she'd seen. So I end up with him, right, it has to turn out better than the train wreck that was my last marriage... with Brad it's going to be different, I hope, because just as the old gypsy had predicted, I really thought that he was my destiny!

Instead of sitting here daydreaming with cups of coffee, I better move my ass. I have booked an appointment today to have a tattoo done bearing his name. Why? Maybe to try to convince myself and Brad that I am serious about staying with him. Hmm. Or maybe am doing it because I feel I am getting one over on his wife by wearing her husband's name on my body, she'd never do a thing like that, probably have heart failure at the very thought... I am feeling unsettled though, knowing that at this very moment he is in that house with her. I ask myself if I still want to go through with this. The answer is – yes! I am sure I do, even though I know it is a bit extreme, I guess, just to prove a point. I get Brad tattooed in Japanese on the back of my neck (to keep the message slightly secret, besides it looked classy). Next, Bradford gets tattooed also in Japanese on my right hip (with little stars surrounding it, each one stood for my children and little dogs. All my loved ones captured in one very important permanent ink statement). So I think the pain has been worth it. I must've been crazy to have gone through with this, but it has been done now, so no turning back. Brad likes to call me his Highland cow, so now I'm branded, am I not? A long time ago on the spur of a moment I'd decided to get 'Coco' tattooed on my other hip, so now both our names sit opposite each other.

I now have quite a selection of tattoos. On top of my newly acquired ones, I also wear my name at the base of my back with a tribal band with a playboy bunny above it. On my bum cheek sits a little lion cub he is stretching and yawning, and he's an adorable character from a Disney movie. Besides, when I pass wind, I just blame little lion accusing him of roaring. Cute. Brad also asked me if someday I would get Bradford Riley Blake tattooed in English down my back, from top to bottom of my spine. *Hmm! That'd be very sore*, I thought. It could be a wedding gift from me, he explained, and he'd pay for it as my present from him. Well, we will have to wait and see. I would say that is way far more of a commitment than wedding vows and so much harder to remove, that's for sure. No mention of him having a Coco tattoo. Hmm! Actions speak louder than words, so they say. That tattoo requested may or may not be done, as the marriage may or may not ever take place. So perhaps was my answer to both of those questions.

I have two other tattoos in a seductive place, Brad knows where they are and likes to kiss my secret tattoos.

When Brad arrives later that night, I show him what I'd got done, which he agrees are stunning.

"Now you belong to me, Coco," he informs me, smiling.

"Oh! Really, do I, Blake?" I laugh back.

"Yes, cow! You do, you're branded mine!" he jokingly responds in a firm tone, leaning in to kiss me until I am out of breath.

That evening we lay out in the garden together on top of those petals. They stick in my hair, and then having to be gently removed as my neck is red and very tender with the recent artwork on display. It is so romantic as silently we watch the clouds go by above our heads; the sweet scent of lilac is in the gentle evening breeze. The cherry blossoms above take me in my fantasies away to a Japanese garden, where I would be Brad's Geisha girl forever. In Japan it is socially accepted among the married men to have a mistress, it takes years of training on how to perfect the whole culture of dress and mannerisms expected of them, which also includes the painting of the face pure white, the making of tea and being able to walk on tiny feet to perfection. Eh! No, so perhaps not Brad's mistress in that country after all, but unlike here, there it is considered an honour to be one.

As reality comes back to me, I wish I am as far away as Japan though, how could the love we have shared make us feel so numb, so scared, how could that be so wrong. Why? Who decides what is right and wrong when you love someone? Who sits on the council that governs the heart? Is it our conscience? I guess it is a sin to love a married man, classed as committing adultery. If it is, then so be it for, your honour, whomever you may be, I am charged guilty of love in the first degree!

"I guess you need to go, Brad," I break the silence, declaring the inevitable, my voice so filled with hurt. He knows I wanted him to stay.

"Yeah, I guess I need to, baby, I wish I could stay though," Brad replies solemnly as he stands up. "I love you, Coco," he assures me, though I can hear the desperation in his voice too.

He leaves. I hear the car engine start up then leave the street. I still lay for a while amongst those petals, just wishing and staring upwards. I watch the night sky turn to darkness. I get up feeling cold, I'd lain there dreaming a lot longer than I'd intended, now my clothes are damp on me from the dew of the grass and my tattoos are beginning to sting and itch on my skin. In the house I feel the air is still warm from the evening sun. I close the door on the sky while tears run down my face as I try also to shut out the pain in my heart. I lift my phone, it is flashing, and it's acknowledging missed calls from Brad. Too late now for me to say goodnight, I miss you so much. He won't come out again tonight to phone me back as he has to stay in that house with her. I put down the phone. I am wrong, as I walk away, the phone starts ringing. I turn around to see my phone flashing, informing me Brad is calling. I smile as I walk away. I don't answer; I and just keep on going. I hear it ringing and ringing in the distance as I close my bedroom door. I smile sadly, now he can be upset all night wondering where I am, why I haven't answered the phone. I have company with me tonight now, both of us suffering upon being hurt because of having an affair. There will be millions out there too, I guess, I just don't know who they are. In my head for now, I'm a film star acting out the role of a mistress in a big Hollywood movie. I'm playing the part very well; I hear the director shout 'That's it for tonight, Coco, and well done you're a superb actress.' *With my life you bet I am!* I'm going to nominate you for an Oscar for this. Oh yes! I sure am doing brilliantly, especially at the part of hurt due to all this shit, so I'm bound to win it, right out the fucking park. I'm wondering how good I will be tomorrow as it gets harder and harder loving him, with each day that passes, it will surpass today; that I know for certain. In my head as I lay in a bath of cool water skimmed on top with a layer of tiny bubbles, I pretend the maid is laying out my silk nightwear, while the butler arranges my dinner to be served with chilled wine. Smiling, I get up, *wishful thinking.* I shall relax tonight, fuck it, tomorrow can take care of itself, which quite cleverly it does, because tomorrow never comes.

5th April and My First Birthday with Brad

Brad phones wakening me up to wish me a happy birthday. Last night on the table downstairs he left a card from him. *Happy birthday to me*, I think before getting myself out of bed. I pull on my robe, and then head down to the kitchen to open it. It's beautiful with messages of love and fifty pounds in it. What a brilliant way to start my day, smiling this morning, no acting that part. I'm happy making coffee to have with cream cake; well, today I'm spoiling me.

My son, River, comes downstairs, giving me my presents (perfume and chocolate). He wishes me a happy birthday, and then proceeds to make me French toast with chocolate syrup and blueberries for a birthday breakfast, which I also eat. Naughty but nice.

After River is out for work, Brad arrives. Kissing me in between whispering that we will be spending my birthday in a very expensive hotel, where he intends to make love to me for hours. Fuck me all night were his exact words. I laugh, informing him that better be fact, not just a birthday promise. I'm excited so I'm looking forward to what Brad has planned, more so about spending precious time with him. Brad has to leave as usual in the morning, birthday or not. Kissing me he is sad at having to leave me again for now. He calls me as soon as he reaches his hometown. I hear the happiness in his voice return as he arranges to pick me up. I will make sure that tonight I look absolutely stunning, besides right now I'm glowing, I feel amazing.

The great thing about making love with Brad this evening is that I don't need to feel guilty about it, not for this one time. This is part of Brad's present to me, so it has nothing to do with anything but me as today it's my birthday. For once I wouldn't actually care that the lies he intended to tell to her could stream to the moon and back, fuck her and to hell with him being married.

I decide just to relax for a while in the garden as the house is immaculate. In a while I'll sort out all my pretty new clothes with some underwear I need for tonight and tomorrow. Bag packed. Tan on with nails painted and I intend that later my hair would also be done to perfection. I spend some self-indulgence time now eating chocolates, drinking champagne that I bought for me, watching a movie in my lounge as I snuggle up with my wee dogs under my wolf fur throw. Now this is my heaven. After a while, the door knocks, it's my fucking ex.

"What the fuck do you want?" I yell at him, not amused at all; how dare he even show his ugly and arrogant face!

"It is your birthday, Coco, I have come to take you out for dinner," he replies as if in his world it's the most natural request to make.

"Fuck off!" I yell, slamming the door shut. *Idiot!* What made him think I'd ever want to see him again? The only good thing to come from that relationship was my child.

He knew about me being with Brad from whispers around town, also he saw us together in the street a couple of times. He decided that I rejecting his dinner invitation was the perfect opportunity to inform my kids and also notify my parents about my affair. They, however, already knew but had said nothing.

With passing time our affair has grown more serious. More and more people are becoming aware of what is going on, so therefore the truth about us can out at any time now, especially with this bastard now threatening to tell Brad's wife. When Brad picks me up, I tell him about what happened today and what he threatened to do to us. His behaviour towards me makes Brad angry but he promises to be supportive, whatever the circumstances are that follow this threat, also that no matter what events unfold, he will stand by me. I completely believe in his words with all my heart when he makes these promises that he will never leave me. We agree to forget about him, no way are we going to let this clown spoil my birthday. Brad comments on my looks when driving, I blow him a kiss loudly, saying about time, thank you. He smirks then he just laughs, shaking his head at me as I open wine, drinking it from the bottle, singing along to the music in the car. An old-fashioned song is playing. (It is also Michaels' favourite song which he sings with so much emotion, reminds me of being in my limo New Year.) As the question is sung once more by the artist, I come back to the present as I shout over at Brad, "No, no, I won't!" This time he laughs out loud; as I drink more wine, I wink at him.

Brad drives for a while through the country until we stop outside a Gothic-looking old-fashioned little cottage. It is so picturesque, it looks captivating, like something you'd find on the lid of a biscuit tin or a chocolate box. This is our hotel actually and apparently it has only three bedrooms for rent, making it extremely exclusive. On going over the threshold, the décor is charming, it took you right back in time; it was as if you stood in times long gone by, which was not only a strange feeling but unusual because everything in the place was immaculate, brand new but in theme of ye olde worlde.

We are led to our room by a mature gentleman, whom I assumed to be the butler due to the uniform he wore. The room is decorated with soft rose flower wallpaper, which sets off the thick pale rose-coloured deep-piled carpet scattered with cream sheepskin rugs around our feet. The room smells of vanilla mixed with fresh cut flowers. The bed takes pride of place in the centre of room; it is huge with four posters and an antiquated rose-coloured quilted bedspread looking so comfy it just demanded to be slept in. I can see it has soft pink cotton sheets under the quilt and huge pillows filled with duck down feathers. The butler shows us everything in the bedroom before explaining to us how everything worked in the en-suite bathroom. It has also captured a nostalgic feel about it as it wore with pride décor colours of cream and old gold. I step forward to admire the woodland view from the little window above the sink, as my hand accidentally rubs against one of the fluffy towels; it feels amazingly soft to my touch. Before leaving, the old butler informs us that he would be at our disposal all through the night; anything we requested, within reason of course, would be brought to us, and all we had to do was ring the bell to summon him. Nearby on a little table, which is rather kooky made with tree branches and old logs, there waiting for me is a little envelope wearing my name, beside it stands a bottle of champagne with a bouquet of beautiful wild flowers. On opening up the envelope, it holds a small delicate handmade birthday card saying COCO in dried rose and violet petals, inside there is a subscription wishing me happiness with a birthday to remember. I now notice a box wrapped in pretty paper with a dried rose tied into the pink ribbons, lying on the bottom of the bed. That is my birthday gift too. Under the wrapping I find a pink velvet box, inside of it is soft rose-coloured delicate tissue paper which looks to be covering with care, in my favourite shade of purple, the most beautiful silk shirt I've ever seen. This must've cost Brad a fortune as I imagined all this had to be included in the price of this evening.

A little later dinner is served in our room as we sit on an opulent dining suite by the window, looking out over the meadows. The butler has placed in the middle of the table an antique vase with a quirky arrangement as it is filled with bluebells and bramble leaves from the woods nearby. He poured Moet champagnes lit candles, enhancing the smell of melting ice cream; the aroma of vanilla already in the room must've been drifting from them. He then brings our food, which is so good, the prawn and fresh cherry starter is exquisite. The lamb is cooked in mint leaves and is so tender, it just melts in our mouths; we both agree the dinner is delicious, even the rose and violet flavoured Eton mess is amazing. This very kind old man did his job with so much pride, treating us as if we were royalty from the minute we came through the door. Little did we know then that he would be the only person we would see during our entire stay there.

After dinner liquors, we retire for the evening as the butler bows, bidding us goodnight. I opt for a deep luxurious bath in the vintage free-standing Victorian tub. As I slip into the warmth of the water, I feel my body totally relaxing amongst the lilac and lavender scented bubbles, which spreads a wonderful smell of nature's flowers through the evening air once more. Afterwards using those cotton wool soft towels to dry myself with, I put on a long pure white silk nightdress, which slips over my head, sliding down my still warm skin it feels cool but refreshing as the material feels as light as a feather. Brad loved the way that type of gown flowed down my body, showing off my nipples; he loved both the feeling of the intricate material under his hands plus the silky ice feel of it brushing against his warm naked body. *I look good wearing only this with wet hair and Channel perfume*, I tell the mirror confidently. Entering back into the bedroom, Brad has his back turned to me but I can hear the pop of the bottle cork followed by a bubbling noise as he pours more of the costly sweet liquid into a champagne glass. Then rustling of the paper as he opens the chocolates, so I sit down with anticipation waiting to taste them both. Brad turns around on his way over, then stops in his tracks looking astonished as he says I am so naturally gorgeous as I sit as if in a portrait. He says he is bewildered as he can't believe I am his. Putting down the tray, he opens a little box which also sat on it, then he takes me by the hand, pulling me back up onto my feet, kisses me so tenderly, then places a heavy necklace around my neck. On feeling his fingers shut a clasp, I look down to see the most beautiful diamond heart necklace I have ever seen sparkling and hanging around my neck.

He promises to love me forever as he picks me up, carrying me towards the bed. Brad removes the silk negligee gracefully. Hungrily, he enters me as his mouth finds mine, my neck then my throat, covering them all with the lightest of kisses that feel like the wind blowing on my skin. He makes love to me on the bed, coming soon as fast he fills me with warm sperm. He lays me down on the floor, with the feeling of the sheepskin on my back, he enters me once more. He then holds me up in his arms, as I hold my arms around his neck with my legs wrapped round his waist, he comes more slowly this time, putting all his love into my as I come too, putting mine over him. Afterwards he tenderly lays me naked back down on the bed, kissing me hard until I feel like I can't breathe. There I sit happily with Brad in the nude, drinking my champagne, eating chocolate, watching the sun go down as the woods grow mysteriously dark on this magical night. Holding the heart in my hand, it sparkles a thousand colours over my bare breasts; tonight he'd made me feel like a real princess. Brad pours me more champagne, whispering secret birthday promises in my ear of more lovemaking that is yet to come. I look over at the little card, it got its wish for me, and this is not only a birthday to remember but a night I would never forget. I had stayed in many splendid hotels but this little place is far by the most exquisite. As Brad makes love to me time and time again, he comes into me as well as all over me, sperm all over my face and eyelashes as he gently holds me by the hair, finishing the rest of it into my mouth, little droplets on my lips, which are by now bruised and swollen from him kissing me. In the darkness, with the only the moonlight shadowing the room, I give him everything a woman can give. I give him my heart in full as I open up to him like a flower to the sun.

6th April

I return home early in the morning. Just as the ex-partner arrives at the house. I don't answer the door this time, so he starts banging on it hard and shouting out my name repeatedly. Then he goes all the way around the back of the house, standing on the bins, he manages to get the height needed to look in the kitchen window. He is now battering on it demanding I open the door. I look through the glass at the demented face, I just ignore him, turning away walking upstairs to my bedroom; he eventually goes away enraged, shouting he's going to kill me if he does get in and he's off to tell Brad's wife about the affair. I accept the fact that the fucking idiot probably will for definite now, as this is the second time in two days he's said this. Oh! I wonder about the neighbours, how much they heard. Oh! So what, I think they obviously see Brad coming and going; besides I don't need to explain myself to them.

Brad arrives at my place a little later, so we sit at my kitchen table talking. We decide to go to visit my parents' house. Whilst we're there a call rings on my mother's phone. She answers; it's Brad's wife. She asks my mother if her husband is there, then proceeds to tell her that I am having affair with him. My mother denies Brad is there, whereupon she then requests that if my mother sees him, he is to be told to return home as soon as possible. Brad has to go, he tells us he'd come back soon. He leaves. My parents just sit with me, nobody says a word. Brad returns, as promised, telling my parents not to worry about it, he takes me home. He tells me that he'd admitted to his wife that it was true what the elderly woman had said about us. The phone call, he tells me, had been made by an old lady, who also gave her my mother's house number. I know exactly who that was; it was the fucking idiots' mother. He tells me that they'd found his house number by phoning all the numbers under the name Blake from the phone directory that were listed in his hometown area. By this time Brad's wife had now told the whole of his family about the affair. The devastation of the fallout news of it being the truth is spreading fast, its after effects started on its path of destruction as in disbelief everybody is supposed to be suffering in shock, except for Brad's mother. She knew her instincts were right all along. Brad arrives back at the house later to find me in the garden just sitting staring, talking to the blossoms on the grass. My friends in my head are back. The voices are singing songs as I blame Brads' wife for it all, not me. On her finding out, she took something perfect and painted it red.

It is dark. Brad sits down beside me. It feels unbelievable that this time last night we were in our majestic little hotel room with all the elaborate trimmings; how that seemed in comparison to this to be a million miles away. The light streaming from the open kitchen door makes a pale pink path across the grass, where all the cherry blossoms still lay. Nobody speaks a word as we sit together under the moon. Time passes, still I say nothing but others are talking. My friends tell me I will never be able to look at the cherry blossoms ever again or think of my cherished presents of yesterday without remembering this night too. They are right, as you walk the past walks with you. I am feeling cold; stone cold right to my heart, yet smelling him beside brings me no warmth inside. The scent of his aftershave I know so well. I wear it sometimes when he is with her. I take the bottle he kept here, I put it on when I feel lonely; it comforts me, making me feel he is close by. *"Another time, another place,"* my friends continue. I look at this statue of a man who sits beside me staring in the dark; he is a silhouette of my Brad.

"You had better go," I say, just hoping that he would before I dissolved in tears.

"I better," he replies as he stands up. He doesn't look at me. "I love you, Coco," he tells me with the saddest tone I have ever heard in his voice.

"So long, Blake." My voice is full of all the hurt in the world. Brad leaves. I close the door. I just sit, not drinking the cup of freezing cold coffee still in my hand. I don't think I even know how to anymore. His ghost is everywhere. I see his fucking ghost everywhere in my house. He is my shadow. My shadow left me. How does that happen? I ask the friends in my head. No answer is given.

They don't know. I don't know. I function yet malfunction, and then I don't even know anymore what it is that I don't know. The black shadow that now stands beside me is hurt. Hurt follows me. I have no peace inside, no friend in calm; my new best friend tonight now is Diazepam. I fling a load of them down my throat. I talk to the broom on the wall. Soon the pills take effect as I begin to float in a world free of confusion; the kitchen clock is now starting to lie too, it is not midnight surely. The three little faces of my dogs look up at me, they look distorted. I don't even remember if I fed them tonight. The broom doesn't answer me when I ask it if I did.

"Where is Brad, broom?" I ask curiously, slurring my words. Still no fucking answer. *Maybe I need to sew my shadow back on like Wendy does for Peter Pan*, I suggest desperately. No reply. Nobody is talking to me tonight now, not even the friends in my head. Fuck them all. Darkness appears, then oblivion as I fall into a deep sleep.

The next few days are absolute hell. Now because Brad's wife knows about affair, she has been made to face the truth about her marriage, she can no longer hide behind denial. She has threatened Brad that he will lose his step granddaughters if he doesn't give me up, and she demands that happens right NOW. She tells him that it isn't love he feels for me, it is just lust. She is in a state of acute desperation, placing pictures of these grandchildren in the jeep, trying to emotionally blackmail him to stay with her, Brad just laughs at this performance. Brad however has all of this to deal with as well as trying to hold us together although he makes it clear I mean more too him than them as he really loves me. I am forced to face the reality of this mess, at the same time being reminded by my hidden friends that I have broken my religious beliefs and committed adultery. Even if we take religion out of it, I've still been doing something immoral. Not giving a fuck because I can use confession to be forgiven and make myself feel better when it suits me or by crossing myself back over again to my religion of witchcraft. I cheat, making the best of them all, by using everything to my own advantage. Protestant and Catholic religions but mostly my witchcraft. My mind is just racing with millions of these unreasonable yet understandable thoughts, which I feel I can't handle anymore.

"You reap what you sow, madam," these words come back to me, they are heard in my head constantly being repeated by so-called friends; they're truth is haunting me.

Brad told me a few days back he is leaving her and coming to stay with me. He arrives back at the house tonight in just as much of a mess as I am… he now tells me that he is not coming, he's staying with his wife, he can't afford to lose his financial stability the marriage provides. He doesn't want to lose me either, but he doesn't know what choice there is. He explains that he's also scared I don't want him now all the secret excitement of the affair has been removed, so I may quickly get bored then hurt him, so if he leaves her now, then I finish with him, in the end he can be left with nobody and nothing. *Aw! Get away with you, Brad looking after Brad!* I agree with my friends here, and I wish they would on my behalf speak out and hunt him to fuck away from me right now but nobody hears them talking but me. *Isn't that the case with us all?* I confirm to myself. We only hear our own friends in our heads but we don't hear what anybody else's friends in their heads had to say.

This results in a massive argument with me screaming and crying at Brad, resulting in him shouting back at the top of his voice. The argument only ended when (as Brad had enraged me so much) I lifted my hand, slapping him hard across his face, knocking him backwards against the chair. (*"Ha-ha,"* my friends say.)

I am shocked in disbelief that I'd just hit him. I had never hit anyone like that before. As I sit down on my floor crying, holding my head in shame, I apologise profusely but I'm not that sorry, not really. (*"Don't be!"* I hear. *"He deserves it, do it again, hit him again, Coco,"* they say to me, encouraging me to fight when I am at my weakest.) Brad is also all apologetic, stressing that he never meant to hurt me either. He doesn't want to give me up altogether (*fucking sweet of him*); he just wants me to wait a little while for him. He expects me bear with him to let the dust settle on the battleground, he tells me. Promising me that everything will be all right again very soon. *Oh! Really, for whom? Him.* After some discussion, Brad says he will take me out tonight for a while in the jeep later on, whereupon we can talk some more. I agreed. Unknown to me though, he's decided that he should take me to meet his mother, so he can show her exactly who I am and show her what his wife is making him give up, then afterwards he has intended to spend the night with me – just for now anyway as is his plan. Brad's mother had known there had been something going on for a while. She'd quizzed Brad many times in the past. Brad is having a carry on; she would tell this story to all who would listen. She told Brad she heard about him at the bus stop when she wasn't even out the house. We just used to laugh about it… we weren't laughing now. No one is laughing now. My usually tanned face is pale and lifeless, my long dark hair just hanging limp, as to my clothes, well a crumpled mess. Brad gets up to go, I don't even acknowledge him, I don't answer him when he says, "Goodbye, I love you and I'll be back down soon." He goes out the house, and I hear him close the door. My friends in my head answer Brad. They shout after him, *"Fuck off you!"* I have no heart or energy for casting a spell. To hurt to care enough.

I wish I was away in a place similar to Kansas City living in a log cabin that would be carried up into the sky by a tornado. It would then fall with bang in my magical make believe city of The Land of Cherry, just like in the old film of Oz. I could go up a purple cherry tree road with all the pink cherry coloured little dwarfs called Cherrykins, with the Witches' broom, the Black cat and the little walking cauldron pot to see if the Wizard of Cherry could make all this love nonsense shit go away. If the Wizard of Cherry couldn't help me sort out this mess of a stupid love affair or free me from the pain I'm in because of it, who the fuck would? Then perhaps he could just give the broom a new handle, give the cat another nine lives and the cauldron pot a new base as his little arse has been burnt out with my spells. Or he could make some arrangements for me instead, to go to stay in a chocolate factory. I could eat chocolate smothered in coloured candy all day, sing and play with the little people who are made out of wooden spoons as we make sweets hidden in a world of fantasy. *"Oh yes!"* my friends in my head say, *"Either one of those suggestions I would consider to be a great idea so let's go up the Cherry Tree Road and over by Unicorn Town to see The Wizard of Cherry City, to see if he can help you all in your self-pity? Fuck off Coco! You're a powerful witch deal with your own shit."* I think maybe, just maybe if I go upstairs to my closet, I could fuck off through those doors and go out the back of it to Coco Kingdom. Right here and now that is the best answer. *"The land of white cocaine! Go to my altar, cast a spell to turn black witches' salt into pure white drug of snow, open the closet doors, open the wall behind, then through the holes I go. Now that is leaving in style Coco!"*

Brad comes back for me; I have sorted myself out to go with him in the jeep. He drives out of town, so I ask where we're going as I can see he's heading for his hometown. He tells me he's taking me to meet his mother, and then to the place he buried his dead father's ashes. (*"Very strange behaviour,"* my friends tell me.) With tears in Brad's eyes, I'm introduced to his mother; she is an adorable elderly woman who is very happy to finally meet me. Brad explains the situation to his mother, including the reason he has brought me to meet her, which is to show her how much he loves me and what his wife, whom he referred to as The Crow, is trying to make him give up with financial black mail. Nobody laughs at the expression on his face as he calls her The Crow as he is deadly serious in his pursuit of telling everyone there he wants to be with me because we love each other very much. His mum is very understanding. I have coffee with her as we sit talking for a while. She tells me how Brad has been so miserable for years in the house over the road with Craw Heed (slang for crow head). This time we all laugh. Then she goes on saying everybody knows he shouldn't have married her ever in the first place. Now with Brad openly agreeing with them about this, it is much too little too late. She is glad at last that her son has found some happiness, which was all due to him loving me. She hopes that we can get everything sorted out; she hopes and prays we end up together. His sister from England is staying there on holiday, and she thought we had sorted it all out and that we were going to be together and that was why I'd been brought to the house tonight. She is now going fucking nuts that Brad has brought me to meet them and say hello but also at the same time to say goodbye. This she couldn't comprehend, no fucking wonder, it made no sense to anybody but Brad as he was under the impression now that he was still intending to stay with his wife then I was off. A decision I had not yet made, as after all it was just an affair I had wanted with him in the first place, but Crow was making him choose.

That night we go back to my house, we just snuggle up on the sofa. It's clear to us both this is a very sad night, so we push that to the back of our minds to try to enjoy our time together. Brad decides to leave early at six a.m. Before he goes back to her, he turns to me, taking me in his arms, kissing me hard then soft. He needs me; in fact, I need him too, more than he knows. He makes love to me with such intensity it feels amazing, yet the entire time I can't stop the tears from falling. As he comes inside me, I grip his ass, and then pull him by the hair, holding him tightly in close to me, but I can't cum… not this time. Afterwards he cuddles me into his chest; tiny rivers run through the hair on it as my tears, flowing furiously, continue to fall. It becomes finally very clear to me that we both knew this day would come; now he needs to leave. *"Goodbye, Brad Blake. So long, Brad Blake, so long."* I hear the voices in my head wish him farewell.

Then all I can hear are soft music notes in my head, the sound of my Grandmother's music box, like tiny tinkling wind chimes, to those little notes in a sing song tune, keeping in time with its melody, these words are silently added, *"He loves me? He loves me not? He made himself my world then he just forgot!"* The voices in my head sing on and on. It is all I hear for hours, a beautiful voice singing to me, *"He loves me? He loves me not?"* now I am just numb.

Sometime later that morning Brad's statement comes back to me. It's Brad's voice I hear now. My friends must've finally gone to sleep for a while. He repeats himself over and over saying,

"I thought I was a man's man, Coco, down in the mines from a young age. A miner. I thought I was strong, a big hard man. Yet here I am, I can't even tell my wife, who is very much aware of the fact I don't love her, that I am leaving her to be with the woman I do love," Brad tells me this, through his pathetic whimpering, in my head, I can still picture his sorrowful face.

I just sit alone with his words ripping through me like knife... a rusty knife, tearing me apart, leaving an infected wound behind. I am broken and don't know what to do. How am I going to deal with this? How am I going to be able to continue to work with him, being in the same building as me? I ask myself, hopelessly searching to find some guidance from somewhere, anywhere, my craft or the world or perhaps advice from the devil himself. *"Perhaps the answer is blowing in the wind,"* my pals say. This is the last thing I hear before falling into a drunken sleep. The wine is my comfort, my hero in a bottle or two, my attitude is cheers to the lot of you who are out there having affairs, *Fucking hope it works out for ya all!*

10ᵗʰ April

Horrid long day. I'm hung over with the alcohol. I walk around in the house wearing dark sunglasses with pyjamas, Ugg boots and my hair all over the ship. Where the fuck is Brad today,

I wonder. Just at that he phones, it's late afternoon. He will pick me up tonight, I am informed. I get dressed, wearing a dark green chunky jumper; the colour is stunning on me. I get into the jeep; he wants to talk.

"I'm listening," I say, looking over at him as he drives towards the beach.

"I am going to Canada in the morning for a month," he says, not even glancing over, he keeps his eyes on the road.

"Let me out this jeep! NOW!" He keeps driving. "Stop this FUCKING JEEP! I WANT OUT!" I scream. He keeps going. I'm not doing this tonight, I'm not hearing this. We arrive at the beach with both of us shouting, me shrieking and very distraught at what is happening. I beg him to stay. He roars at me: "I'm going!" He then pleaded with me to wait for him.

"WAIT FOR YOU? YOU WANT ME TO FUCKING WAIT FOR YOU? WHO THE FUCK DO YOU THINK YOU ARE? YOU CAN'T BE SERIOUS!" I rage hysterical even louder.

He is; the expression on his face tells me he is before he answers. "Yes, yes, I am," telling me that he is very serious about it, and he loves me more than ever. Bullshit! I ask stupidly if she is going with him; he says no, he is going on his own. He needs space to sort out his head. He needs space, fucking class.

Oh! I see it all very clearly now, her plan is to send him away to her sister in Canada, hoping I will go with someone else in his absence. Or he would come to his senses, as she put it, when we are apart, trying to get him to change his mind about loving and wanting to be with me. She is praying he would realise that he had made a mistake in going with me, then stay with her. This scenario was set up to split us up. Yet, he is conforming to her wishes, he is leaving me. Her plan is already beginning to work.

"You need to go to Canada to think things over and decide what you're going to do about us?" I ask him sarcastically.

"No, Coco, I want to be with you. I love you so much, Coco, I don't need to go to Canada to know that," he replies tearfully. I looked out at the waves. I've sat here a million times in the past with Brad. Him begging me to go out with him as the waves rolled in. Him coming in his pants, kissing me on our very first

96

date, promising to love me forever as the waves rolled in. Now tonight as the waves hit the sand, he is telling me he is leaving me to go to Canada and begging me to wait for him to return. How dare those fucking waves just roll in to the sand as normal when my world is falling apart! *("The sky coming down on your head, Coco,"* my friends in my head say as they torment me, laughing.) There is no point in arguing anymore. *FUCK HIM!* I think. His mind made up to go, mine made up not to wait.

"Take me home," is all I say. He drives me home crying. I can see that he is agitated, I sit in total shock, nobody speaks a word, and you can cut through the atmosphere with a knife. On arriving back at my house in the car, he leans over to me and frantically pulls at my sleeve, taking a piece of green fluff off my jumper and puts it in his wallet; he is taking it with him as well as my thongs (the ones he kept the very first time we made love) inside his jacket pocket. With huge tears rolling down his sad face, he keeps on saying how beautiful I am and asking himself how he can leave me. I kiss Brad once on the lips, and then I sit back, offering him my hand for him to shake his goodbye. He refuses to take it. Casually, I get out of the jeep.

"So long, Blake," I smile at him through the falling tears.

"COCO! I LOVE YOU!" are the last words I hear as I close the door. I am aware of him watching me walk away, I don't look back. As I turn the key in my door, I hear the jeep leave; next I hear Brad peep the horn as the jeep leaves the street. Brad left me. He left me to go to Canada.

I don't remember entering the house. I am stunned and in deep shock at what has just happened. I am so numb, not being able to accept any sensation of disbelief. Reality begins to hit me slowly as I start trembling. He said he was just scared of us being apart, what about me? I am absolutely terrified. I sit outside amongst the cherry blossoms, my thoughts go to the recent times we sat under them together; we were supposed to be so much in love. I get up, go back inside, banging the door. I hate cherry fucking blossom trees. I hate all the trees, especially more so the oak ones, as an old gypsy had lied to me long ago under one of them.

"Well what did you expect? You went with a married man. Now you are suffering the consequences of that action." Action – *fuck the consequences, I fell in love with him. I just let him walk*

out of my life with all the dignity I could find. I let him go! I told myself. As it all comes back to me, once more a feeling of calm enters my body, then covers my whole being in a blanket of bewilderment. I refuse to acknowledge that it is the end of the road for us; all my earlier strength and determination of not needing him has somehow in this lonely house disappeared. I put my arms out, throwing my head back to look at the ceiling as I start spinning around and around; I spin in my kitchen like a spinning top.

"I will someday be his wife, in another life, in another land. Why not? In a land that time forgot. Perhaps in a thousand years in the wintertime, he will be forever mine, where it will still be today and he won't have gone away. I will marry him in a land of snow."

"Remember the snow, Coco? Brad loves the snow – and you, of course. Where would that be your land of snow, Coco? It would not be Coco Kingdom tonight! Fuck off! Would it be Canada Coco, Canada all covered in snow?" the voices in my head sing.

Still spinning I ask the wall and broom out loud: "Is Canada all covered in snow right now?" They don't answer; from my friends in my head I receive no answer. I should know the answer to this stupid question, yet I don't. Feeling dizzy, I lie down now on the cold tiles of the kitchen floor. The tears flow like the Niagara Falls, or the Angel Falls, which is perhaps more appropriate, as my guardian angel seems to be a fallen angel now. Your guardian angel is supposed to stay with you, be constantly by your side, it should never leave you. I would say he should be dismissed, as the bastard did exactly that. To Canada he takes an invisible trunk, filled with love, which would fill this universe, so such a lot of extra baggage. The hurt he left behind, however, doubles that. As Brad packs his case right now to go to Canada, I pack too. I pack the memories of some happiest months of my life and put them in a box.

Take the sun, the moon, the stars and the rainbow from the sky, put them in the box. Take all the colours from the world, put them in the box. Shut lid tightly, pack it all away in the back of the unused cupboard under the stairs. Switch off all the lights, tell the glow worms to glow no more, put the world into darkness.

For as Brad leaves, the tenebrosity of this world is all I know, my dark world, which will follow me wherever I go.

I think perhaps, no I know, because I am the one who made it, pitch fucking black. The pain rips right through me as I hold my tummy, yelling. I can't stop the hurt inside me, my head is full of floating misty grey clouds and I can't see his face anymore. I try to get up but I can't as I slump back down, feeling the ice-cold tiles of the floor on my legs. I hear his voice in the distance saying only one word, he is calling my name. Coco. Gloom takes over me before I blackout.

Sometime later, I wake up. I have no concept of time or how long I lay there. I must've fainted, I guess. My hair is all tangled with the tears, and my eyes feel sore, swollen with crying. I struggle to stand. I can't walk. I crawl on all fours to the bottom of the stairs. I go up them, crawling the way a monkey would. I lie on the carpet at the top of them as the pain and murkiness of night smothers me once more. Struggling into bed, I pull the duvet over my head. Screaming, crying in black obscurity, distressed, I continue to weep with more agony inside causing me to vomit out the side of bed onto the carpet. I howl into the night like a wounded animal, as excruciating thoughts of him cause me, this time to regurgitate the stinking contents of my stomach and spew all over the bed. Lying in the vile liquid, praying I was dead. Sombreness comes back this time, bringing with it inevitably sleep. Shortly, I wake up cold and shaking; I've had a nightmare. Reality hits, not a bad dream as I smell the sick on me. Squealing, soulful wailing of an indistinguishable sound echoes through the empty house as in tears I uncontrollably suffer with the sharp daggers stabbing at the mental torture of suffering returning deep inside me. I crawl on carpet, feel stairs and cold floor, sleeping pills. Diazepam. Drink strawberry milk, *he always brings me strawberry milkshakes in the middle of the night, not tonight though Coco!* I feel pain, burning me, scorching me inside, hollowness deep within as I swallow more milk with a lot of hard pills. Crawl, feel carpet on stairs, yet again puke over the bed, green bile soaking right through to the mattress, pull the already stinking, wet quilt back over me. Absence of light, torment and anguish, manic delirium arrives. Now floating around and around on a silky cloud. Numb. I feel nothingness settle in, with my acceptance of the present all gone, just as is my existence for now in my head all disappeared. BRAD GONE! Peace in the calm with oblivion but not in DEATH!

11th April

My phone ringing wakens me. I stretch out to reach for it, I get it, and then drop it as I realise my hair is now all stuck to my face matted with sick. My phone rings again. I get out of bed desperately searching for it, on finding it I grab it, shaking I try to answer the damn thing as well as pull my sticky hair off my skin.

"Hello? Hello?" Nobody is there. I press buttons.

"Coco darling." *Oh my God, it's him.* "Coco, I'm leaving for the airport in a little while, please wait for me. I promise I will come back home again to you. I love you so much." His voice is breaking, he is extremely upset.

"Brad? Brad, please don't go. Please stay, Brad?" Nothing, he has gone. The phone is informing me I have no new voicemails. I have missed the calls. I was listening to his voice on the answer machine. I try to phone him back, it goes to his voicemail. I try demonically frustrated to call him continuously. Shouting out his name, I fling my phone at the wall and still all covered in the bitter, rotten substance my body projected leaving dishwater like concoction everywhere. I lie down on the bedroom carpet amongst it, hollering at full volume, as I am destroyed and tormented mentally all over again. I am back in the jeep as I re-live last night once more, with everything said word for word. I am deranged as I lie there smelly and dirty still wearing the green jumper, thong and Ugg boots from yesterday evening, which I have slept in. Somewhere in the far distance I remember getting into bed last night with the boots on as I play the voicemail repeatedly for over an hour. I continue to play it, this time on loudspeaker non-stop. Each time I do this I am being charged as Brad is on his way to the airport, this message is costing me a fortune, yet I don't care – I don't want too.

Suddenly, I stop. I get off the floor as if I have been struck by lightning; of course, he won't go to Canada the voices in my head inform me. He will be here soon. Fuck sake! I put phone on charge and happily singing now I flee for a quick shower to rinse off all the filth from me. I fling jumper and thong in the wash, the Ugg boots, ruined, go straight in the bin *.Fuck them, Brad can buy me a new pair!* Next, I run and strip the bed, scrub the carpet then the quilt with Dettol; hurrying about cleaning the mess, I have to work fast; to help get rid of the stench, I fling the window wide open. I light candles and plug in an electric diffuser air freshener. Quickly, I burst open the packaging on new sheets and quilt set. I have no time now to rinse them in fabric conditioner, I need to get them on the bed now. Good, all finished, perfect room prepared for Brad. Next, scampering to the shower hurriedly I shampoo my hair washing all the disgusting dirt thoroughly away. Blow drying it quickly with the hairdryer as I hold my head upside down. This creates a lot of volume, making it look all wild, *fuck it!* That will do. I rummage demented through my drawers, and then pulling out of the clothes my old jeans, his favourite pair, he likes me to wear them for him. With those I fling on a white T-shirt, no bra also I wear no knickers. No make-up either but spray loads of Coco Chanel perfume on myself, now I am sorted I wait. I wait for him.

"Brad won't get on the flight!" I tell the broom. "Brad will love the new purple sheets!" I tell the wall. "Brad will make love to me under my new purple sheet!" I confirm out loud. *("Yes! He will,"* says the voices in my head. *"Maybe not, eh! Not today, YES, yes today he will, Coco, and he will again tonight."*) For once I don't want them to shut up.

I wait and wait, as the mauve shades of evening falls he doesn't come. The sky is becoming the colour of the sheets. I don't feel very well now, so I just put on my purple silk negligee made of lace all down the back, his favourite one. Feeling pleased and pretty proud with how I look, I wait some more knowing he will be here soon. I check my phone, no missed calls. Strange, he must just be running late, so I will wait some more, it won't be long before he arrives. Midnight. I realise Brad isn't coming; he has left the country by now. I play the voicemail; listening to it I wet myself turning the purple silk material also the colour of the sheets, into dark wet patches clinging to my legs. Shaking like a leaf, I throw up only bile. I realise I have pissed myself. That won't do. I strip the fucking thing off trailing the urine right up my body and over my face. I fling the negligee in the washing machine marching starkers to the shower. *Fuck run, Coco!* I wash for the third time, and then still naked I go looking for my Diazepam. I fling wet towels in the laundry basket, standing in the nude looking out the window at the shadows of the cherry blossom trees; I want to shout at them how much I fucking hate them. I don't shout out. I stand silently hating them, hoping they lift their roots and walk away, go, fuck off into the night. Brad won't come tonight, so he won't see my new purple sheets. *"Brad won't come tonight, Brad won't come tonight Coco; he is in Caannaaddaaa with his wife,"* my friends in my head say. They sing *"Caannnaaddda"* drawing the name of the country out in a singsong form of torturous shit. I reach into the cupboard for my pills; I take my bottle of innocent calignosity, my vulgar friends of the night. I swallow them, washing them all down with coffee, long gone cold as I had made it earlier waiting for Brad, he didn't come so I didn't drink it. Now I do.

I go to bed under my new purple sheets. I am alone feeling as if I am just drifting. As I sink further into the smooth cloud of indifference, my friends in my head sing me a lullaby. *"Where you float like the bubbles in the champagne glass in a world trees are made of marshmallow mass, float above the chimney tops on a carpet made of lemonade pop, in a world somewhere afar, where everything is made of bubbles like the Aero chocolate bar, where the sun melts chocolate and pain away. I'll stay there with Brad forever and a day."*

"Brad will come tomorrow, then make love to you *under the new purple sheets!"* I hear the voice say in my head just before the music box tune plays on and on and a beautiful voice sings "He loves me? He loves me not?"

12ᵗʰ April

I wake up wishing that I had not. I had no idea that it is Easter Sunday. I go out to the supermarket for shopping this is when I realise what day it is, so I buy River chocolate eggs. I make a nice Easter Sunday dinner, making promises to myself as I eat the chocolate egg I bought myself, whilst drinking wine to forget Brad Blake. It works for an hour as I look over and there on the kitchen table sits the huge egg I bought for him. I will give it to the bastard when he returns from Canada. *("You are a clown, Coco, the clown,"* is what the voices in my head call me.)

The weeks that follow are the worst of my life. Usually, there are highs and lows, fucking days of drama with Brad but this; this shit is just weeks of being constantly depressed. I mostly feel anger now, which is usually followed by tears at my own stupidity for allowing me to fall in love with him, that wasn't part of my plan way back then, though I convinced myself that being with a married man would be totally different from this. I am now mentally at breaking point, living in a world of tears, which is then accompanied by a complete non-acceptance that he did perhaps want to go with her. All in a cycle with absolutely no happiness, I start to think I may end up a patient in the mental health unit rather than an employee. I become addicted to Diazepam pills. I need them to help me get through the day as well as the night. Sometimes I see myself taking eight at once, hoping perhaps they will make me sleep forever, as sometimes I wish not to wake up. I just function wandering mystified around in a haze of everyday life. Everywhere I go, I'm reminded of Brad. Everything I see, I am reminded of him. At work, in town, at my parents' house, at home I see him standing everywhere about my house, his ghost haunts me… Everywhere I go, I think of his dark green gypsy eyes, his curly hair or travelling in the jeep with him. I just can't get him out of my mind or the witch chant I wrote as my friends in my head continue to repeat it, *"I close the circle turning from the light, I offered my soul to the devil tonight, in return I damned Brad Blake to me, so it was worth it don't you see? Don't you see? Don't you see?"* The music box melody follows: *"He loves me? He loves me not? He loves me? He loves me not? He promised to me love forever, leave me not, fucked off to Canada, all promises forgot. Bastard. First class bastard."*

As the time goes by my work colleagues notice that I am devastated, when supposed to be working, I am found on a sofa in the corner of the duty room tucked up under a little blanket he bought me to keep warm on the night shift. Under my blanket, I just sit in a trance. They offer me words of encouragement and assure me that Brad clearly worships and definitely loves me. I get that they are trying to help but it just makes me feel worse. *Bull shit!* If Brad truly worshipped me, loved me indefinitely, then why the fuck is he in Canada with her? I know she is there with him. I know he lied to me. Always listen to, always trust your instincts, besides Bobby and me, we phoned her house from work in the middle of the night, no answer. *Surprise! Surprise!* Why not? Because she would surely have answered the call at that time in the morning because of the time difference it could be Brad phoning from Canada. No answer. No answer. No answer because she was with him. The next time he phoned me at work, I mentioned the call to him. "Oh! She flew out a couple of days after me to try and sort out her marriage," was his explanation. The lying bastard, she flew out to Canada with him. I know she did. Of course she fucking did! The fucking voices in my head won't shut up telling me so.

Brad continues to make every effort to contact me at work when he gets the chance. Listening to his voice filling me full of promises made of shit are the only moments of joy I have in the time that he has been away. He reminds me he has pictures of me hidden on his phone, which he informs me he has been using to lose sperm over while he can't be with me, and I am supposed to be happy about the fact he's not sleeping or having sex with her, he is pleasuring himself over my photographs, yet he chose to go hundreds of miles away with her, leaving me behind. *Get to fuck, Brad.*

River notices the condition I am in, stating that he thinks I need help. I need help. *"Fucking understatement,"* say the voices in my head. I laugh hysterically. He has started to help me with the housework. *"Too little, too late,"* my friends remind me. *At least River is trying.* This morning he made me hot pancakes with maple syrup for breakfast. A known Canadian breakfast, the last thing I need. I ate wistfully thinking, *God bless River.* Then with a great deal of sadness I remembered the time not so long ago when staying over at a hotel, Brad explained he had to leave earlier than usual. Brad on his way out ordered this breakfast to be brought to me in bed as a wonderful surprise. *"Now he is in Canada taking her breakfast in bed,"* my friends in my head shout out at me. I wish they would shut the fuck up just for an hour of the day. I don't know how I function, mostly I just do. Being without Brad time seems to go on forever. I just survive it. My little dogs were my saviours. I owe them my life, as they are the reason I have to get up every day, they need me most of all and I need them more than I would ever need Blake.

Fuck him! Fuck this month too, because this year with it April brings Canada.

Chapter V
Pleasure with Pain

1st May
Beltane: May Day

Ancient druid fire festival celebrating the return of the goddess. Dancing 'round the maypole with coloured ribbons to symbolise the union of male and female. Beltane Eve we light huge bonfires on the hillsides to light the way for summer.

Fuck all this. I am not celebrating anything do with light or summer or male and female. Fucking Brad is still not here with me. As my world stays in darkness and I am angry and lonely, however, I do eat witches' honey bread that I had baked earlier on today and I do drink May punch so I suppose that this year that is my contribution to Beltane. I should celebrate it after all as it is very much my religion to do so. Besides the reunion of male and female is not that long away, after all? He is due back home is he not? But for a fleeting moment, I consider doing the opposite tonight, instead of celebrating light move to the dark side. Casting an evil curse spell upon him, distant makes no difference, I am a very powerful witch. I just sit staring then decide not too, he has fucked everything else in my life, am I going to let him take my craft too?

3rd May

"BRADFORD RILEY BLAKE ARRIVES BACK IN THE COUNTRY TODAY!" my friends in my head whoop and whoop, bawling, *"HE IS BACK! BACK! BACK! BACK!"*

I have to get up off this floor, now! I tell myself sternly. I know deep down inside that he does still really love me, even though he left me. Nothing pains me more right now than the thought he left me with – that he may never return; however, he did, and I'm trembling feeling both nauseated and excited. I am lying on the carpet holding my head, which hurts badly, as my tummy does, hurt real badly now cramping with nerves. On the floor when he left, on the floor when he returns.

"Coco, get up, don't let this bastard keep doing this to you. Stop doing this to yourself over him, recognise he is a waste of space, and don't be sick also don't push your pants please."

Seriously. The thing is, if you play little houses with someone else's husband, much like fire, you will get burned. In the game of being a mistress the stakes are always high. "Thou shalt not commit adultery." The commandment rings in my head… but I did commit adultery and none of my white witch spells could stop him from leaving me to go to fucking Canada with HER! You didn't try though, did you, Coco? My friends in my head silently torment me. (*No! I did not lose the fucking plot by playing little houses. I lost my sense when I felt I loved him, do you hear me? I allowed myself to love him so much. I lost the will to live, never mind trying to do or make spells to keep him. Would that have worked? Yes, yes probably, you stupid bastards now just go away all of you.*) I clamour silently back at them, knowing the real reason I did not use my magic was because perhaps that maybe he was the magic, my fucking real pure perfect magic.

Finally, I realise this can't go on. Fuck Brad… Fuck Brad Blake, I don't need him. I move my ass, getting up I go looking in the mirror, which reflects my deep tan, tired eyes, shadows under them but shiny messy, un-brushed hair, toned body, skinny now, far too thin, but at least the fantastic orange-coloured glossy nails compliment the colour of my skin perfectly… I still look good on the outside of me, *"Do you really think so? Hmmm! Coco,"* even though I'm so much falling apart inside.

I decide to make today about me instead of him. Believe it or not, he was controlling me from a distance by the way he was making me feel. I head into town for a sunbed in a salon, where everyone knows my name and I'm good friends with the manageress. As I lie in the warm glow of the sunbed, I relax to the scent of coconut and calming sounds of the easy-going/upbeat music, which lifts my mood, making all the worries of the world fade away. It makes me want to get up and dance (even when I'm lying on the sunbed, I find it difficult to lie at peace).

After my sunbed, I take my tanned arse to buy all my favourite food before heading hurriedly for home, now a storm is brewing out. I get my new PJs on then snuggled up on the sofa, time to watch a movie cuddled with my Chihuahuas and a hot chocolate. For dinner I decide on ham and pineapple pizza that conjures up happy memories, reminding me of day trips out with my children when they were young. For dessert I intend to have meringues filled with cream, which for once remind me of when I was a teenager and first fell in love. I smile, wondering where he is today. He was an ice hockey player who went back home to Toronto in Canada to play for Toronto Raiders, the ice hockey team. Oh my God! Whatever made me think of him today after all those years? Maybe, maybe because that makes two of them who fucked off to Canada and left me. How fucking ironic is that! I'm shaking as I make my coffee, I remember Gary told me if he had a ladder he would climb to the sky to pick a special star for me and make a necklace with it, and then I would never forget him. He went to Toronto. It hurt me so much; I willed my heart to stop beating. Brad fucking leaving hurt me even more. *Forget about them both*, I tell myself. I try to hold a bag of truffles as my hands tremble; they're made by Thornton's. When I worked there, I was only nineteen and being manageress was some of the happiest days of my life, things seemed simpler way back then.

Just after ten o' clock I decide it is time to get my arse to my purple silk crib. How appropriate I feel like a lost child. Lying there, alone in the dusky room, as thunder rolls in the distance; my mind begins to fill with painful thoughts. I know I'm still missing him… needing him as much as ever. I am crying thinking about how he is now, yet again, back in that house with her, wondering if he's in a bed with her! The little voices in my head keep telling me and they continue repeating themselves, *"He left you, Coco. Left you to be with her, to fix his marriage with her." Shut up now, PLEASE.* I know he left me. He actually really and truly did go because he wanted too.

Later after midnight my phone is ringing. It's flashing, Brad is calling… No way. No ghost of a fucking chance. It's not done that for weeks, not since the last phone call he made, leaving me a voicemail in tears, begging me to wait for him, saying how much he loved me before he fucked off that morning to Canada with her. I don't answer but the phone just keeps on ringing and ringing, it won't stop. I go downstairs, make witches' tea, and drink it sitting in my lounge. He keeps on calling. His wife must be sleeping now he is sneaking to phone me, *bastard of the highest class!* Still he keeps on calling. I retch and bring up pizza all over my sofa. I wipe my mouth, and then with my unsteady hands I shakily turn my phone off. Well, Brad can call but this time Coco won't fall, I'm not having it. *"Phone off ha-ha! Not having it! Phone off, ha-ha! Not having it!"* This time Brad Blake can wait. Like he made me wait for him. I clean up then go back to bed.

Unable to relax at all, as heavy rain rattles against the windows, I get back up to look for Diazepam. Searching for sleep furthermore to kill this pain inside me, I need my No Way Josie pills. Finding them I spill out the bottle, those little tablets to me look like a million dollars' worth of sparkling diamonds They are my peace, my world of obscurity,; they make me fly away to a place of pessimism… they eclipse my soul to fucking none existence, no more Brad Blake.

Six? Maybe eight should be enough, I think to myself, lifting the glass of orange juice to help me swallow them. At that moment for some unknown reason, I change my mind. Spitting them into the sink, I turn on the hot tap, trying to melt and rinse them down the drain; diamonds don't dissolve and are easily retrieved from water I grab at them collecting the broken chalky white wet pieces. I run upstairs fling them in the toilet and pour the rest down the pan too. I flush it, standing watching the last of them disappear, I suddenly realise my golden nuggets of blissful sleep have gone forever. (My friends in my head are shouting at me: *"Are you fucking daft, Coco? Why did you do that? You need them if not for Blake, then to help you from suffering withdrawal symptoms, which you will get, Coco, yes you will, given the amount you took."*)

In this moment it becomes horribly clear to me that I am an addict. I just have to force myself in a minute of madness to get rid of the stuff I need to get me through the fucking day and night, but that is only one addiction dealt with, I'm also physically and mentally needy of Brad Blake and the withdrawal symptoms suffered upon him leaving me must surely be infinitely worse than going cold turkey from drugs. The voice in my head chimes in again: *"You need him too; you made him your hero, alas he also became your demon. Your married man left you, he destroys you and yet you still crave him. He will suck your blood like a vampire, but then again you stick to him like a leech."* Why must they say shit like that to me? *But is it really shit, Coco? No chance of peace now!* Music box starts to play soft music notes and that ethereal voice of an angel starts singing, *"He loves me? He loves me not?!"*

Monday, 4th May

Another unsettled, sleepless night, so I just get up out of bed and stay up after fretfully tossing and turning. I am beyond ill at ease, agitated and troubled knowing Brad Blake is back.

It's still very early morning, yet my phone starts ringing, flashing Brad is calling. Here we go. I answer the phone this time, mustering the courage to stay strong, "Hello, Blake."

"Coco, oh God! Coco, I'm so sorry I left you. I missed you so much; I will never leave you again ever. I'm back like I promised, please believe me, Coco, I would never hurt you."

Brad's voice rambles on with apologies, my mind phases out of the conversation. I start thinking about the last part I heard 'I would never hurt you'. Never hurt me! What planet is he fucking on! How can he be so insensitive! Does he even realise what misery he has caused me? How much hurt I've suffered, the pain is beyond control; he has absolutely broken me resulting in me being unstable and disturbed.

I try to regain my focus on the present whatnot back to the phone. "Brad, Brad!" I yell down the phone to get him to shut him up for one minute. "When will I see you again?" I ask as I'd managed to stop his pish talk of making more promises he absolutely wouldn't keep.

"I just told you, Coco, I'm going to pick you up tomorrow night for work. I will pick you up early as usual, because I need to talk to you, she asked me at the airport on the way home if her marriage was in trouble. I answered her question by asking her 'What do you think?' She asked me to tell her that I love her, and I couldn't say those words because I still love you." Silence.

"Truthfully, I always have and always will. *Whatever!*" I hang up.

After that I switch my phone off. , I speak softly to myself, "I need to speak to you too, Brad, but only to say one word… Goodbye. No, two words actually, three words, Get to Fuck!" Tomorrow night I will be in control, I will change my life. I've already been through the worst, so surely it can only get better from here, right? Get rid of second bad habit. Won't give him the glory of addiction.

Tuesday, 5th May

The next day is a blur for me, trying to decipher what is real by what is happening in my life. Brad comes to pick me up for work. I look out my window and there once again sits Brad Blake in his silver jeep. Just as he'd never left.

I walk out with my head held high and get into that jeep. I act robotic. I only function with severe coldness, without knowledge of anything, except what I'm programmed to do, which is to hold it together. Brad looks at me, he has tears running down his face; I ignore him. He's very nervous. He tries to make small talk by telling me that his wife no longer wants him to come to take me to work, I'm not allowed to be in the jeep. Yet here I am, Brad. She wants to put all my CDs in the trashcan. Brad tries to reassure me by saying that he has kept my CDs at his mother's house so that won't happen, and he will be continuing to collect me for work without her knowledge. *How fucking sugary sweet!*

I can't contain my emotions any longer. Robot malfunctions. "Well, it would seem you've fucking sorted your marriage out then? With her? Stupid me!" I burst out in anger.

"No, Coco, I sorted fuck all out, it is over. I never had sex with her in Canada; she makes me feel physically sick. She knows quite definitely that the marriage is in trouble and that I love you. She was told that straight to her face by me when she said I lusted after you but didn't love you. When she called you a tart, I defended you as I told her I loved strawberry tarts, being sarcastic as I also told her I asked you out, I fell in love with you. I wanted you sexually, that I wanted you full stop. Her brother-in-law Felix said you were just a piece of ass, but I told him it was different not like that, because I have fell in love with you

111

the moment I met you, besides I do want to be with you, Coco. I just need time to sort all of this out; I need a little time to think it over," he sincerely begs me. I have heard those words somewhere before, those very words I once said to him a while ago, *"I need a little time to think it over!" That is exactly what I did back then, think our relationship over, and that is what I for fucking sure should do right now too, only this time decide to hunt him, hunt him to fuck out my life for good.*

As I look up into his eyes, I can see the fear of the realisation dawning on him that I am going to leave him. Memories of all the times Brad and I have had in this jeep come flooding back to me and I start crying. "I need to go, Brad, I need to leave; you know that I have to go," I whisper to him through my tears. He obviously knows I am being serious as he goes pure white with shock when I tell him. He takes me in his arms; feeling him against me, I feel so light-headed I almost faint. I still feel way too much for him.

He undoes his seatbelt and pulls me towards him, kissing me hard with his tongue in my mouth. "God! I have really missed you so much, Coco. I want to make love to you, I need to be inside you," Brad pleads to me, knowing I can see how hard he'd become.

This is the hardest part… to resist. It would be so easy as the temptation is unreal from his promises and kisses. I am fucked again: my addiction has returned. I have surrendered heart and soul; head and clitoris, I need him inside me as much as he needs to be there.

I manage to pull away "Brad, Brad we need to go, we are going to be late for work," I force out from my breathlessness. Brad starts up the car, heading in the direction of the unit. We are back at the beginning of the game.

As we pull up at work, I decide I need to get a final answer from Brad. "Well, Brad… so, I'm to be your mistress once more then?" I ask hesitantly.

"No, long-term relationship. I love you, Coco, I don't do mistresses. In my eyes you are my wife, even if she is on paper. You're the woman I love, the woman I make love to, and I will marry you, Coco. I will never leave you again; I promise you that, Coco. I will never go anywhere again without you by my side," Brad reassures me in a comforting and loving tone. *"Fucking stupid Highland cow,"* my imaginary friends say.

I believe him, because deep down I want to. We agree to continue the affair; he kisses me before we walk in to work. Suddenly, he made me feel that all the hurt is not so important anymore, it has all been laid to rest. *"Stupid witch, Coco. You have learned nothing. You let the bastard win, are you really going to continue with the affair? Are you really that fucking daft? You might as well go and take down your White Witchcraft altar and reset it back up in your old Black Magic ways. Go follow Satan because on following Brad Blake, you are already half way there. Fucked in the dark and desperate side of this world!"* the friends yell in disbelief. Brad leans over into the back seat, handing me a package, in it is little brown bear with the cutest face wearing tied round his neck a chocolate-coloured tartan ribbon. He had brought me it back from Canada. He explains how she tried to get him to buy a different one, a cheaper one as she thought it was for a patient at work. He says I told her no because unknown to her I wanted this one for you so I bought it. Then he explains he had also got me a large bottle of Canadian maple syrup but customs at the airport took it off him. He apologises he couldn't get me some of the duty-free perfume as she was there. He, however, tells me that he'd buy me some perfume and maple syrup in town tomorrow. I am delighted with the little bear, I call him Toffee.

I enter the ward with a sparkling smile on my face, I can't contain how I feel, I am so very ecstatically happy for the first time in weeks. The staff are looking at me mesmerised.

My charge nurse Bobby asks me with no surprise in his voice, "Is Brad back, Coco?"

I look up, replying enthusiastically, "Yes, Bobby, my Brad is back."

The following week the affair finally goes back to our normal loving way, just as it was before he left for Canada. Brad sits me down, explaining to me that everything he was doing at the moment was so that he could remain in the house complying with just enough of her ideas, or so she thought, to be able to deal with her financial blackmail whilst also staying in a relationship with me. He would remain sleeping separately from her in the back bedroom of the house, there would never again be any sort of sexual relationship as that had finished years ago anyway. He would not go out socially with her, not even for the shopping now, in fact not go anywhere at all as he was affronted to be seen with her anyway. I make my rules, which he has to strictly follow, too. He asks that we both come to an agreement that we are to remain faithful to each other. I acknowledge that fact, agreeing but warning him if I ever find out he is behaving differently with her then he is finished for good. I mean it and he knows it. At least now we both understand where we stand. I can walk away at any time if I want to, I suppose; we both can, I guess, but for now I choose to stay, as does he.

The people at work continue to keep their mouth shut on our behalf, even defending the affair when she phones his work checking whether he is there. We have a system in place, if she phoned work when he was with me, they'd say he was on a constant; they would get him to call when he was free. They would notify us and he would call her back. He takes a lot of overtime; he works shifts half the time then staying over in hotels with me on the rest. On those nights sometimes he'd go into his work on the way past to phone the house, asking her to tape football, showing the works' number calling into the house phone. Game sorted, he made, we made a total arse of her while she understood I was out of his life, or so she thought.

Sometimes though I still feel raw as remembering everything that happened is a heavy burden for my heart to carry. He hurt me really bad on leaving me. I try moving on as we go about our happy lives together as if we didn't have a care in the world. As far as I am concerned, to him I am his wife, fuck what the law says, we love each other! We often go out to Greenan Castle in the jeep, making love under the stars in front of the lovely view over Arran. But we are as fucked as that castle it stood in ruins.

12th/13th and 14th May

Brad phones me constantly, saying he misses me so much. One night he phones me at ten thirty, telling me he needs to make love to me so much that he asks me to take a taxi out to the Ailsa Hospital to meet him at midnight. Cinderella runs away from her prince at midnight, I am running to meet mine. I am so happy he is back to his normal self, our love is rekindling like a bonfire being lit. I buzz about getting ready, wondering how he managed to get out the house at that time of night, he must've said work phoned, so that means I have him for eight hours. I am glowing with happiness.

I take out some clothes, throwing on my jeans, thong and chunky cardigan (no bra). I style my hair all wild, put on my favourite Coco Chanel perfume and pull on my new Ugg boots Brad bought just as my hired transport arrives to take me to him.

As the cab pulls up, I see Brad has arrived. He is standing at his jeep. I fling money at the driver then jump out the car. I am running fast towards Brad, squealing loudly as I leap up into the air, Brad catches me in his arms; I kiss him hard on the mouth. We get in the jeep laughing; fuck knows what the car driver must be thinking as he turns to drive away! Well, it is on the grounds of a psychiatric hospital this took place I supposed, so perhaps he made an allowance for that in my behaviour. As Brad pulls away, he can hardly drive as the air is electric between us. He can't keep his hands off me whilst driving with one hand. By the time we reach the breezeless luminescence of the unruffled beach, I am desperate to have Brad make love to me. It feels like is has been forever!

As we head into the back of the jeep, Brad takes off my cardigan and starts kissing my neck taking light kisses down to my nipples, sending tingles down my back dancing around my breasts. His breathing is hard and slow as I gasp with pleasure. He slips off my boots, undoes my jeans and thrusts his finger past my thong (already damp with excitement), straight into my secret place. Brad covers my lips with his, flicking his tongue in and out of my mouth as I grip his hardness, taking it out of his pants. Moving away from his mouth, I slink down level with his penis, which is rock hard, dripping sperm when take it in my mouth. "I want to be inside you so much, please sit on me, darling, sit on it," Brad demands through his gasps and moans of pleasure. I take him out of my mouth, then straddling him, I lower myself down slowly, taking every inch of him deep up inside me, and my eyes are glistening with pleasure in the moonlight shining through the window.

"Coco, oh Coco," he says as he begins to climax.

"Fuck me, Brad," I am begging him to fill me with every drop of his sperm. "I want it all!" I seductively whisper as my body shudders with excitement. He fills me with warm liquid; he holds my hair, pulling my head back as we climax together.

He is hard again within seconds, so both of us, naked in a jeep, make love again as I climb back on his erection and we move into each other once more Brad ejaculates again. The sunroof is opened to the sky as we make love on and off for hours as under the stars we share an erotic loving act all night long. It is such an amazing, yet debilitating feeling. Daylight starts to filter through the jeep window as Brad spurts sperm in me for the third time; it is so romantic despite both of us naked in the backseat of a car. I feel that the past few weeks of turmoil have disappeared, no kind of buried themselves from dusk to dawn in pure, raw sexual passion. He tells me that I have no idea of how much he missed me; perhaps not, but fuck I know how I missed him. *Understatement of the century.*

"Coco, thank you darling, I just desperately wanted you so much tonight," Brad says so lovingly whilst gazing into my eyes.

Now that it is early morning, we decide we better go as Brad is supposed to be finishing a night shift just as I thought, but I want to go to McDonalds for breakfast. The place is empty as we plonk ourselves down at a table holding hands drinking coffee. We have to hurry Brad has to go. I wish we were going home to bed together. He drops me off at my house kissing me goodnight. Ha-ha good morning more like. When I get in, I don't shower because I don't want to wash his scent off me. I just cleanse my face; putting on my night cream in the morning, I smirk thinking everything is upside down today. Getting into bed, I smell him on my skin as I pull up the duvet; I pretend he is beside me as I go to sleep. For the first time in weeks, I feel calm, as a tranquil veil made of love descends gently over me. This is so much better than Diazepam. (*"For now!"* my friends in my head say. Where the hell have they been? I haven't heard from them in a while s but then I am not likely to when I'm happy or of sound mind, well that's a lie because I am never stable am I?) All I need is Brad to fuck me all through the bewitching hours, and then I sleep like a baby, because I got another one over on his wife or perhaps I am just the cat that stole the Devon cream.

The Rest of May 2009

May passes by so quickly; we are both actually working a lot of night shifts just now and spend whatever time we can together. We have lovely romantic walks through the trees at night when it is pitch black in the forest, which I love, I'm nocturnal, so on being with him out there I suffer no fear. As the moon is full tonight, I tell Brad, laughing, "All the werewolves will be out roaming the woods." He nearly about shit himself at the thought of them hunting us down. I was not one bit scared out there raking about in the stygian darkness (I was actually wishing to meet Edward from the Twilight movie, yet him probably if he knew me, like Brad would nearly shit himself at the thought) as his love acted as my shield of protection. *Right Coco!* As our intimacy grows, we also begin talking about everything and anything. Nothing feels awkward or wrong, it is just easy to say whatever is on our minds. We share the same dreams.

I start sending even more sexy photographs of myself to his phone. *How pathetic is that? Seriously Coco!* This time the one I send is one of my favourites. It is me standing wearing only tiny red pants with black lace and my finger seductively just above my clitoris. Brad would now store these photos in his second secret phone, and then he would send pictures back of his hard cock dripping with cum after wanking to my photos. I would pretend to Brad to masturbate moaning while looking at his photos, wishing I could be there in person. This becomes our game. *Eh! My game, for what? What was I trying to achieve with this nonsense.* I love to watch him doing this. *Did I?* Cow, he'd say. Eh! Highland Cow, please Brad.

I however love the intimacy we share, both when we together also when apart. There is no doubt we both have serious feelings about us. We belong to each other, he is mine and I am his and together we are special or so we believe. (*"Are the two of you together really so special though?"* I hear my friends in my head question.) You know what I say in reply. Two words. Fuck off!

June 2009

June brings the summer and Brad is down cutting my grass in the glorious heat. We would share many an evening over some wine and then make love. We are living pretty much like a real couple, other than the fact that he doesn't live with me yet. We make love everywhere, in hotels, at our castle, on the warm sand at the beach. Everything is awesome. For now.

21st June

Summer Solstice also known as Litha is here again. It is one of the lesser Sabbats and the dates can vary slightly from year to year. Summer Solstice, we celebrate the Sun God at her highest. Night time is now being dominated by the daylight, and the days are at their longest. It is also celebrating the beauty of our planet and all she provides for us. We share and eat honey, fresh vegetables, fresh citrus and summer fruits. Use herbs like lavender and fennel, lemon verbena and thyme and fresh basil. Drink ale and homemade mead and be thankful for the season of wonderful food and life. We cook with all the fresh foods and bake with all the sweet berries.

One hot day during Litha, I am baking in the kitchen wearing tiny red shorts and a small white top showing off my flat stomach. Brad turns up out of the blue. He comes in and kisses me, smacking my arse. "Ouch! Brad," I laugh. He then licks his finger dipped it in the bowl of dry icing sugar and puts it on my nose. He laughs, so funny he thinks. I take a handful of the icing sugar powder then fling it over his curls, as it lands it sprinkles the dark hair on his head pure white. This time I laugh, shouting, "Hi! You salt and pepper head." Picking up the bowl, he empties it over me. I lift the box and fling more over him. A fight starts as he lifts a strawberry and squishes it on my nose. I try to get some strawberries too but he is too fast so I put the cookie dough on him instead. What a state we both are then; I scream on seeing the mess all over the place, including our clothes. Brad steps forward kissing me again as behind my back he puts his hand over what is left of the cookie dough and rubs it into my hair. "Bastard!" I scream.

"What did you call me?" he asks coming towards me with the rest of the box of strawberries. "What, Coco?"

I run around the table. "Nothing, I said nothing!" I shout back as I run around the other side again to get away but he comes across the top of the table so he catches me shouting, "OH! No, please don't." He picks me up and lays me top of the kitchen table. He kisses me, putting strawberries from his mouth into mine. He pulls off my top and takes the box of icing sugar, shaking the remnants of it onto my nipples. As tiny drops of pure white sugar land on my nipples, making them look like little snow-capped mountains, he sucks it off. He pulls down my red shorts and gets so excited when he realises I am not wearing any underwear.

My body is sun-kissed, covered in coconut oil due to the summer heat, so between that the sugar, strawberries and the chocolate dough in my hair, Brad says I taste and smell so sweet. Like his own homemade strawberry tart (as in, once he told his wife he loved strawberry tarts when referring to me. Hmmm!). *Cute!* He lays me back naked on the cold hard table as he reaches over for more coconut oil as he massages me; it all just melts into my warm skin. Brad opens my legs and slowly pushes every inch of him inside me. He then lifts me onto the worktop, spreads my legs and starts licking my clitoris, flickering his tongue gently over it, then puts it in and out of me so quickly until I climax. He gets up, then kissing me he carries me over laying me back onto the table once more; he holds one leg right up over his head, enters me again, pounding me hard until he comes, jetting deep inside me loads of hot liquid as my legs tremble in excitement, I come again. Contented and smiling as he lifts me down from the table kissing me, I feel so in love I can hardly walk.

"Guess what, Blake?" I ask him in shocked amazement on discovering that anyone in the world passing could see what had just taken place.

"What?" he asks, laughing at the expression on my face. Before I answer, I looked around at the kitchen at him and you would think a food bomb had exploded. Then I look at us standing naked covered in stuff and oil, him with his cock still semi-hard, all of this and the fact no cookies would be baked today are the least of my worries. As I point over to the other side of the kitchen, Brad turns to see what I mean; my back door, which is at the side of the house facing out onto the street, Brad had accidently left wide open. Oh my God! He leaves soon afterwards. I finish cleaning up the mess. As it is a lovely night with just a little chill in the air, I decide to go for a walk. On walking through the trees by the river, I notice a stone table. I stop, smile, back track then I point my wand at the table casting a spell to set up my witches' altar. I walk round the tree in my beautiful long cream coat, and I come out from 'round the other side dressed in my witches' cloak. I draw the pentagram softly in the air, differently for my candle spells. I curtsy to my altar before casting a candle spell of love, asking the goddess to convince Brad Blake that he wants me and only me. I close my circle with my wand and black salt, for protection of all on ending the spell, then I just walk away in the dark, in the opposite direction as my altar clears itself behind me. I appear again, dressed as before in my cream lace dress and long cream cloak, I now get up on the stone table that I used to provide my altar. I stand on it under the tree in the moonlight, holding my wand as I stare out over the water, thinking, I smile sadly to myself; knowing that along with all this love it includes a lot of doubt, that there is also a lot of pleasure with pain.

Chapter VI
Memories Lost in Time

The calendar months seemed to go very swiftly by as we continued to grow closer with passing time. Lammas: August Eve came and went as quickly. This is a Sabbat to pay homage to Lugh, the Celtic Sun God. Brad celebrates it with me, lighting yellow candles to honour the death and rebirth of the god. His fucking face is a picture, I think he is so glad when it is all over, but he likes the cranberry muffins and the alcoholic nectar of the gods that follow, but refuses to eat the baked squirrel, a traditional dish, which I don't have. He doesn't know that though and almost shit himself when I said that was what is being served for dinner. Just another playful game of mine, he laughs nervously at me, I can see him contemplating if this is so, he is still not sure what to think about, dinner or me. The relationship we shared had worked so far despite that under certain circumstances we were not being completely truthful with each other – not yet. Let's say you wouldn't class us as being an honourable couple who were forthright in this affair, but is this not what the scenario is though? Stories and lies? Maybe, but there were still too many dark, deeply hidden secrets between us. Both of us very much aware this needed to be addressed, but it was easier to stay in denial than deal with it, I suppose. Neither one of us wanting to approach the subject first, yet hoping the other wouldn't bring it up. Due to this undeniable fact of the silence of this situation between us the fighting between us had increased as did the sex, both were becoming more extremely intense. We fought with the passion we made love with; then perhaps some. I went from a conscious spirit of ecstatic happiness to feeling morbidly depressed as I felt trapped in a place of hopelessness. That was followed by hatred of everything, which then went on and blossomed into a kind of sad sorrowful love for him. I walked around carrying a cloud of guilt above my head, for living in and exuding physically such an emotionally unstable love in my commitment to Brad. Which was what exactly? I decided to go out tonight. Back to the place I cast the candle spell of love. This time I am dressed in my witch clothes to perform Black magic. It is dark and very late so no one will see me. Besides, I don't actually care that much. I hurry back to the stone table, I am so hell bent on cursing Brad Blake. On arriving there, I turn my back on it, angrily I glare out over the water once again as I chant with my back to it, asking for a demonic presence. Swiftly I turn around, feeling it has arrived, angrily I fling my hand in the air and bring down my satanic altar, where it sits in front of me on that same fucking cold concrete surface. I fling black salt everywhere as I protect nothing. I curse Brad Blake to hell with all I got, acknowledging for it to come back to me times three – FUCKING NOT! I dance with glee. I hear no music box. Or voices saying, "*He loves me? He loves me not?*" I dance with all the invisible witches that only my eyes can see. As I lift my dress kicking up my legs to the devil playing the bagpipes. I dance all over the forsaken land before I clear my altar with one swift swipe of my hand. Done. I precedent over that empty witches, pulpit. Mission accomplished. Fuck him. Over and done. Complete but not delete. Ha! Ha! Ha! Ha! I go home. I say nothing.

The next day as I sit in the garden pondering over my childhood dreams of making a fairy-tale love story of my own, I was left with little hope. As by now all my expectations of this happening had been broken and justly so, with his haunting lies. Amidst it all is my black and white, dark and light spells. Yet, it would seem, he was still a senseless addiction I couldn't be without. Dark days were returning, bringing lost hours in which I found myself creating in me a whole new obsession with Brad Blake. My invisible friends were back. Their voices shouting in my head were warning me not to trust him. I found myself crying out loud at them, insisting they shut up whilst refusing to listen to their advice, because trust him is exactly what I did. I stupidly went against all reason and common sense, deliberately forgetting everything I'd ever been taught in lessons of love, because I wanted too. This false security in a chosen fantasy love, in which I had been pretending to be comparable to

Shakespeare's Romeo and Juliet, but the fact they both took their own lives in the end, which in reality is absurd, so this drawn out fantasy love story along with everything else it too eventually took its toll on me. I decided on something which I truly believed to be the ultimate sacrifice for him, a mistake that cost me very dearly in the end.

Early one morning out of the blue Brad arrives with some of his clothes. He said he wants to stay with me for a while and that his wife was aware of the fact he was with me. I just looked at him questioning nothing. I decided that this was a good opportunity of finding out if this is what I had really wanted.

It is late as daylight is fading in the hot season of the year; the warm breeze of summertime blows the cherry blossoms about in the garden. I sit on an old wooden bench (which my father handmade out of tree trunks and logs) with a glass of red wine, watching them being scattered in the soft wind, I think it looks a beautiful, dreamy enchanted place of tranquillity to be. It was my magical world, a garden I created with all the trees and tiny flowers amongst which sat solar powered fairy houses which glowed lights from little windows in the dark. I loved this place. Yet the beauty of this picture, however, with the scent of the nearby roses lingering in the air evokes memories for me, which disgusted me for disturbing my perfect haven also I contemplate how those memories hold bitter hurt for me certainly no happiness. Now, tonight perhaps all that would change as I feel it is the perfect time to act out my plan.

Brad said he was going to visit his mother. He was only gone a short while when he returned saying he had changed his mind now he sits quietly beside me amongst the cherry trees, as I turn around he smiles. I remember how I hated those cherry trees with a passion more than ever felt for Brad. I ask him to close his eyes; on him doing so, I lean over towards him, playfully dropping kisses ever so lightly on his nose, so delicately that they can barely be felt. On wondering what is tickling him, he abruptly opens his eyes. My explanation to him is that the garden fairies came over to kiss his beautiful face. Laughing, he takes hold of me by my collar of my shirt; he pulls me into him now kissing me full on the mouth. I wear no bra, this shows through the white silk as my nipples have grown hard on rubbing against his body. On us pulling apart, he notices this; he takes one of them between his fingers, gently massaging it through the soft material before whistling in appreciation at how erect it now stood. Putting my hand down between his legs, I can feel him throbbing; I know that he also wore no pants, which is beginning very clearly to show. I whistle back. I stand up, pulling him to his feet as I take him by the hand to get the car keys. Brad asks where we are going, winking at him, I explain to our castle so he can lay me on the sand. We drive out to the ancient derelict castle, where below it he slowly makes love to me on the beach. Then as he fucks me again amongst the old ruins, I feel something has shifted in our relationship as I sense that once more our love is invincible. He has returned to the status of being my prince crowned with adoration as he urgently empties his sperm into me, greedily I share his orgasm with all the ardour in the world. I promise myself to put his ghosts of the past to rest, praying that's where they would forever remain. I hope the lies would no longer keep resurfacing. But then again even after the love we have just shared, on buttoning up my shirt, I feel no composure inside me, with certainly no promise of my final wish being granted as I pull my knickers back up.

On leaving the old historic place that Midsummer's night, I glance behind me as I walk away, on looking back at the dark castle which is open to the rafters, it holds no shelter whatsoever from above and its' very old stone walls are now actually all tumbling down; it stands very proud on the edge of the cliff with its broken, but once regal silhouette against the deep hues of purple worn by the twilight sky, it looks eerie, sinister even. I am convinced I feel something evil in the air back there, so slightly confused by this, I just go on hurriedly back to the car, saying nothing Brad. I tell myself now not to be so fucking melodramatic by putting a bad omen on our love, had the sex not just been amazing, sealing our love eternally? After all, I had pretended dreamily for so long that it was our romantic happy-ever-after castle.

"Conceivably, Coco, in another life! The fact is, it was a castle once but that was a long time ago. In the 12th century it was known as a fortress then by the 15th century it was a stone castle which was used as a home. But by the 17th it had become a three-storey watchtower, one of many that sat along the coast! I guess so on this we can agree, Coco, as now it is as fucked as

124

a castle as you two are with each other. So perhaps it is better this way for you, a watch tower to live in rather than a castle, because the tower after all would be much more useful when looking out for the enemy, you could very quickly see in advance, therefore be warned of Brad's upcoming arrival," my imaginary friends sarcastically state to me, ignoring what they say I disregard their facts intentionally. Staring out the car window, I watch the remains of the castle fading into the distant duskiness of the night. In my thoughts though I am trying to be more realistic, but I honestly still feel that something somewhere out there was warning me that I was terribly wrong in my decision to go through with this idea of mine tonight. Perhaps I should wait for now, just maybe the timing was all wrong. I choose, however, to ignore my instincts, which goes against what we are taught as human beings, that one of the most important given rules of survival in the protection of ourselves is – to follow our instincts – I do not. On this occasion, it leaves me with the result which is – I have fucked myself.

Later that night Brad lays naked on the bed watching me walking around the room. The atmosphere is strange, he looks nervous, frightened with anticipation of something about to happen but worried on not knowing what. I feel neither love nor fear, just numbness with a readiness to do this. I lie down beside him, rolling my nakedness on top of him, as I start slowly, softly running my tongue over his lips, darting it in and out his mouth. He holds me to him, kissing me desperately, his erection, throbbing on my thigh, is now leaking out sticky fluid onto my tanned skin. His breathing becomes heated as he moves his warm mouth down onto my throat. He starts sucking on my neck, biting it sorely as I moan. I slide my hand between my legs playing with myself for him, making the gentle slushy noise he likes to listen too. I whisper in the darkness asking him to fuck me, he groans that he will. It is difficult to see the expression on his face as in the dimness of the room there is only a pale shaft of light coming in from the outside street lamp, which barely lights the place. Running my fingers gently through then around his hair, I grab on tightly then all of a sudden pulling hard, I harshly jerk his head backwards while tenderly biting on his bottom lip, thereupon searching his face; I find his eyes staring blankly into mine. I hold his gaze for a while, before I order him very clearly to follow my instructions

"I want you to fuck me up my arse!" I demand roughly, pushing him away from me freeing him from my grip. I slip my body back onto the bed as I proceed onto my knees, offering him my little bare derriere high in the air. He gets on his knees behind me as I reach over to the table and handed him a bottle of scented lubricant, which he takes from me saying nothing. He lays it on the bed beside him as he roams his hands over the cheeks of my backside, massaging it, kissing it, whispering,

"Oh! Coco, your bum is so firm, your skin smooth, Oh! Coco," he speaks with a rasping tone in his voice. He is dripping more sperm out of his penis as by now I can feel it landing on my flesh. He opens the bottle of strawberry gel, massaging the fruity oily substance over my bottom half and thighs to relax me. He concentrates next on my little tight hole, he puts more gel on there, massaging it in, then he starts to gently open me up by pushing his fingers inside it, then he opens me up further by using his thumb. I hold the pillow, closing my eyes as he enjoys playing with me. I lie trembling in the shadows, where the smell of strawberries hangs heavily in the air, listening to how excited he's become as I wait, terrified of the hurt I am destined to suffer when that huge, hard-on goes into ass for the very first time. He massages more cool gel on me; I feel the warm tip of him pulsing at the outer circle of my anus as he gets ready to enter. He pushes in gently, kindly protruding only a little way up to begin with, and I hold my breath, feeling my skin stretching to accommodate him. He slides slowly back out, and then he pushes back up in again, this time his cock goes deep inside me, right up that sacred, tiny narrow passage. Gripping the pillow furiously, I bury my face into it to stifle my scream, the searing pain I feel, is as I had expected, and unreal.

"OH GOD!" he says in a deep gasping tone to the darkness. The same two words he used when he touched my soft, smooth pussy for the very first time.

He continues to ride into my little hole as I buck up my behind to meet him, ignoring the discomfort. I clinch my cheeks together, lifting them high in the air, as I move with stealth and speed, keeping his rhythm with the accuracy of a dancer. I shake my behind for him, and then draw circles in the air with it, thus creating an amazing sensation on his manhood. This pattern I continue until the sperm comes hard and fast, shooting up my rear while he pumps it out of him time after time.

Lying in his arms afterwards, I am significantly glad it was over. He is unaware of the throbbing ache or how tender and inflamed my body feels. He tells how much he loves me, that he finds sex extraordinary between us, besides he whispers clinging to me; I am the best lover in the world. In the gloomy grey space in the room, I lie staring at nothing as he talks away, my mind wandering as his voice drones on; I am rudely aware of this so he catches my attention just in time for me to hear him saying that he'd honestly never even thought of having sex that way before, which he'd enjoyed immensely. He appreciates the experience. He mentions also that he won't take it for granted on knowing how much it must have took for me to do that for him, he says he thanks me beyond words. I comment back that I thought he was worth it and I love him infinitely, which is how I truly felt at that moment, but not a few minutes before. *Well! Coco, which one is it? Love him or love him not?* I see a black rose in my head with its petals being pulled off one by one, the voice which continues teasingly, love him or love him not? Love him, love him not? Along with the words, the music boxes' melody plays in my mind as I get up shaking my head to block out the image, what the last petal would reveal or confirm the real resolution of the flower puzzle to be, well, I do not care that much not really. On moving my neck, I feel like it is burning, it hurts as I delicately touch the skin. I am sure it would be bruised, leaving a mark often referred to as a love bite or a hickey. It was a strong possibility, I consider, by the way Brad had sucked it. Knowing it was more a probable fact, I am mortified, so on deciding to hide it with make-up, and I just dismiss it for now. I think about how I'd always contemplated having anal sex with Brad as a given pledge of my love for him. That was exactly what I had done. I feel I gave myself indefinitely to him as a woman in the most scared way I knew how, which I feel was the optimum thing to do. More so than giving your virginity to a man, as it is something all women eventually lose, but this, in my opinion, was the most sacrificial gift of all. Is the feeling of regret for my actions already setting in? Maybe. As it begins to dawn on me that the leader has more regrets than the follower and the scholar makes more mistakes than the fool.

Later, actually, it is the next day; I find out (from his mother) that he had sneaked out to phone his wife hours before we went to the castle. He had lied to her apparently about where he was staying. She drove by and found his car parked outside my house. His wife texted him informing him she knew where he was, who he was with, telling him to stay there with his whore and to keep away from her. He'd been in tears at her finding out, besides he was worried for himself at being caught. I was not aware of these events taking place so all of this was unknown to me at the time. I questioned nothing when he came earlier that evening to tell me that he was going to visit his mother. I had just taken for granted when I'd noticed he'd been recently upset, that perhaps the reason for being so had lain there. It was only him on returning twenty minutes later after he left, I enquired if everything was all right he told me that he'd changed his mind apparently and decided to spend time with me in the garden instead, which he did. So idiotically, I accepted this was the actual case when he had in fact gone out to contact his wife. He hid the information from me by not disclosing that he had made calls to her. He made excuses to her, covering for himself by telling her stories of where he was and that he had left because he just needed some space to sort out his head and their marriage. Thereupon he had also made some detailed arrangements over the phone to visit the house they shared to speak with her in person. He claimed that I was only a friend, whom he was renting a room off for now because he was in dire straits as the other guy he was going to flat-share with had moved in his girlfriend. Now therefore under those circumstances he'd nowhere to stay or go so that's why he'd come here to me. Despite the fact that she'd known about our affair in the past, she chose to believe him because she needed to be compliant with his pish for her own financial benefit. Yes, this time she had one over me; give her credit where it is due, but for money? At least my foolishness was for love, or so I thought. "*Fucking told you Coco, but you wouldn't listen!*" said all the whispers in my head.

Me, I wasn't buying his fucking lies any more when he tried to deny all of it. After shouting and swearing at him, I retreated deathly calm. The pain I felt, however, was as if a surgeon had just sliced me wide open while still conscious and was ripping the heart organ right out of my body whilst I was still alive. He was, as always, talking his way out of his shit; I refused to listen anymore. I just looked at him coldly with tears running down my face, as devastated, I brokenly whispered

"I thought you were my hero! I trusted you, Brad Blake."

A few days later, he came to me explaining he had to stay over with his mother at her house. He promised to phone later but did not call all night. That was because he spent the night in the marital home with his wife (as arranged earlier per phone call, unknown to me). Late on, in the following morning, he walked in the door, looking guilty. His face went bright red as he said, "I am leaving to go back home." I did not look up. I replied, "Well go!" He wanted to take me to lunch first. *OH! Do you really? Fuck off!* "GO!" I yelled at the top of my voice. So he did. He took his stuff and he was gone from the house as quickly as he had arrived. First you don't see him, and then you do. He is there! Then you still see him, and then you don't. He is not! *Fucking magician!* In his absence, all that is left behind is a bag of presents lying on the kitchen table for me. Expensive crap he bought earlier that morning. I open the back door and fling the fancy presents one by one at those fucking cherry trees. I cry no tears as a cute teddy bear gets stuck up on the branches of one of them, and the bottle of Elle perfume skelps another, just as the last black petal falls and the music box tinkles in my head, the last notes whisper the words, *"Love him not!"* I know now for sure; I have made a complete arse (*Cynical Coco, you fucking bet! That fucking word is burning through my body like acid raining down on my skin*) of myself. Deep down I had always known this would happen. *You should've trusted your instincts, not that bastard. Hell will mend you Coco! Oh! No it will not, unfortunately.*

I remember the day I thought he would never hurt me, he was my hero, then again perhaps now that is just all that is left of those thoughts, just memories lost in time.

Chapter VII
Disillusioned – You Were My Hero

The daylight has long since filtered through my blinds in the bedroom. I realise it is New Year's Day and I have been lying awake all night thinking about the past. I question myself whether it had all been worth it or not. Did I truly get what I wanted or what I deserved? I set out all those years ago to have an affair with a married man because I wished for the power and freedom which I thought that kind of sexual relationship brought. The bonus of it came in the form of a glamorous lifestyle, which I was led to believe is what a mistress lives. I expected to be treated like a spoilt princess, who received expensive presents. I would jet away on romantic rendezvouses whilst making love in exotic places without a care in the world for his spouse or give a fuck he was married. I would have all the unsolicited sex I wanted on tap but without the hassle of sleeping around or the pledge of marriage vows or having to behave as expected like a loyal, boring, devoted wife. Is that what I got in the end?

I lie about it to me, because if I am to be true to myself, the correct answer would destroy that make-believe realism. After all, I committed to him in a form of marriage did I not? Albeit without legal documents, but by wearing a wedding ring, making promises of loving only him for eternity. In the end, I kind of contradicted the whole fucking thing of being in an affair with this fake marriage.

The married man, who is lying sleeping beside me now, is classing me as his wife. By law or not, he states that I am by the terms and conditions of the definite love he feels for me in his heart. This is fact, Coco, he lovingly informs me. Exactly, ditto! *Bullshit, Coco!* I inform myself, changing my mind about it as I get out of his bed or rather my bed with him in it.

We would have many moments where we lived quite happily like a newlywed couple. But that part of us could change instantly, tearing our love to shreds, we could be as unpredictable as the weather, as destructive as a cyclone storm coming in from the ocean, ripping apart a beautiful tropical island, shattering the illusion of a perfect hot, Indian summer's evening.

As it is New Year's Day, we are going to spend the night at Port Patrick. Dressed expensively we arrive at our destination. The place where we stay is classy; we are welcomed profusely as we are known to be regular customers there. After a few drinks in our luxurious bedroom, Brad pushes me backwards onto the bed, hungrily making love to me, ripping off my silk knickers. Literally tore them off me, I go berserk at the price of them now ruined, which he promises to replace. That is followed by us sharing a shower. We get dressed quickly into another set of fancy Dior clothes for dinner. What are all these designer labels about? I fucking hate it. I am much happier in ripped jeans with a T-shirt. We sit at a candlelit table overlooking the harbour, drinking pink rose champagne whilst reminiscing about our first date. Brad takes my hand, he tells me he'd asked his wife for a divorce so he could marry me, but she'd refused. I smile sadly back. He explains it doesn't matter what she said or did, or how long he had to wait for a divorce, because he loves me more than anything or anyone in this world. He promises me that we would be married as soon as possible, no matter what it costs him. I am the most important thing in his life, so fuck everything and everyone else, because if we have each other then that's all that mattered. I agree with him on this that we stand together. We raise our glasses to the future, toasting the memory of his mother, to whom we gave our word to comply with her wish that someday we would be married. I look out the huge glass window, noticing how beautiful the moon shining above the bay reflected on the water. I smile, aware of Brad wistfully watching me. I think about how much my opinion of us has changed yet again since this morning. As I glance at the stars above, I think of his mother way beyond the darkness as I mentally make note to never forget her wherever she was.

4th January

Brad's mother's funeral is today. Fuck. This I very much would have been dreading under any circumstances, and I am trembling in anticipation now of what the day ahead holds. How do you say goodbye to someone whom you had only known a few years but loved as if she was your own mother? Brad's mother wanted so much to be there on our wedding day, when I married her son. This was not to be, so she had me making promises to her, some of those I would be unable to honour as they were out of my control but the others I hold onto my given oath. She particularly requested that she would very much like me to attend her funeral with Brad; this was also one of her last wishes. But the family rows which this was causing were making it extremely awkward for me to do so, which was very upsetting for Brad and me.

One of Brad's sisters had made it clear to the family that she did not want me to be there, while instructing the family to tell Brad of this being her position. She further stated to them that on my attendance, only if it was necessary, in her opinion I should absolutely be told to stand at the back on my own and this was her final decision in the matter. Brad was determined this was not going to be the case, if so, then that is exactly where he would stand at the back beside me. All this shit had made it extremely difficult for Brad to go and say goodbye to his own mother. He should have been up at the front standing with the family near her coffin, rightfully so; this is where he belonged on one of the saddest days of his life. Instead, he was torn by his sister's horrific orders, which went against his mother's wishes and his love for me.

We get dressed to go; Brad demands of me to appear stunning. Shaking, I have to have my nails, hair and tan perfect. He not only wants to make sure he makes his point by having me there with him as his mother insisted but he also intends to show me off at the same time. He informs me that the only reason I was asked to stay away in the first place was just out of pure jealousy in case I stole her thunder, which Brad states I am very much sure to do. I stand in my designer coat, which alone cost three thousand pounds, with the rest of my clothes priced over the same. The jewellery I wore was taken from my safe and is insured for sixty-five thousand pounds. It was a very extravagant birthday gift from extremely rich friends, who consider me to be an adopted member of their family. No gypsy trinkets tinkled on me. I feel uncomfortable as today isn't supposed to be about me, but Brad I guess had his own reasons for making that an issue. Brad and River also dress in designer attire as we leave to go to the crematorium. Brad informs me his mum would have loved the drama of all this, the fact that against all odds I am still going to the funeral with him taking me fucking spirited style, not only that but I am dressed in the rich rags of Vogue magazine. I laugh at Brad's description of my clothes, which he had once got from my father. Dressed in those beautiful rags this witch stops laughing though when Brad tells me he refuses to go in the family funeral car. I am shocked as well as extremely upset by this. I feel so sorry for him; he has done nothing wrong and look what it is costing him to stand by me. Yet a long time ago apparently the same sister once told Brad if he ever needed to talk about the affair, then she would always be there for him. He also said something about a pot calling a kettle black on her dishing me for sleeping with him whilst he is married. He informed me, yes, he was married but when I slept with him, I was not; therefore, she definitely had no stake on that matter. Brad held his ground firmly and chose instead, in a very self-respecting manner, to go to his mother's funeral driving his own car, in which sat River and me.

On arriving the place is very busy as a lot of people have turned out for the ceremony and to give commiserations to the family and even more so to pay their last respects to his mother. All three of us stand where we were requested, noble as if royalty, we hold our heads up high. I had kept my word to Brad's mother, just as Brad standing proud beside me had assured his. Brad's mother's nature was one of understanding; if only she had known what had taken place that day, she would have stood by her son in his dignified decision, not only was she strong but she was the wisest and fairest of them all.

Brad makes sure that we stand as far to the back of the building as we possibly can, so we are the very last people in the queue to go in; therefore, in that order we would be very last people out. Brad turns to me then River and says, "Let's go," just as soft music begins to play and the velvet curtains start to shut around the beautiful coffin in which an angel lay. We head behind us towards the back where we had entered, an undertaker standing nearby notices us leaving early and follows suit, probably wondering about the circumstances of our sudden departure and our chosen route. On noticing Brad's face stained with tears, he nods despondently at me then unlocks the door and sadly lets us out. I acknowledge that Brad is a very proud man and I contemplate how he had just made a total cunt of his sister in front of everyone, because everybody there knew what she had requested this of me out of pure jealousy. Brad's actions clearly stated to them all, "Fuck you!" as Brad chose to leave his own mother's funeral using the back door so we are the first out. Brad tells me, "She knows why I have done this, as does my wife along with the fucking whole of his hometown who are standing there, and I shall never ever forgive her for this today, Coco, if I live forever." He means every word he says as he swears on his mother's soul. River and I say nothing. River touches Brad's shoulder and takes my hand as we walk to the car. Brad drives past the glass doors at the front of the crematorium just as the family and Matts' wife comes out; Brad sees them, and they see us in Brad's car as he just keeps on going.

Brad drives for a while through country roads as we all sit in in the car in complete silence. Each of us deep in thought, then a little while later as he turns the car around, Brad backtracks down the road we come up to the old-fashioned inn where the post-funeral reception is being held. On arriving some of the family come outside to greet us. They are so glad Brad has come after all. On entering the premises, Brad has no intentions of sitting near the family as to avoid a negative atmosphere or confrontations. Megan, however, is having none of it; she came to greet us crying and drags us over to where they all are seated. She insists that we sit down amidst them at the family table. Brad's wife isn't there so at least that is something. The food is delicious, bravely we ignore the certainty I am far from welcome at that table. The sister sat opposite with her husband turning his back to the whole table. How rude. Brad said the sister was staring at me, taking in everything about my appearance. He said the jealousy written over her face was not the colour of one green tree, but a fucking forest full. The full reason I was not allowed anywhere near her in the first place. I was once mistaken for being a little fat woman with short hair, on the sister being informed by other members of the family this was not the case, she turned coat very quickly after inviting Brad to talk. Brad said she hated the fact I was slim, Italian looking with extremely long and thick dark hair. Apart from that, all the family loved my personality. The nieces loved my style and makeup and nails. The jealous one thought she was the beauty of the family, wrongly so. Her face was very much haggard, I was stunned by her appearance, Megan could easily wipe the floor with her. There is some lightness though that breaks through the heavy air that hangs over me, as Brad's niece is over the way, she smiles at me. I know she can't come to speak to me due only to the fact of who else sat nearby. It would get her into trouble. She waves to me mouthing, "Love you!" Megan is very, very close to me whom I refer to as my sister and she doesn't give a fuck who it suits or doesn't suit rather. Brad said, apparently because of this, I steal more stars from Brads' sisters' jealous sky. The rest of the family say the same to me, even Brads' brother, "It is pure fucking jealousy of you Coco, and now you can see why!" *Her problem.* When my son, River, and Megan's grandson offer to buy her and her husband a drink, they are also very rudely ignored then informed to go, so they do very much to the tables affront. Honestly how pathetic. Earlier on some sunshine had shone through the dark cloud as Brad's best friend Liam and his wife arrived to attend the funeral. Brad noticing them getting out of their car, took me over to greet them. I met them for the very first time under the most awful circumstances; Brad introduced me to them as 'his Coco'. I especially loved that phrase; Brad's mother had also referred to me as 'Brad's Coco'.

That evening after the day is eventually over, I feel only emptiness. As I sit with Brad in my dark lounge, I speak softly to him, "Brad, we promised your mother to make this relationship work, so let's try. We owe her that much, besides I love you."

He smiles, "Yea, I know, Coco, I love you more."

Today we have said goodbye to an amazing little woman, she was one of a kind. I whisper "Goodnight" to her as I light the candle she bought for me. I lie in Brad's arms watching the flame flickering, wishing she could be here with us right now, just like she had been on so many winter nights before. Wishing she could have still been here to see my wedding day. I smile at the memory of the look on her face as I told her I was getting married to Brad in Sherwood Forest in my bare feet, wearing no bra and no knickers. I described to her how all the forest would be lit with tiny sparkling lights and candles and among them we would all dance until dawn, along with the fairies and elves. I also whispered to her that my wedding dress, which lay half made, was jet black and would be covered in glistering jewels and I would wear snowdrops and black roses in my dark hair, on my mouth, black shimmering lipstick and black glitter eye shadow with deep purple jewels under my eyebrows just above the black eye makeup… Her expression you could see was one of disbelief as horrified, she tried to picture it. Yet she just smiled, nodding her head just sufficiently in the right places, just enough to convince me that she agreed with my plans.

"That will be nice," she said. "Yes, that will be very nice Coco!" she repeated when clearly what she was thinking was *fuck sake!* definitely not the same as what she was saying.

I come back to the present and cuddle up to Brad as I say out loud, "Yes, perhaps it would have been nice, very nice back then. With my cake designed in the style of a trifle with the base made of a real butter sponge soaked in brandy, with a blackberry flavoured liquor jelly, covered in thick fresh cream and topped with wild berries from the forest." *Fuck traditional wedding cake, been there, done that, besides this was more my kind of thing really.*

"Coco, what the fuck are you talking about?" Brad inquires at my random statement as he moves back on the sofa to look at me; I lift my eyes to his face.

"The past, thoughts of the past spoken out loud. But you wouldn't understand. Once upon a time our love was rare like a Briar Rose, soft and delicate, a spectacular beautiful fragile flower, with only the time of the season before it dies. Now beneath its jagged thorns, it is slowly wilting away and I don't think its roots are strong enough anymore to hold through the winter until it's time to bloom again. The trees of the forest can wait though; they will always be for a hundred years or more. But storms, however, may blow them down or man may cut them to the ground, but they stand strong until then and that can be for a very long time. But the roots of the roses, they risk being suffocated and starved of oxygen by the awaiting trees as perhaps their roots will grow around about them? We should have embarked on our journey earlier, and then maybe the rose planted in the forest would be strong enough to last the voyage and search for light and air in the darkness. Maybe it was the right time back then with me wearing a long black dress, standing in my bare feet and bare arse, perhaps it was the nice time, the nice time for a wedding trifle with berries from the forest, but not for wedding cake, definitely not traditional wedding cake," I answer with a strange sadness in my voice.

"Knowing my inner voice was informing me that could not be really, would not have taken place, even in those bygone days, because Coco after all, he was already married. So the other make believe wedding ceremony you shared taking place at the pond, in the forest at midnight with him standing mesmerised as you both make vows to love each other forever, with you stood only in your bare feet wearing nothing except buttercream silk underwear would have to do for now." I remember that night afterwards we shared champagne in a candle-lit bath. We made love as Mr and Mrs in our world. In the morning he went home to his real wife.

"No, Coco, not just for now, maybe do forever," I repeat, talking to myself audibly, copying what the friends in my head had silently yet clearly stated.

"Coco, what the fuck are you talking about?" he distinctly asks me for the second time

"I don't understand you!" he says, appearing even more confused than before.

"No, you don't, I already told you that," I say, getting up, going off on my trail to make some coffee. As I pass Brad hobbling with only one slipper boot on, he notices and I am uncomfortable as my other foot feels cold on the tiled floor on reaching the kitchen. On searching along the way back, I find the other boot lying in the hall, which I must've already walked past. I pull it on, continuing my short journey to the lounge with an air of self-control. I smile thinking there is a solution to every problem, I recognise you just have to find it, like I had just done; I laugh glancing down at my feet.

Later whilst back in my kitchen whilst baking a witches, cake , I think back to the phrase his mother used, referring to me as 'Brad's Coco'. Everyone agreed with her that he was besotted with me, he worshipped me, and I was the best thing that had happened to him and him to me. Him to me? Eh! What fucking planet are they all on? They are disillusioned – I am fucking even more so Brad Blake on wishing, on even thinking it at one time, how wrong was I? For a long time on and off I was so disillusioned you were my hero.

Chapter VIII
Wakening from a Fantasy Slumber

The rest of January and February is filled with a bad karma between us. February arrives with it bringing one of the witches' Sabbats. A major one, Imbolc, pronounced Im-bulk, also referred to as Candlemas. It begins 31st January and ends sunset, February the 1st. I don't go to the coven meeting to celebrate, which is a really big thing for me not to attend. I light candles to celebrate the Goddess of Fertility. I consider casting a spell to bring love and harmony back, as in taking out the old, bringing in the new. I just leave it. He is not worth it then again, I am not sure if this is exactly what I want with him now anyway. I half-heartedly decide, smirking, perhaps I should take my broom but not to sweep the magic circle as in "sweeping out with the old", not to sweep the old, hurt out the door but to sweep him out fucking door, down the path, out the gate and sweep him right out my life for good. The rows escalate despite my good intentions at the beginning of the year. I hate Brad one day, and then I love him the next. We argue even when I am only trying to comfort him in what he is suffering on going through this heart-breaking loss. We both try to fill the void left in our lives on losing his mother by using our own coping strategies. Brad wanders about in a trance, as I speak to him, he doesn't listen. I exercise non-stop while the voices in my head spoke to me, I did listen, and I didn't listen. I did listen to them telling me this is not working with Brad Blake. Then I didn't listen to them as it is just lies they tell me. So I blocked them out because ultimately they spoke the truth to me, Stupidly I then decided that they didn't, not really. The tension in the house is becoming violent and very destructive. We physically fight, with him slapping my face in anger just because he doesn't want to acknowledge the truth in what I said about us. That is just Brad. My reaction is hitting him back even harder, usually with some sort of heavy ornament; that type of retaliation would leave him bleeding, with me devastated. He always hit me first but I always drew first blood.

There were several times I thought that the relationship should be ended immediately. He had to go, leave; it would be the best thing to do for both our sakes. He was always going to leave tomorrow in the morning, but tomorrow morning never comes. The mental torture I suffer lasts, I keep repeating things over in my head due to the awful things said by both of us. Words we shouted at each other haunted me for days and nights, way beyond the time it took the flesh wounds to heal. Brad couldn't let it go either, so in jealous rages about my past, which to me were invalidated but he would question me on yet again. Whereupon the answers I truthfully gave to his stupid interrogations would enrage him further, thus causing the fights to start all over. It seems the mental games we played held no winners or losers as we both mentally fucked each other over time and time again. I also questioned whether Brad was staying with me because he wanted to, or because it was one of his mother's final wishes. Nobody but him knew the answer to that.

Valentine's Day came and went, leaving behind no romantic meals this year or him being tied up to the bed while playing sex games with food, no licking cream off his hard-on under twinkling red heart-shaped lights. No bottles of champagne and no boxes of chocolates. No rose petals sprinkled all over the bed. No definite sign of a hero dressed in a fucking pilot suit carrying me upstairs to bed, slowly making love to me, teasing me so much until I was begging him to please put his cock up me. We never argued on the day though, so I supposed that was something. Brad kissed my cheek, handed me two bottles of expensive perfume, and then just walked away. An envelope lay on the kitchen counter with my name written on it. I opened it to find a beautiful card which read 'To my wife on Valentine's Day'. *How fucking sweet*, I thought sarcastically. I sat the card on the dining table but I put it bottom up as that is what I perceived my life to be, crazily spinning upturned out of control. I felt as if I was a rocket NASA was trying to send to the moon only I was upside down going through space watching the world disappear. Little did I know though at this point that was exactly what was going to happen to me in my world on the twenty-eighth of this month. Or perhaps maybe I did, I felt something was seriously wrong, otherwise why else would I sit the card the upside down other than because my fucking instincts had told me to do so and this time it would seem I had listened to them.

28th February

It is a cold, bleak February day. The icy wind racing through the bare trees in the garden create soft tunes, a melody which I close the door to shut out. I am in the comfort of my lounge with hot chocolate, lost in thought about nothing particularly just the weather and what was happening in my day ahead. Brad is at the doctor's; he would be back soon surely, as by now he'd been gone some time. Just at that the door opens, bringing in the cold, and then Brad bangs it shut. Brad is on edge as he comes in looking stricken as well as cold. He is shivering as he sits down beside me.

"Coco we need to talk; I'm going back to stay with my wife. I need to go into the hospital next week for an operation on my foot. I can't manage on the stairs here, so I need to go back there as all rooms are on ground level. I love you. I am coming back to you, Coco. I promise she means nothing; it means nothing; this means nothing. I will be in the back bedroom sleeping again in the bed in there. I won't be sleeping with her. I won't be able to drive either. I will come back as soon as the plaster is off, as soon as possible," he struggles out his explanation.

Oh! Will he? Coco, we need to talk, he said. Well, it seems to me he is the one doing all the talking whilst I listen. He is the one talking. Not me. Will he come back, really? Not just his fucking decision to make that, now is it?

I sit numb as I hear the words tumble from his mouth. His mind is made up, it would seem. No point in attempting to change it as he is making statements rather than leaving the conversation open for discussion. He then goes back out to phone his wife, stating he is now going to explain to her that he will be coming back to stay at the house with her on the given date because he needs to go into hospital for an operation. This is not the first time she has heard this, which is what he was trying to convince me was the case. He told me first, he says, then her about the hospital and the operation. *Fuck off!* I am very much aware that this has been discussed between them at one point. He is just now making and confirming the final arrangements with her as it had all already been planned earlier than today. He would probably have gone to the house to see her after he had left the doctors this morning the phone call will be her final acknowledgement of his return. *How cute is he?*

The rest of the week the wind continues to blow through the trees, just as Brad continues to go about his tasks preparing to leave me. He stocks up the cupboards with food for me. He buys gifts of expensive chocolates, perfumes, make-up and underwear. He is as particular as a little squirrel collecting winter food for hibernation. He leaves no stone unturned on this bizarre shopping spree. Another mind game but the game being played is in whose head though? Mine? His? Buy Coco plenty so she has enough of everything until I return. Or is he thinking, give her no reason to leave here, leave him, hoping on doing all this that it would guarantee for him in some way that I would wait for him and he would be able to return to me as if nothing out of the ordinary had happened. *"He won't come back!"* the whispers in my head say. *"Please he has too!"* my heart cries. *"Eh! I think not, not anymore."* Buy Coco everything and secure myself a place to return when it suits me. Give my pawn a guaranteed winning place in a game of chess. Buy stupid Coco? Whatever it is he is thinking fuck knows, but one thing I do know for sure, all the stuff just keeps on coming and coming.

7th March

This is our last night together before he leaves, so we have sex three times. Nothing, just sex. I gave him the best sex he ever had, feeling fucking zero. It is my goodbye present to him, his fucking last gift from me. Another sexual sacrifice of myself, *Stupid witch!* This time and for the last time though the bastard is taking my heart with him. Actually, he is welcome to it. I want it no more. It is so broken; it just keeps me in pain. *Broke my heart and destroyed mentally. Now would he not love to know that Coco?* Fuck him and his wife. Let him go back and physically fuck her too, in fact. Me, I have no desire to make love with him ever again, I am done chasing his fucking rainbows, tired of looking for silver lining in an old fucking teapot. I lie with my eyes closed whilst he lies on top of me for the very last time, as he comes moaning my name, I feel oblivious to the moment and my surroundings. I just feel dirty. As he takes my body, my mind is far away, I picture myself lying in the warm sunshine, and I feel its warmth on my skin. I imagine the smell of perfume in the air from the Cyprus trees blowing in the breeze. A pure white chateau with pale pink tiles on its roof stands behind me and that is the place I intend to go to, when this night is over. When he has finished the sex, with his ejaculation emptying sperm into me, it is over. I open my eyes to find he is looking at me closely. I lie silently watching him just watching me.

"I love you so much, Coco," he says, tears running down his face. From my tear-stained face, I say fuck all.

8th March

The morning arrives as if it has no place in this nightmare. The day of his big departure has arrived, yet again. He offers to take me for a farewell lunch yet again, this time I go, to a restaurant by the beach. I recall that sometime before those waves rolled in as he was leaving me. The meal is lovely and he promises me that on the day he returns to me, we will come back here to do this again. This time he will stay with me forever. I listen to the sincerity in his voice, look at the honesty in his face and believe fucking none of it.

We go back to the house, Brad packs up most of his belongings, leaving behind some of his important personal things with me as proof that he is coming back. It's time to say goodbye, then he leaves, just like that. Gone as quickly as he came. He is becoming real good at this disappearing act. He phones me on the way up the road to her, promising to love me forever. I glance around the quiet, empty house. As I sit on the stairs crying, my little dogs all come to sit at my feet, trying to comfort me. I pick them up one by one, kissing them. I appreciate all their love so much. They never hurt me, never let me down, this, I realise, is what real love is in this world and them leaving me will be when the darkest days in my life will once again be. *"Not today,"* my friends in my head say, *"not today, Coco, because you still have all of them."* I stop crying, and then get up putting my music on.

I sing, cleaning and re-arranging my furniture to have my house right back just the way it was before Brad Blake arrived. I wash and polish, removing all memories of him away quite happily. The hell of all this mental abuse makes me crazy, making me wonder half the time if I am in New York or New Year. I smile at my own sarcasm as I keep cleaning. I sing to myself, "I'm gonna wash that man right out of my house!" instead of hair.

The door opens; there stands Brad in the hallway, so Brad is back. His hands are full of more chocolates and flowers he bought for me. He kisses me crying, saying he is so sorry to have left me and that he loves me so much. He has been away less than three hours. He looks around the kitchen then back at me. He tells me he has just made the biggest mistake of his life and perhaps he should come back, as in right now. Just cancel the operation, go back up there this minute to get his belongings and bring them back here straight away. I say, "No!" He looks shocked. I tell him to just keep arrangements as they were, just as he had planned. This time I'm calling the shots, not him. He goes back out still crying, he is begging me to let him cancel it all, and he wants to come back here within an hour and he is confused because I won't agree to it. On him returning back up the road once more he phones me yet again, this time he is pleading with me to wait for him. A while later, when it is still early in the evening, he calls me back once more, this time from the shop. She walks in behind him, so he hangs up on me, pretending to have been talking to a work colleague. His second secret phone is hidden as before and I don't hear from him again that night. It is one of the longest, saddest nights of my life. The voices in my head keep me company and all the earlier bravado has now gone. I feel myself slipping slowly back into the darkness. Once more I hear the friends in my head returning, singing the same song over and over to me:

"You made something perfect, so perfect with your spell." But it was far from perfect though, wasn't it? I ask of them. *"No!"* they say, *"It was perfect, you know it was perfect Coco, so perfect with your witch's spell."*

It was hell.

"Yes, but it was your perfect spell, that made Brad Blake your perfect hell."

9ᵗʰ March

The day of his operation. A lot of strangeness today. Brad phones me very early morning as soon as she drops him off at the hospital and before his operation. He tells me he missed me very much last night and he will call as soon as his surgery is over; he tells me he loves me and I am his world and that he detests being with her. I exercise all morning then I phone the hospital for information on Brad, whereupon they ask me if I am his wife. Knowing she has taken him there and is returning to collect him, I cannot say that I was. He is using her and we both know it. So I state in confidentiality that I am his mistress, whom he has a very close relationship with and I am very concerned at this moment about his health as he just had surgery. The nurse says she understands and releases the information I asked for. She informs me that he is doing well at present and out of theatre. He phones me as soon as he comes around from the anaesthetic. He asked the same nurse, who had by then informed him quietly that I had called. He asks her to dial my number for him on his secret phone and on listening to his conversation with me, she hears him telling me how much he loves me. The nurse, who is also very much aware that I am not his wife, is at the same time looking out the side room door in case someone comes along the corridor to visit him and he gets caught talking to me on his hidden phone. Apparently, just after he finished the call, the nurse came abruptly back to inform him that was good timing as his old mother had arrived to take him home. The nurse was then shocked as Brad informed her that this woman was not actually his mother who had come to collect him but that the old aged woman was his wife.

Sometime later his sister Megan calls me to ask what is going on. She informs me that she already knew Brad was going back home as Brad's wife had told her a few nights back. *Well, well, well there is another shock statement for me. Not!* She goes on to tell me that Brad's wife is under the impression he is back for good. *Really!* This apparently is the arrangement that has been made between them, with him also promising her to have no contact with me ever again. More hurt and devastation, but no surprise here, by no means. A huge commotion ensues with me screaming and swearing at Brad when phones back later. He persistently informs me this is not the case. He is coming back

145

to me, and his wife can think what the fuck she likes about the situation but he is leaving her again for definite as soon as possible.

Over the next few days Brad phones me as much as he can. He has to attend a funeral one day so he has the chance to come by the house for a short visit. He has company in the form of a driver, so he doesn't say much and he can't stay long. The following day when I am in town, he phones me, begging me to trust him, saying he is not sleeping with her and he informs me for the third time that he has made the biggest mistake of his life on going back there. He feels like a caged animal being kept in that house, and she keeps on checking his white phone like an idiot and she is making plans for them, hoping to keep him there with her. I hang up on him with my own thoughts on the matter being she won't find anything because she is checking the wrong phone; not only that, in her desperation she is making him dislike and use her even more.

16th March

It's wild out tonight. The wind rattles through the branches of the trees in the garden and rain hits off the glass on the windowpanes. I stoke the log fire, now the place is so warm and cosy, with only the fire glow and light from the candles making dancing shadows on the ceiling. I snuggle up, enjoying the fact the only company I would have tonight is my little dogs. Brad has been phoning but I have been ignoring his calls. I wonder if the weather is as bad where he is, probably, but I don't care that much really. I am just curious, so be it if he goes out in it to phone me, yet receives no answer to his calls, his problem not mine. I have my own plans tonight, however, which do include him but answering his calls is definitely not one of them.

I go for a ritual cleansing bath, and then, donning my robes, start to mix all my unusual ingredients needed for the preparations for my spell. I plan to cast a spell at evening tide, and then at midnight bury the magic of it under the willow tree. I would make sure that Brad Blake this time, under this spell made tonight would be bound to me forever. His love for me will be his downfall, as I intend it to be used as the tool he will be tortured by. He will suffer torment at the depth of it, causing him to feel so bewitched by me; he will not be able to live his life with or without me in any form of peace.

On completing the chant and formulation of the given spell and as the torrential rain falls from the heavens, under the old tree I bury my sacred object, believed to hold the supernatural powers of my craft. Wrapped in both a lock of his hair (I cut awhile back) and my blood, it is planted deep down into the earth. So now that symbolises that he bears the burden of his love for me until the end of his time, death is the only thing to set him free or if I unfold the magic conjuration to remove the curse. In the darkness, there is very little moonlight as I crawl out from underneath the old willow. I am damp from the mist of the weather but with its branches bowing to the ground, they provided some protection from the elements while I was under them. Now, however, with the wind and heavy rain blowing right into my face, I put my head down as I hurry back towards the house. Tripping in my haste, I stumble over my heavy robes, which by now are suddenly soaking wet in the storm. They were already all covered in dirt, which is turning to pure mud on being drenched with the icy rain.

As I enter quickly in through the door, I wonder for a second if Brad Blake is worth this? I strip off the layers of the gown and cloak, stepping out of them; I stand naked, shivering with the filthy garments lying at my feet on the wet stone floor. On looking down, I think perhaps a spell now to clean them is in order; I smile wistfully to myself at the thought. I shake my head hopelessly, then wrapping my arms tightly around my bare breasts, I shudder again as I am chilled to the bone. I step over the damp clothes, running naked upstairs to have a hot bath. I sink into the hot water, allowing the cold to leave my body; eventually, I begin to feel relaxed and warm once more. Brad Blake, however, shall be the worse for wear than I am tonight. If I have regrets on falling for him, the price he pays has just been ten folded on him for falling in love with, then attempting to leave me.

18th March

Brad arrives unannounced. Now I know the spell yet again has worked. He says not last night but the night before, he woke at midnight feeling very unwell. Since then he hasn't been able to stop thinking about me twenty-four hours a day plus he can't sleep with the loneliness his life holds now without me. He says that the uncertainty of him not knowing where I am or what I'm doing is driving him crazy. He goes on to explain a kind of longing inside, missing me while desperately feeling he needs to make love to me to fulfil the emptiness. He walks around with a hard-on at the thought of me. Peculiar, I smirk, that part was not in my spell. He emphasises more, elaborating on the fact that he can't be without me much longer and he needs to be here, with me. Well, today I am not surprised by him appearing at the door of my house now, am I? But I am shocked he is driving his car with a plaster on his foot. His insurance would be void, apart from anything else. He states she had gone out, leaving him home alone for once, and he wanted to come; in fact, he needed to come to visit me as he desperately has non-stop urges to be with me. He went outside with his car keys to see if he could handle the car and voila! Here he was. *"Well! Well! Well! Coco Houston, do we have a problem?"* No, not yet, well perhaps.

This is only the second time I have seen him since he left me to have the operation, with it being the very first time we are alone. After living with him for months and being with him almost every day for years before that, I found these last ten days had been extremely heart-breaking for me. Canada all over again. It takes a very bad situation to make you stronger though, not only that, I am extremely angry. No tears. No running and jumping into his arms, no kissing him, no sex, and I am not going to be giving him any declarations of undying love on missing him. He sits down. Shaking, I go and make him tea for him, coffee for myself, trying to hide how nervous I am. I find it stupid pretending I am fine, working hard to keep my true feelings under control. I breathe deeply, exhaling slowly, then repeat this procedure to calm me before entering back into the lounge, handing him his drink. He is sitting on the sofa, as I stand over by the window, he is watching me

"I want to talk to you, Brad," I say in a matter-of-fact tone to him, which causes his face to literally pale in front of me.

"Okay, Coco!" he replies meekly. I stand a few moments in silence, staring at him as he waits anxiously listening for what I have to say.

"Just recently, when you went behind my back to discuss with your wife about you returning to the marital home, I believe your wife told you a few things, Brad. One that she loved you and that she wanted you, but she didn't need you!" I say in a smart tone used when being arrogant and rude. He looks at me with surprise showing in his eyes, I can see he is astounded by the accuracy of the information my informant had provided, by the expression on his face, I can see that he is quickly trying to calculate who could have possibly told me this. I know this to be the truth about the conversation they'd held and I had just repeated word for word because his face turns pure red with shame and embarrassment at being caught out with his lies. He can't answer me, he is speechless; I stare right through him before I continue talking.

"Well! Guess what, Blake? I have my own opinion on the matter too. You see I loved you. I wanted you and unlike her, I thought I did need you but you know what has happened now, Brad? These last ten days I have learned to live without you!" I very confidentially brief him.

"Oh Blake, and by the way, I don't give two cents what you do with her, actually make that phrase two fucks, more appropriate choice of words I think, don't you? After all, you sleep with me and her!" I say sarcastically, knowing he didn't have sex with both of us, but sharing our beds, well that he fucking did, so I know I got that part right.

"Now go! Get out. Go! Get back to your wife and out of my fucking life!" I speak in a very calm voice to him.

Seriously, I feel nothing. I am just glad it is finally done, it hadn't been planned, it had just happened that way. The picture on his face is a rainbow of colours; believe me it tells a thousand stories. He sits now wearing a look of surprise and shock of not quite being sure of exactly what had just taken place as I walk out the room.

I hear him get up, shuffling along the wooden floor behind me as he stumbles after me with his foot in plaster. I go marching back into the kitchen; he is closing in on me from behind with his face pure red in temper. He is shouting and swearing, saying it didn't take me long to get over him, then calling me a whore amongst other things. I ignore the name-calling, walk to my back door, then holding it wide open, I gesture for him to come to it, as he does, I wait then I put my face right up into his, ordering him out as viciously I spit in a voice full of contempt:

"GET OUT NOW! I CAN LIVE WITHOUT YOU! I DON'T NEED YOU ANYMORE!" the words are spoken softly, in a cold voice that registers as full of deep hatred, hurt and anger. He understands all too clearly that I mean every single fucking word, as still I hold that door open.

He lifts his hand and belts me so hard across the face that he knocks me into the tall American-style cooler. I put my hand to my cheek, my face is stinging, burning red hot with the slap, my eyes begin watering and I lose my balance with the force of the blow. I regained my composure, then slowly move back towards the door, as I struggle in pain, I hold it open once more, repeating the request.

"GET TO FUCK OUT MY LIFE!" I demand from him. This time he goes. As he stumbles down the steps, my legs also give away, after banging the door shut behind him; I lock the door just before I collapse to the floor.

No tears. No fucking tears this time for me. I unsteadily head upstairs to bathe my face, my eye hurts and I feel physically sick. I throw up down the toilet, realising my whole body is trembling in shock. I go to my bedroom, where I sit on the bed wondering why I had just wasted the last five years of my life with that bastard.

I come back down a while later, astonished to find him standing in my kitchen. I had no idea he was there, I never even heard him enter back into the house, I must have been so lost in thought I forgot he has keys.

"Brad," I say; he has his back to me, filling the kettle with water. I notify him with all the dignity I have left, "I can't do this anymore. I just can't handle the pain of this relationship; I don't need this or want you in my life now." I stop talking. Sighing, I sit down at the table, holding my head in my hands as he continues to make tea as normal, as if he never heard a word of it.

"Coco please, Coco, I'm so sorry for all the hurt I've caused you, but I can't bear the thought that you don't need me anymore. Please, Coco, I need you to need me because I need you darling. I need you," Brad cries in an anguished voice as tears roll down his face. This time it is him that stands breaking his heart, begging me to reconsider giving him another chance. He stops crying after some time, I look up as he is wiping his eyes and he starts to smile over at me; the big hard man, the hard coal miner he portrays himself to be now stands whimpering like a baby in tears over me. Pish! In tears at what he'd done to himself is more the case. I glare right through him. Revenge is sweet so they say. I just felt washed out as I remembered all those times he threatened to leave me, including the time he called saying he was at the airport and never coming back. As I pushed my pants with fright and fell to the floor hysterically, he sat right outside my house in his car. *BASTARD!* I take my coffee from him; I just sit thinking, watching him, I say nothing. He speaks first.

"Besides, Coco, you have to stay with me because I bought us a donkey. You a donkey. As back at Christmas time, I asked you what you wanted and you were told you could have anything you wanted, preferably something you didn't have. You chose a donkey. I couldn't get you one then, but I have one now for you. It's in a field just outside of his hometown. It can't stay there much longer, so tomorrow it's moving to live on a farm out by the holiday park just past Dunure. I will come for you and take you to see it. Okay?" he asks, smiling through his tears. He wins again. How can I resist? I get up, going over to where he is, holding him close to me, I try not to cry. I reach my hand up, wiping away his tears as he covers my swollen face in tender kisses.

"Coco, you're so beautiful, and I love you so much, so much more than you will ever know," he whispers into my hair. Shortly afterwards, with my face still smarting, swollen and bruised, he leaves me as usual to go back to his wife. I shut the door on his back and enter the kitchen again. The loneliness I feel is awful once more. His presence is still felt and I can still smell his cologne. I turn around to find that on the kitchen table, beside my one of my spell books, he had left an old-fashioned book with an inscription on the inside page. It was also signed and dated the 8th of March, the fucking date he left me. Why, I wonder, would he sign that date, maybe to show me he done it that night and was thinking about me and was alone in the back bedroom after all. The memory of that time still haunts me. As I hold the book, I remember how on walking around the bookshop the other day, I was touching all the covers of the books and thinking of my own manuscript. I sat down with a coffee in the bookshop and was determined that despite everything, I was going to do my very best to have my story published.

The next day I go with him out to Dunure to meet my donkey. It is a bastard of a thing and it hates me from the moment it set eyes on me. I call it Gucci. It chases me through the field, and then it bites me. I have to run like fuck in my wellie boots, and I get stuck in the mud while I am running and it nips at my arse through my jeans. I go home with my bottom sore and all black and blue, matching my face, and that is that and this is my donkey.

For the rest of the week I decide that I shall go to visit and feed my donkey myself rather than the farmer who has agreed to do it on a daily basis and check up on him if notified nobody is going to be around. I go the following day and on him seeing me coming in the gate, he runs at me, chases me, and then bites me. It breaks my nails and tears my clothes, while Blake continues to stay up in that house with her, breaking and tearing everything else that is left of me after Gucci is done. That is the relationship I have with him and with my donkey, which he fucking bought. I go back and forth twice a day to the farm to visit Gucci, which results in me getting hurt. Then Blake comes back and forth to visit me at my house, with ditto results; I get hurt.

21st March

Date is of one of the Witches celebrations. A lesser Sabbat known as Vernal or Spring Equinox. There are many ways to celebrate this, as with all Sabbats.

Today I celebrated the flowers coming out of the ground, the weather getting warmer and thanked Ostara, pronounced Ost-ara the Goddess of Dawn, also known as Spring Maiden. I thank her for the beautiful blossoms growing on the cherry trees in my garden. We witches celebrate the season of rebirth and renewal. I bake poppy seed bread and poppy seed cheese biscuits which I have with fresh green salad. Later today, I took some of both the salad leaves and the poppy seed biscuits to Gucci. He loved them. When they were finished though, once again I had to run like fuck for the gate as he chased me back out the field. *That's what I get, after fucking baking biscuits for him all morning.*

A few days later when Brad comes down to visit me, a row starts between us over money. He felt I spent too much on clothes. He tells me I need to be more responsible with my income. I tell him that my finances are none of his business, yet he still argues on, causing things to escalate to the point of him breaking my temper.

"Listen you, what have I to do exactly? Are you suggesting that I take financial advice from you? Big, sensible, reliable, responsible, financially sorted Brad. Who bought a fucking donkey, by the way, not just any donkey, but a donkey with a fucking personality disorder, which is costing a fortune to keep, and like you, does what the fuck it wants to me!" I scream in temper. He bangs out the door. Argument over. He has no answer for me. Case closed. He lost.

26th March

It is raining very heavily and almost midnight. I can't sleep, so I get out of bed and go downstairs to make some coffee. I seem to be doing this a lot lately, I realise, getting up late, just sitting in the dark lounge watching the last glowing embers of the fire dying. I light a candle as I consider whether to add more logs to the small flickering flames. The log basket is empty, the logs are stored outside, but not only is the weather wild out, the stove needs to be cleaned, which I had planned to do in the morning, so I just decide to leave the fire as it is tonight. Drinking the strong coffee, I look around the room, this time though its décor takes on a different form as I make pictures in my head out of the shadows on the wall. I create some fairies out of the shapes, and then see one which can be considered to look like the silhouette of a wolf, strange how this image made me think of Brad. I begin to wonder where he is sleeping now. *In her bed or in the spare room*?

In the silence of the night, there is only the lone noise of the wind whistling through the trees in the garden. The storm is becoming worse with the winds getting up, at that there is a huge crashing noise coming from outside at the front of the building. I recognise it to be the sound of something breaking. It had to be a plant pot breaking, getting blown from the step. I sigh at the mess that would be left behind, as this has happened on a few occasions in the past. Luckily, all my other pots which grow the delicate herbs which I need to use in my spells are in the kitchen or my shed, so at least they are safe from these gales; well, if the old rickety shed doesn't get blown over the rainbow that is. I smile at this thought, reminding myself there is a wicked witch over there too and that perhaps she can probably find use for them. My mood changes to one of gratitude, as I love being inside on a night like this; when the weather outside is untamed, it makes you very humble to have shelter from it. I feel there is something magical in the power of storms, as dangerous as they can be, I am fascinated by them. I have not been tired at all this evening, I find it hard to unwind; I am mentally tortured all over again on him being up the road in that house with her. I have all this shit in my head once more. My friends try to talk to me but I've managed to shut them out of my head completely tonight, for the time being anyway.

I rise from my comfy seat, passing by the shadow fairies as I dally to the kitchen with a little of the bitter coffee left in the bottom of the cup. The air is cooler in here, with the tiles on the floor below my bare feet also stone cold. *Ironic choice of word, Coco.* I reach up to the rack overhead, lifting down a bottle of wine from it, contemplating with surprise at how many full bottles are still there; usually it would be half empty. On opening it a smell of fruity red berries rises from the bottle as I pour the red liquid into a champagne glass, not a wine glass, before taking it to my lips to down the glass in one go. I let the sweet spicy liquid run down my throat, and then shake my head, one at the strength of it, then at the pleasure of the taste. I take a swig from the bottle then refill the glass, lifting it along with the bottle; I hurry back to my lounge. Passing into the hall you feel the temperature rising in here, as the warmth of the lounge walks out the open door into the hall, with the scent from the vanilla candle following behind it. I put the bottle on the table; plonking myself back down on the soft leather sofa, I empty the glass for a second time. This time the strength seems milder and the taste of the fruit softer. I play with the smooth stem of the empty glass as I sit holding it for a while, as I try to look once more for the picture of my wolf in the shifting shadows. On finding it, I think of Brad once again. In a shadow of a wolf he haunts me, why? Sitting staring at it, I find no answer. I put the glass down beside the now almost empty bottle I acknowledge before leaving the room. This time I am going to change into my robes. I have told myself quite reassuringly now is the right time to cast another spell. Perform a magic ritual to make Brad Blake very uncomfortable, make him uneasy inside, causing him to feel he is losing me.

On returning downstairs and whilst during the preparation for the spell, I realise that one of the herbs required for recipe is locked up outside in the shed. Fuck! I do need this ingredient, so I will just have to go out to the shed for it. I pull on my boots, rushing out into the night in the rain. I struggle to open the rusty lock on the old door, but after a few attempts, I manage it eventually, but only just. On entering the dark shed, the musty smell of damp hits me, the door bangs closed behind me, leaving me in total blackness. I search about, feeling along the shelf as I try to find the shape of the jar I'm looking for, my fingers touch it, just before the door, catching in the wind, and flies open again. In the grey light now filtering in, I notice a spider out of the corner of my eye running for cover. Eww! Yuck! I don't like those horrible things. Oh gads! They make me shudder in disgust at them having eight eyes. Ohhhhh! Turning back towards the shelf, I grab the jar I want, and then get my arse quickly out of there. I have no knickers on, what if the spider went up my fucking robe? I let out a scream in the night at the thought of it as I grapple to lock the door with as much difficulty as I had in opening the thing. Angrily, I turn the key, and then also flee for cover, just as did the spider. Back inside, shaking myself down, I shiver thinking witches are supposed to like spiders; well this one, she does not. I wouldn't harm them but sure as fuck couldn't be friends with them. I finish my mix, then lay my table as per spell indicates before lighting all the coloured candles required. I then proceed to cast my spell over Brad Blake; I finish my chant with, "AN HARM IT NONE, DO WHAT THOU WILT." Now with no evil done, I convince myself that I'm just teaching him a lesson in love. I bring my spell to a closure with

"MAY THE GOD AND GODDESS PRESERVE THE CRAFT, SO MOTE BE IT." Now my work is done. I open my eyes, on rising from the floor; I snuff out all the candles. As I do, I put away all the fairies, along with the wolf, as now I have put all the shadows down to sleep. I just sit in my robes by the depraved fire flames; slowly the glow from the dying embers of the fire disappears. I drink the last of the wine, smirking to myself. As I wait for the spell to take hold of him, sheets of rain hit off the windows, with the wind howling loudly in the night. It shall be my only witness that Brad Blake shall be waking shortly from his sleep. Very soon he will be looking out his window at the wind, which will confirm to whoever listens to it that she has awoken him. Very sorely tonight he will be missing the person he loves most. The one whom he now feels he doesn't want to be or rather now thinks he can't live without. I am satisfied at the feeling of a soothing peace inside me as the anxiety I felt earlier now belongs to him. Finishing off the wine, the alcohol takes effect, relaxing me further, making me feel sleepy as I curl up on the sofa, pulling my wolf skin throw over me, I feel the soft warm fur of it on my cool body, I think of the shadow of the wolf again. I snuggle deep down under it thinking of the wolf and it's comparison I make to Blake. Then whispering to the moon, I say, "Goodnight, Brad Blake, may you have sweet dreams in the time that is left of your night. In the light of the morning, may you be desperate in your haste to come to me." Glancing at the clock, taking note of the time before closing my eyes, I have my final pleasurable thought of the red roses he shall bring. As the sand man comes for me, Brad Blake should be just getting up out of bed, whichever one he is in.

27th March

I sleep late this morning as it is three minutes to noon when I wake. I have slept all night on the sofa down stairs. As I wander to the kitchen I find that Brad has been and gone. On my table, wrapped in tissue paper, lie the red roses. Beside them there is a handwritten note done in childish writing, mostly with capitals, saying, MiSS YOU CoCO Blake, LOVE brAD. 'MiSS YOU, COCO, Blake LOVE, brAD. Xxx'. I lift the roses from the table; smelling them, I lay them by the sink; lifting my black vase, I fill it with slightly warm water then add brown sugar to help preserve the flowers before neatly arranging the flowers in it. I put them on display in the lounge, and then go outside to the garden, where I sit on a garden chair in the rain drinking my coffee. As the raindrops land on my face, they blend with the fallen tears, as two become one, they run down my cheeks, landing on the already soaking wet grass but I hardly notice. I reprimand myself for not requesting chocolates and perfume to be included in my spell. Smiling sadly, I decide I shall remember to do so next time. The conclusion I come to is no matter what presents he brings, without them I still love him. I sit crying for ages in the still pouring rain, which has been fallen now for three days non-stop.

The bad weather continues as the weatherman informs me floods are everywhere. The television is on low in the background, so I don't take much notice. But I look up once again when the presenter talking catches my attention as he mentions donkeys. I turn up the volume to hear him ask for money for the donkey sanctuary as they are apparently among, if not the most, neglected animals on the planet. I am shocked by this news. I think of Gucci out in the storm and for the first time I wonder if he is all right. Penitent and crying I phone a taxi, grab my mobile, pulling the quilt cover from my bed in a panic. Into a polythene bag I fling some carrots with dark chocolate mints to take with me for him. I cuddle my little dogs down for the night into their baskets before leaving the house. I have my wellies on, with my pyjamas and my thick winter jacket. Behind me I'm trailing the huge quilt. Fuck knows what the taxi driver thinks, especially when he drops me at a barn with a quilt in the middle of nowhere on a wild, dark night.

I enter the barn, finding much to my surprise it is quite warm inside. Gucci is comfortable in a bed of clean straw, looking very cosy indeed. He looks up at me as I enter the pen as if considering to get up and nip at me. I wait before venturing further in, he doesn't get up. "Don't even fucking think about it," I warn him loudly. For the very first time ever, he doesn't move. I lie on the quilt near him, feeding him the carrots and mints, telling him stories. He gets up and wanders off after a bit, bored listening to me, I presume, so I just lie quietly on the straw under my quilt, wondering about Brad Blake.

28th March

I must have fallen asleep. Daylight had appeared when I open my eyes to find Gucci standing above me, gently nudging me awake. Slightly disorientated at first with my whereabouts, my memory returns, whereupon I try to get up as quickly as I can before Gucci kills me. As I do, his ears go back and he runs, I run fucking faster, just getting my arse over the pen in time but with the quilt left inside. I decide not to chance trying to get it, so I will just leave it there for now, I confirm to Gucci. I phone a taxi to take me home. It's the same cab driver who took me to the barn late at night that comes to pick me up; he is just finishing night shift, I am his last hire. He looks at the state of my clothes. He is calculating my scenario. His beady eyes take in the mess of and, unknown to me at the time, the straw in my hair. He asks just one question or rather makes a statement of the obvious. "No quilt!" the driver says.

"Nope!" I reply. I get in the car. Driving on the way back, he keeps on glancing at me in his mirror, looking at me back and forth with a look of wonderment in his expression. I think he is confusing himself more than he already was, as mostly I think he is trying to work out what happened to the fucking quilt.

Later that day, when I am downtown, when I am in an exclusive chocolate shop buying Gucci candy, Brad phones. I listen to him half-heartedly as he rambles on about how much he misses me. I hardly answer him or can even be bothered to listen to his shit, so I just hang up on him. Seconds later he phones me back. "You don't want me to come back, do you, Coco?" he questions me, to which I gave no reply. I disconnect the call.

Honestly, at this point, I have no answer for him. Perhaps due to the fact that by now I do not really care that much whether he comes back or not, or maybe it is because I am planning on leaving him the next day anyway.

He calls me again. This time he is begging to come home. "I want to come home, Coco; please this is not my home now, I know I don't belong here anymore. I hate it. My home is with you not here with her. I should've never have left in the first place and I miss my little boys." (My dogs.) He says the magic words. Home. I needed to hear him classing my house as home. He goes on promising he wasn't making a cunt of me, he hadn't slept with her, and he was still in the back bedroom on his own. *Really? Really? Really? Fuck off!* He goes on about how she was eating popcorn noisily, which was annoying him as he watched television. An argument started over it and then she told him to go back to where he came from. Brad tells me laughing at her, that little did she know that is exactly what he intended to do. I listen to so much then just hang up on him. Once more I am not that interested in what else he has to say as it would be just more lies, no doubt.

29th March

Clothes all packed up, my little dogs all ready to go with me, and Gucci is all sorted out until I return home. Today I am going to London for a while, I am leaving Brad Blake. First though I need to get a few things in town. On the way home in a taxi with my purchases, Brad texts me, which I ignore, so he then calls me, asking me to meet him. I refuse explaining I am in a taxi on my way home. He calls the taxi firm, requesting the driver to take a detour with me to a particular coffee shop as there is surprise waiting for me. Upon the taxi driver's doing so, I arrive there to find Brad Blake standing in the doorway. I get out of the cab while he pays it. Trapped, I angrily inform him he has ten minutes of my time before I leave again. During that given time we have coffee then Brad, in front of his niece r, begins to make the arrangements with me to leave her aunt for the final time on a certain date. He begs me to wait, to stay in the relationship with him, just to trust him. *"Fucking trust in him, yea right, don't make me laugh!"* the voices in my head whisper to me as he promises me that for definite he would be coming back for good this time, with him returning on the fourth of April, the day before my birthday.

His niece drives me home, she tells me that she wishes he would make up his mind, which he now has done and hopes that he sticks with his choice as she is fed up of being in the middle of it all. I agree with her as he puts her in such an uncompromising position time after time. Once again in my haven, I lie down on the rug by the fire, as usual the wind and rain batters against the windows and my little dogs cuddle up beside me. I decide not to go today now as it's late, besides I have missed the train which I had intended to catch. I shall stay put for tonight, in the shadows of the candlelight once again, I look for my wolf as I decide what to do tomorrow morning, whether to stay with or leave Brad Blake.

31ˢᵗ March

I'm woken up by banging noises coming from the kitchen. I come downstairs to find the place covered in lots of chocolate Easter eggs left for me, my son and daughter. I had no idea it was Easter Sunday yet again. There is also a lot of expensive food to make a complete Easter Sunday dinner. There are more gifts for me, including suitable wine to accompany the meal. A card lies on the table, it simply reads, 'I love You Coco. Brad'. The house is empty once again, so he must have just left. I open the door just in time to catch the taillights of his car leave the street. How romantic of him, I think. If it hadn't been for Brad bringing all these gifts, then we would have had nothing on Easter Sunday. He makes a brilliant Easter Bunny, I smile. Besides, this just proves again how much he loves me, so maybe I should stay and give him another chance after all; we all make mistakes, don't we? Besides if it's Easter weekend, everywhere will be extremely busy, and I think perhaps I should have booked the train in advance. *"Bullshit! Making your excuses stronger than you Coco! Pussycat Coco! Fucking not got the audacity to leave him? Have you?"*

I remain put yet again. Pathetically. Later that evening, after a wonderful dinner, I head to the barn to give Gucci his chocolate egg. I stay the night once again falling asleep, this time outside his pen. The farmer had hung my quilt up on a peg near his stall, so he must have been thinking that for whomever the quilt belongs to or whoever sleeps with it, this will keep it dry for them. Maybe in the loneliness of the night as I sing to Gucci he is glad I am here after all.

3ʳᵈ April

Brad comes by the house today to check I have everything packed up ready to leave in the morning. On top of the bed we lie cuddled together, making plans for our future. Brad is sexually aroused so I take him in my mouth. On doing so he comments that he had been a full month without this. Just this, I question him, what about the rest of the sex. To which he replies there has not been any. He is shocked and disgusted at the thought of it with her, then even more so at me for just assuming there had been a sexual relationship between them, albeit only now and again. *Well,* I question myself, *I wasn't to know what went on for sure, did I?* I ask myself this again, confirming to me that I did no wrong as I am quite perturbed by the look on his face. He explains that if he ever did go into the bed, it was only when she got up. He also states that was a long while ago. He explains that when he was staying there, she got back into bed beside him one morning, and he lay just there for a little while before getting up so it wasn't too obvious to her that he didn't want her because he still had to stay in the house and convince her that he wasn't still seeing me. He says he felt weak and he'd let me down. Weak in what? I question him. Let me down in exactly what? As in what had happened in bed? I ask again. It just makes matters worse as he is now asking me of exactly what am I accusing him of. He tries to explain what had happened but I just laugh and poke fun at him for being in bed with an old age pensioner. His face is bright red and he is pretending to vomit as he says, "Oh! I'm going to be sick, Coco!"

Later that evening I prepare myself to leave with Brad. Well, most of my stuff still sat packed anyway plus I had made sure my hair and tan was perfect for the runaway jaunt, which it was once again actually conceived to be. Brad phones saying he loves me very much and he can't wait to be back with me again. My thoughts are contradicting his, as I am far from sure about that or anything else right now for that matter.

4ᵗʰ April

I am up, dressed and waiting for Brad. He phones to say he will be a little late as she decided to do her hair before going shopping. The minute she leaves, he phones back informing me that he is packing the car with everything belonging to him, along with other personal things he wants to take from the house. He had all his clothes prepared days ago so he could remove them with military precision. He could carry out the task without delay in case for some reason she returned to the house. The events that take place that morning ensure that this time he can never return to her. Last of all, he takes the most important thing in the world down from the wall – the original wedding photograph of his dead parents, which had hung there for years. He then hurriedly checks the house for the last time to make sure he has everything before he leaves. Brad follows that by locking the doors then he putting his keys through the letterbox. Brad's game plan is that when she comes home, she would find them lying on the carpet behind the door, clarifying cruelly that he was gone.

He goes from his house to his stepdaughter's house to inform her he was leaving now; this she had already known and had been expecting. As soon as he leaves her home though, she makes a phone call to her mother, telling her that Brad had left. His wife had apparently driven home like a bat out of hell to try and stop him from leaving. On arriving back home, she picked up the keys, realising she was way too late and he was long gone. Crying, she went to her daughter's house; she was very upset, wondering where he was. Then realisation of the situation began to dawn on her, regarding what could have had happened. She came to the correct conclusion when she said that Brad must have gone back to that Coco. There must have something been going on there, as you don't go back to a person time and time again just to rent a room. Brad said that she always blocked out the truth of their marriage and hid behind denial so she could save her own face each time he went back to stay because she wanted him there but mostly for financial reasons. So now she had admitted to herself out loud what she had known deep down all along.

While all this was going on, I too have my own issues to deal with. I do not put myself in her shoes as you can imagine how awful that must be plus I feel Brad dealing with her in that way is all wrong. He showed no respect at all when perhaps he should have done. It is not, however, my marriage so at the end of the day, it is up to him. He feels she deserved no better as his life was hell with her from day one. No love. No winners today or losers, just time standing still for a moment as we all accept the place that we were all in for now. I am more concerned about my little dogs about them being left behind, with them not knowing or understanding where I have gone or when I would return. Everything is just fogged over in a cloud of horrid hurt, it should have been an ecstatic time for me, but it is one of the most horrible days I have had or rather we have ever encountered, believe it or not. I feel physically sick, mostly at the thought of my little dogs. What his wife must have felt that night is awful but to be honest, it is the least of my worries. I am more interested in me than her, I guess that is not totally true as I struggle with trying to shut the thought of her alone in that house that night out of my head, nobody deserved that, I know that. *"You reap what you sow, Coco, reap what you sow!"* my unwelcome friends clarify.

5th April

We wake this morning to a text on Brad's phone from his wife. "You lying, cheating, deceitful bastard, don't ever come near me again," Brad reads this out to me, pissing himself laughing, then he deletes it as he then ignores the text completely and how she felt; I feel sorry for her as once I felt like that when he left to go to Canada. Fuck knows what the future holds for me either, so I don't gloat, I just felt numb and say nothing at all. He says to me, "I love you so much, this and her mean nothing to me!" he kisses me and flings the phone down as hand in hand we go down to breakfast. I look at him thoughtfully and his attitude is that he can't care less what the fuck she thinks.

I have a brilliant birthday with Brad spoiling me as usual with loads of expensive gifts. He makes love to me with such love and tenderness; we have the most amazing sex, with him making me feel the most beautiful and the luckiest woman in the world. That night he takes me for a birthday dinner with champagne. Brad tells every single person we met, who passes or would listen to him, that I am his wife.

We continue to stay with Megan on our hideaway holiday for a few days longer. Everyone notices we were inseparable at this point, we are constantly flirting with each other and kissing, touching, being very affectionate in public, not exactly an appropriate way to behave especially at our age but we do it anyway. As usual Robert wakes us at dawn with the fucking hoover, which was very funny and Megan goes nuts about it but he continues to do it anyway. We both have a nice time together despite everything that has happened but it is all over too soon, then it is time for me to return home with Brad, the difference with him is that now he is considering my house as his home too.

The next few weeks both of us take time to settle into a routine suiting me and Brad. It is different from the last time he was here to stay long-term – it felt more real, the love felt more intense between us and that kind of scared me a little. Brad is determined to make it work as he seriously thinks of me as his wife.

As it is my birthday, Brad has also booked a log cabin as a surprise. We go and stay there with my mum and dad and my daughter Jet comes too. We have a wonderful time full of fun and laughter as we all live in a little house in the woods, just like the television programme called The Walton's. Which is what I used to tease Brad about, saying that is what he played at with his wife in back in their so-called marital home, to which we would both crack up laughing as she sat knitting and he did the cooking. Our relationship is in a brilliant place. Brad gives me some beautiful jewellery which cost a fortune, with embedded sapphires and diamonds, to remind me of the stars in the night sky. That is so romantic and we all share a lovely hotel dinner. But on arriving back home, my feelings just change again for no reason and I cry a lot as I just want us all to be back there at the cabin once more as I relive every day spent there in my head over and over. I miss my daughter and I refuse to admit I am possibly depressed but a lot of unhappiness takes over my days and nights as sadness sets in my life. I become very much aware I need to change this, yet I did not know how. My little dogs and Gucci become even more so my world.

May

First of May brings the celebration in the witch's calendar it is Beltane, pronounced Bell-tane which is also known as May Day. It actually begins on the 30th of April. This is one of our very important Sabbats. It is where we welcome the summer. Large fires are lit to give tribute to the sun and the ashes from the fire are believed to hold magical influence. I burn rose incense and sage in my cauldron to mark this occasion. I don't particularly like the summertime much, but my little dogs do and I am sure my donkey will also love to lie in the sun. My little dog, called Versace, he especially loves the warmth outside He lies at my feet in the sunshine as I write my manuscript, only moving when I do, to follow me but only as far as the door, Goddess Bel love him! I smile at this as I think to myself that I much prefer autumn time of the year; however, summer is an important time for Mother Nature, therefore I celebrate the coming of it anyway as part of my religion. Nonetheless, I prefer winter, I am more nocturnal; I am up late at night. I love the dark.

9th May

Another stupid row starts where he hits me again. This leads to him packing his clothes and leaving once more. He is back an hour later and I am just tired now of all the fighting and the abuse; it is clear this is only working for short periods of time. I want us to finish for good but Brad wants to try to rebuild the relationship, so here we are again, both of us with hope and me willing to give him yet another chance. Stupid me.

The rest of May passes with us more like a regular couple than ever before, so perhaps it would work out after all. I am very confident now, convincing myself that he is here for good, especially under the terms he had left his wife, it was shocking yet he had made sure to guarantee me that there was no return ticket, not this time. I learn also that he chose to leave his wife in that way to show her that she meant nothing to him plus he felt it important to make her very clear on the fact he loved me. Kind of a bittersweet way, I think, of showing us both exactly where we stood.

The cherry blossoms are back on the trees in my garden, sitting under them drinking wine, I think how much has changed since the time he left me for Canada. These last few weeks together we took romantic walks in the woods, ate candlelit dinners in fancy restaurants, made love sharing our fantasies, at the early hours of the morning, we were dancing naked in my garden in the light summer rain. We had been extremely happy and relaxed living together. I have a special surprise for him this evening though. I am going to teach him a new sex game which I made up. A game of our very own fantasy sex, which would be played with fruit-flavoured jellybean sweets.

Darkness falls as I take Brad by the hand upstairs to bed. The room smells of fruit as I had lit fruit-scented candles adding to the sticky sweet aroma coming from a huge bowl of jellybeans by the bed. Brad is laid on the bed, whereupon he is blindfolded with a silk scarf, and then tied up at the wrists and feet with silk ties. He is then fed jellybeans one by one and the challenge is to guess the flavour for sexual favours or forfeits, either by personal choice or from handwritten cards I had made. He tastes the first one, answering correctly – strawberry flavour. He is offered a token or he can have a sexual favour of his choice or pick a sexual favour card, the details written on it was my command. He chooses his own favour and he requests to lick me. As I spread my legs either side of his head, his tongue flickers in the air, trying to find my little clitoris. I watch for a minute, letting him search for me just as a snake tastes the air, before I lower myself gently onto him, allowing the warm tip of his tongue to flicker over me. He moans in his desperation to do so, but I let him lick just for a second, then it is time to try another jellybean.

He gets the flavour wrong, so this time I chose his forfeit, plus he would receive no token. He would do as I ask or I can use a forfeit card to decide his punishment. You needed six tokens to be freed or you could buy yourself free from my game with whichever present I choose or by the reading of a gift card which stated the gift to be delivered. I make the decision to play on. His forfeit is I choose to play with myself for him with the punishment of him not being able to see me as he loves to watch, though tonight however he can only listen, so at this point he would have to just to imagine what I am doing as I whisper to him, informing him seductively that I am pushing the tiny silk panties aside, gently touching myself, then deeply pushing my finger up inside me. I let him taste little droplets of my juice as I put my finger from my sweet pussy to his lips. The sperm shoots right up out of him into the air. Game over. He loses immediately when he ejaculates. He is untied and his forfeit is my present, my decision. I order him to lick me for hours until I can take no more; at that point I cheat, adding a massage. He has to comply with the first, allowing me to come and come again in sheer pleasure but not the second but as the rules of the game are new to him, he doesn't know that so I get both. My game is then boxed up and put away. On the bed, still laughing, we feed each other the jellybeans, trying to guess the flavours. "Better to be prepared, Brad," I say to him, "try to learn all the different flavours for next time as in my own special game I made up to play with you, these rules are the art of the game. The better you are at tasting the flavours correctly, the better you can play the game. The better you are at playing game, the better the sex is you receive. Last of all, Blake, the more you play and the more you learn to hold out longer from ejaculating, the higher the chances of you winning.

With the bonus of the longer you hold on the longer you will get fucked." This I promise him sincerely as I get up from the bed to go and run a bath for us to share. He goes downstairs still eating and trying to guess the flavours correctly. While he goes to get the bottle of wine and order us some pizza, he continues to eat more jellybeans, still getting them all wrong. I laugh so much, this game is way too much to my advantage, and I smirk with delight.

June

At the beginning of the month, I still sit in the sun most days, writing my manuscript. The other little dogs come and go as the heat is too much for them. But little Versace lies at my feet and both of us would be there in the garden from dawn to dusk. My skin is a gorgeous sun-kissed colour of deep rich wood as the sun tans me while I sit writing with Versace; those hours we spend together are so precious, in fact priceless to me, I think they are worth so more to me than this book, if it ever makes it.

20th June

The Midsummer Sabbat Solstice, sometimes known as Litha, pronounced Lith-a which is another celebration on the witch's calendar, we celebrate the light and honour the sun, between the 19th and the 25th. We make flower crowns and we hold fire rituals at night, building bonfires and dancing. We also decorate our altar with summer fruits and flowers, and leave candles burning all day long. We make lavender cookies for love, protection, purification, peace and happiness. Oat cookies with lemon zest for love and friendship and vanilla ones for lust and love. This is the longest day and the shortest night and is the time to celebrate the completion of the cycle that began with winter solstice. There are also so many different ways to celebrate this time, dates and days may also change due to calendar year. I don't see Brad tonight, he is at work. Thank fuck. I just do all my witchy stuff quite happily wondering if he loves me. Do I love him? Music box. The real love I know is what I feel for my children and my little dogs. Later I cleanse myself and wash away negativity, moisturise as I renew myself with a charge to improve my life. I am therefore creating beauty in soft skin and mostly promising myself to stop reaching for moon dust because most days, all I am getting is sand from the beach in my ass.

22nd June

We go to Port Patrick for a night out. We have dinner at an exclusive hotel at the harbour. The food is amazing, I have duck in blackberry sauce and the wine is a rich dark fruity red, which compliments the dish perfectly. Brad has fish and white wine. We meet up with friends who are on holiday there for the weekend. We have a lovely evening, going in and out of all the different small bars which sat along the front promenade for a drink. We listen to the live bands playing modern and Celtic music.

Afterwards back at our hotel, Brad starts an argument with me, which leads to him slapping my face hard. I tell him to get out of the hotel room, which he does. He sits in the jeep for a while then he returns to the hotel by the time I have removed my make-up. I am in a silk chemise making coffee in the corner of the suite when he enters through the room door. He apologises as I look at him, I say nothing. I know I am in an abusive relationship that now would never change. He would never change. I would have to either get out of the relationship or live with it and him for what it truly was, the decision was mine and mine alone to make. I turn away from him, he comes to bed; as he tries to hold me in the darkness, and I pull away. Later I wake up cuddled up into him; I get out of bed making more coffee while he sleeps. I sit in the cool room by the window overlooking the bay, as I watch the sun come up on the horizon, I know and I admit at last to myself that my friends in my head are right for sure, I am fucked and this relationship is as fucked as me because I cannot live with him or begin to imagine what it would be like to live without him.

The next five days are perfect and full of blissful love as Brad pampers me with presents and is so sorry and treats me like a princess once again. It won't last though, I know that. I sit in the sun writing some more as wee Versace is as always by my side. He listens to me as I talk away to him, I tell him all about my life and he looks up at me as I explain my dreams. I pick him up, his fur is so warm as I whisper to him that the relationship I have with his daddy is so destructive, so harmful, but like an addiction

I keep on living it but then I ask him, for how long? He looks at me with dark brown eyes as tears run down my face; he licks them to comfort me. I smile as the friends in my head answer the question. They say it will be for as long as you want to, Coco, for as long as you want.

By the end of June though the tide is turning again, well, just a little at first. The problems start again, although not too serious at this point as they are just more stupid arguments about particularly nothing which end usually with us making love. This pattern continues. We are back in the position I call Mr and Mrs Blake, as in the movie where husband and wife fight all over the house, then make love as the same. Well, that is fast becoming our routine. At times when I fight with him, it feels like I am sleeping with the enemy but the romantic evenings and lovemaking we share outweigh for now all the other shit. We are just so explosive together, like a hurricane meets volcano. I sing made-up song lyrics to him, *"I am gonna put a spell on you, then watch you burn,"* as I crawl naked up the bed onto him after yet again another pointless row. Never on an even keel, we would be either deeply in love or happily cut each other's throats. I just continue to sing, *"Make love to you under my spell, then watch you burn as in hell."* My song is so appropriate in comparison to my life with him. I love him then I hate him. Music box. *He loves me? He loves me not?*

Though to be fair, in general in our own sadistic way, we are happy I suppose because when it is good between us it is brilliant, but when it is bad it is fucking awful.

July

July had arrived, keeping the warm weather. We share a lot of ritual sex acts, which as a witch I perform on him, also with him. During the long afternoons of that time, we make love in secluded woods amongst the long grass. We go for naked picnics there together, feeding each other the food then drinking wine from the bottles before pouring it over each other's body, followed by licking it off and fucking each other roughly, wildly under the hot sun.

I book dinner for two at an exclusive hotel in a very historic part of town. I also book a room to stay overnight and request that the bed is made up with my own new purple satin sheets, which I supply. The hotel staff willingly do so. He is asked to come dressed in his white shirt to meet me there. He arrives to find me not waiting in the lobby as was planned. He phones me on his mobile phone asking where I am. I tell him to come up to room one. He enters to find me wearing black underwear and a black and white silk robe. I blindfold him with black silk knickers then with him only wearing his white shirt he is sat on the edge of the bed and fed jellybeans. I remove the blindfold whereupon he thinks it is party time. *Oh really!* Then I get him to lie on the bed, I strip off the robe, taking the silk belt off my robe and put it beside him. I walk away from him in underwear casting a spell with my wand, I make the black and white silk belt move, wrapping itself 'round his wrists, tying him up. He is terrified. I put on high heels now with my long black and purple silk lined witch robe followed with the lightening of my vampire candles of red and black wax. Little does he know that dinner is not on the fucking menu. Whilst he is still wearing his white shirt, I unbutton it then drip the hot candle wax on his chest. I then tie him to the bed as he watches me walk around chanting spells, swishing my robe back and forth, thus showing off my black expensive lace and velvet top stockings. I untie him whilst keeping my underwear on, I refuse to make love with him. He sits on the edge of the bed as I lie behind him, I put my hand on his shoulder as I instruct him to leave, just go. I just wanted to punish and hurt him, I guess. He leaves quite upset. He is quite broken actually. Game over. I won. Let him feel what it is like to leave me behind in a hotel room on my terms this time, not his. This is what he has done to me sometimes, as he headed home to his wife after sex, leaving me to spend the night alone in plush surroundings. I was used to it, but that is not the point. Sometimes it hurt me so much, not tonight though. He goes back home to our house alone. I choose to stay myself, go for dinner on my own. I have my photograph taken wearing my beautiful long witch dress whilst standing on the ballroom staircase amidst all the sparkling fairy lights. Then I go back to my room, light candles, enjoy a relaxing bubble bath and happily, not in the least bit feeling guilty, under those soft, silky purple sheets I eat my expensive chocolates with champagne from room service. *Fuck him!* Besides it does not bother me being in hotels on my own and I intend to do it again very soon. He phones me a lot during the evening, but I don't answer him. I sleep peacefully and the next morning after a sensational breakfast, the menu is one of the best, very exclusive choice, bringing in London, showing up some of their top hotels. I have my breakfast afterwards Brad comes to pick me up, the only thing he said was that he hoped I enjoyed my time alone. Which I did, apart from missing my little dogs, a bonus was that I was nearer actually to wee Gucci. I don't tell him that.

At home though, we still bicker on and off, Brad is still hiding things from me. We are not being honest with each other yet again. I know this is very true on my part plus I am sure it is in Brad's case too. I hide from him that when he is working nightshift; I still a lot of the time spend the night with Gucci in the barn. He would have gone mad about it, putting a stop to it for my own sake. Not for keeping me safe from my donkey but you could never tell who was wandering about out there at night; I guess he had a right to be concerned; after all he worked in a forensic unit. He could not, however, understand why Gucci did not run biting at me anymore, which I pretended in the car was not an issue. I kind of dismissed it as if it was neither here nor there, treating it casually so he would not catch on to what was going on as I always made sure to be home before he came in from work. I was delighted with my secret still being hidden from him even more so that Gucci now was my little friend.

Brad and I mostly fight during the daylight, which I find very strange. While at nights behind the closed door, we engage in more unusual sex, still performing evil games using ties with blindfolds on each other, which we use as some kind of restricting yet punishing torture in a form of sex. Using hot candle wax or ice cubes which melt uncomfortably on our bare skin. We play with slimy foods, use objects and sex toys during our lovemaking, which goes on for hours and hours. We live out different sexual fantasies and on doing so we still share ritual cleansing baths before and afterwards. We make love outside in the dark garden in torrential rain where he fucks me in freezing cold showers, naked under the tress, I cast more witchcraft spells, it is as if we are looking for something completely different sexually together, something way beyond human understanding yet we don't know what or where to find it.

We have a terrible fight near the end of the month which results in him raising his hands to me yet again. I retaliate, slapping him back hard whilst yelling at him to get to hell out. This time he goes without much of a performance. I get drunk on wine, and then falling all over the ship, go to bed. I wake up to find him in bed beside me. He is hard in his sleep, so I roll him over onto his back, I climb on top of him, sitting on his hard-on, just as he wakens up he comes right into me. I kiss him smiling, he whispers back, "Love you, Coco, by the way that was an amazing dream I just had." So this is us right back too square one. No apology given either way or on any count about the earlier commotion but that is cool with me because I am buying time, only he just doesn't know it.

The next day comes with me being ill and hung-over with the alcohol, then I am totally devastated and broken beyond Brad's belief as when I go to visit my donkey, I find he has gone. Just gone, he has disappeared just like that, into mid-air. Gucci is not to be seen anywhere. I search all day and night with him not being found. I can't find any trace of him at all or even of my quilt. The farmer says when he went into the barn that morning to put him out to the field, it was empty and he assumed I had come and taken him away. Now though the farmer states the obvious that since I do not have him then maybe he has been stolen or has just got lost. Fucking stolen or lost. I am in hysterics, screaming at him and Brad to find him or else. A few days back the same thing had happened to my little dog Versace; he wandered out the gate, and then got lost. I was so distraught, it was unbelievable, I was so frightened he would die or get killed and I would never see him again. I searched for hours, looking for him in shock and hurt, praying so hard I would get him back. I was screaming absolutely terrified in case he didn't return. He was found safe, and my son brought him home to me. I was delighted beyond words to see his little face as I broke my heart holding him tight into me. Now the little donkey is gone too. I hope he is all right wherever he is. Stunned and shocked, I am numb for days as I wonder about what has happened to him, where he is and I am sure someone has taken him away but why? I search everywhere for him with no results and still with no idea or understanding of what has happened to him.

August

The first of August is 'Lammas', it is the celebration of the first grain harvest, a time for gathering in and giving thanks in abundance. I celebrate with the rest of the witches the Sun's life – giving energy reborn as life giving bread. Thanking the goddess, the Grain Mother all with a heavy heart. I hurt deeply more so, all I really want is Gucci. I don't make corn dollies, I don't bake bread. I make spells for Gucci to be found and for him to be well wherever he is.

2nd August

Still I search for my donkey.

I hate this fucking month of the year, although it is my son's birthday month; it never seems to hold any happiness for me other than that. But this time, this month kind of changes things of the past a little. Brad and I share so much happiness despite all the sadness on losing Gucci. I will never forget this year, I shall remember for as long as I live the love we shared the August of this summer.

The weather stayed humid while Brad and I made love in the river under a waterfall, which was an amazing experience. He built a den in the woods, pretending to be my Robin Hood, and we stayed in it all night making love, looking up at the sky, making wishes in the stars. I spoke to our ancestors beyond the night sky, asking them to grant my wishes of keeping us all safe and well. I asked them that night to bless Versace, keeping him in the gate, to look after all my other little dogs keeping them well and to make sure Gucci was happy and safe wherever he was. I called it the 'fairy den' as Brad had decorated it with flowers, rose petals and solar fairy lights. He had wine, chocolates and perfume waiting for me in this little tumbling down homemade house in the woods. I wore the pretty pure white underwear he bought me as we slow-danced under the moon. It was so romantic the way he removed it from me, kissing me all over, and then when I was totally naked, he laid me on the forest floor, entering me with such passion, we both came together so quickly. We walked in the woods at midnight laughing as he tries to scare me in the dark, pretending to be the shagging monster that was going to get me, shag me all night, and then eat me. In the blackness of the forest we went singing and dancing through the trees before screaming in fun, pushing each other into the freezing cold river. Fuck knows what the forest would have said that night if it could have talked, I smiled to myself. I wished we could have stayed like that forever, in the den, in the woodland just me and Brad with my little dogs.

The next day and night, however, I spent yet again searching heartbroken for my donkey. I found nothing.

It was this month that we shared what I called the Strawberry Summer Nights, where all the food and wine was strawberry flavoured and together we bathed in baths full of strawberry-scented bubbles. It was on those special nights that I wore sensational sexy underwear in shades of pink as we made love at least three times a night under strawberry-coloured sheets. Some of those hot August days we made love in the sea at little private beach we found and claimed as our own. We called it Coco Beach. We camped out there at night in a tent on many occasions, where we lit a bonfire burning the driftwood, and then we would make love again by the fire on the sand or at the edge of the sea as the waves rolled in over us. We drank wine and toasted marshmallows on the embers of the dying fire as we sat hand in hand, planning our future together, watching the sun coming up on the horizon. It was perfect.

The happiness of our love continued as did the non-stop sex. We made love one night up a dusty old loft with me wearing an old wedding dress from times gone by; it felt as if we were in a different century. We bought a new buzzing battery operated toothbrush each. We had the most amazing sex with one of them, which I intended to fling away afterwards; however, Brad wanted to keep it to brush his teeth. This remark, as you can imagine, I found to be hilarious laughing at him, thinking no way, I smirked shaking my head in fun yet at the same time screwing my face up disgusted even at the thought of it. Whatever would his dentist say? I wondered about this as she was so far up her own tight arse as it was, I could imagine the look on her dour pinched face if only she had known. I laughed out loud as I informed Brad of this, and he had no choice but to agree with me on this truthful assumption. My own dentist, however, would shake his head laughing as his personality would show amusement as I don't think anything I did anymore would surprise him, well perhaps not really. I need to inform him to stock up on buzzing toothbrushes because if my book makes it, then I reckon he is going to need them.

One of those August nights we visited Loch Lomond. We went into a little place called Luss, just not far from the start of the loch. It is a little village where all the time gone by small cottages are all painted in the same colour, all with matching tiny windows and flowers in abundance in the front gardens. There you will find a few cute cafés selling home baking with excellent coffee and old-fashioned little china pots of tea. The few tourist shops sold all the Scottish gifts and keepsakes from handmade soaps to tartan boxes of shortbread and Loganberry wine. The pier, which you can walk along, goes into the water with the view right up and down the loch amazing. The water is so clear and at the side of the pier sit small boats, who take you out on trips up the loch. A beach sits to the left of the pier, with an old-fashioned shop down at the beginning of it, which is like entering a little cave. It plays Scottish music, selling tartan cashmere shawls, Harris Tweed handbags and unusual presents that you can buy that are made with deer antlers and the most delicious butter tablet that melts in your mouth. There they also sell butter tablet ice cream, which is totally to die for.

On leaving Luss, we headed further up the loch. I was surprised the first time I went at how long the loch was and admired all the wild flowers that grow along the banks of it. The scenery along the way is of trees and little beaches on the side of the road you drive up, with the mountains on the other. The loch stretches for miles and miles and is so calm. Whenever I see that loch, the picture it creates is different each time. The sun sparkles on the water, shimmering like a sheet of pale blue glass, and the mountains so near you can reach out and touch them. Other days when the clouds hang over it, the loch is a dark shade of sapphire blue, rich and mysterious-looking with the backdrop of the mountains looking different yet again and as if they are calling out to you to come over to them. In the middle of the loch all along the way sit little islands on which dark green trees grow the colour of which complement the shades of blue in the water. At the top of the loch is situated Scotland's oldest pub. The Drover's Inn. It has real log burning fires either side of the bar and is full of stuffed animals, with tartan shawls hung on the walls along with swords. All the staff wear kilts as their uniform. The premises are thick with dust and stour from the coal and logs they put on to the open fires, this also creates a smoky atmosphere, which adds to the already old-age look of the ancient floor and décor. The food was excellent and the place added more character to Loch Lomond as it is just as famous as the loch and was very much worth the visit.

The Scottish poet and folklorist William Lang in 1876 wrote a poem based on the song titled 'The Bonnie Banks o' Loch Lomond'. The title has sometimes been known to date back to 1746, the year of the defeat of Bonnie Prince Charlie's rebellion with different lyrics at the start of the poem. The more modern version of it, however, is more known and sang today rather than the traditional one, with the loch being as famous worldwide as the song and rightly so.

Today the sky is a lighter shade of the palest blue with white fluffy clouds behind the mountains, with the loch to the forefront the picturesque view is stunning and one of a kind. There is something magical here that makes you feel proud of your country to have such heritage known for what it is. We book into an exclusive hotel which stands grand back from the road on the banks of Loch Lomond. The bedroom is luxurious, very opulent, decorated in dark rich colours with a four-poster bed. The views of the loch from the window of our bedroom are magnificent. We share a wonderful dinner at night in the restaurant, which is expensive but the quality and presentation of the food is unbelievable. Traditional Scottish dishes like Haggis and Clootie dumpling deep-fried in batter with added double fresh cream, scotch whiskey and wild blackberry and bramble liquors. The chef recommends the wine to accompany his dishes which compliments them completely and the dessert is so light you can almost imagine it floating in air.

After dinner, we walk along the edge of the loch hand in hand. I remembered the other time we stayed here in an exclusive log cabin at the edge of Loch Lomond. It had a four-poster bed all dressed in tartan drapes, with a Jacuzzi hot tub and a separate sauna. The patio doors opened right out onto the loch, where we danced under the moonlight and made love in the water. I have keepsakes in my lounge of washed up logs from the lochs' waters' edge. I glance up at Brad smiling at the salted sugar, bittersweet memories, remembering how it hurt afterwards, as once again he went home to his wife. As Brad tells me how much he worships me. I look at him, slowly deliberately taking in the expression in his eyes and I can see that he sincerely means what he says. A little further along, he stops to take off his dinner jacket. I watch him wonderingly as he lays the jacket down, smoothing it out on the grass. He pulls me towards him laughing, asking me to sit down. As I do, he gently pushed me backwards and lays me down on top of it. My head is in the grass as he kisses me, then he lifts my expensive tartan dress, as he removes the tiny red tartan thong-style pants, he kisses my mouth again, then he proceeds to go down and cover my clitoris in millions of tiny delicate kisses. I feel so much love for him and pride for that beautiful place that night as I lie back looking up at the sky beyond the mountains. Listening to the water of the loch touching the shore, under the moonlight and with the famous song words in my head, I feel the most honoured woman in Scotland, with my traditional Scottish gown held up at my waist, I lie with my bare arse on the expensive silk lining of that jacket as Brad Blake fucks me 'On the Bonny Banks of Loch Lomond'. For the second time.

The end of the month brings more sadness though as it is the anniversary of my other little dog C.C.'s death, I look back down at the floor and I see him still sitting there as if it was yesterday; sadly I wipe the tears away, I still miss him every single fucking day.

September

Today is the first of September. Brad hits me again today hard and has his hands around my throat shaking me, calling me a whore. An argument starts and as usual, I challenge him; I never back down from anybody in a fight and especially not from Brad Blake. I don't really like confrontation at all and by now I am so tired of all this fighting with him. When Brad goes to work later at night, I cast spells of happiness for our future. I pick up little Versace, cuddling him thinking he is getting so old now. I carry him down the backstairs into the garden as I let all my other little dogs out before bedtime. The sky is so clear, with all the stars twinkling brightly tonight. The month has come in slowly bringing with it a change in the weather. You can feel the crispness of the autumn chill in the air. The leaves are starting to fall from the trees and the nights are drawing in. It is coming up to my favourite time of year, which is also Brad's. So perhaps this would change our mood. A few days later on a clear, early September morning, I find my donkey. Gucci is standing in the middle of town with a woman holding a bucket collecting money for the donkey sanctuary. I approach her claiming that he had been stolen because that donkey had belonged to me. I look under him and the unusual white marking on him confirm he's mine, He looks up at me with his big sad eyes, he puts his ears back, opening his mouth to bite me. He was not doing that to other people just me, so t that alone confirms for sure that it is him. After the commotion of an argument with the woman, I phone the police, who ask me for a description. I say she is a big fat cheeky cow who is wearing a red jacket. He says he had wanted a detailed description of the donkey, not the woman. On waiting for them to arrive, I phone Brad's mobile.

He turns up first looking ashen, admitting to me in quiet tones that he and the farmer had given my donkey away as they had been under the impression that I no longer wanted to keep him. On realising the mammoth mistake, they decided that it would be better to keep their mouths shut as to his whereabouts. I am so angry, hurt, totally shocked with the deceit that I can't fucking believe what I am hearing. I had suffered mental hell on not knowing anything about Gucci's disappearance or his safety. Brad watched this happen to me, all the while fucking knowing exactly where he fucking was, as did that bastard of a farmer. Yet they had both helped me search for him for fucking days and nights, for weeks on end, with their sincere promises of doing all they could to find him, which had just been all lies and pretence. Disgusted, I am shouting out loud in the street, where by this time a lot of people had stopped nearby to listen. I scream at Brad explicitly in public as I fucking tell him to stay away from me. He is so embarrassed by my behaviour that he shows his official name badge (which he still wore from his night shift at work) to the gathering crowd, claiming that he is a mental health nurse with me the psychiatric patient and his position is to take me back to the mental hospital. He pushes me forward, locking my arms in a tight grip painfully on my back, I scream with the pain and looking up with tears in my eyes, the last thing I see is Gucci's sad eyes looking at me. Brad is hurting me and marching me head down towards the car, pushing me into the back seat. As he drives away from the scene, I have to phone back my friend in the police force, explaining what had happened to my donkey. He is stunned by my revelations but tells me at least Gucci is being well taken care of. At least that is true.

Arriving back home I am raging at Brad and totally distraught as I get out of the car. He comes in the house behind me, trying to apologise as I pack his clothes. I order him out of the house so he takes the clothes I fling at him and leaves. Only though for a few hours does he stay away. He comes back to the door with a peace offering; he has brought me chocolates with a bottle of Gucci perfume. I snatch the perfume bottle from his hands and clonk him hard on the head with it, then fling the fucking perfume with the chocolates following it down the full length of the garden at the cherry trees, then bang the fucking door shut in his face.

The middle of the month the relationship deteriorates big time, the arguments are horrendous. This time the fighting has escalated so much that no amount of passionate sex would even out the hatred in the betrayal I feel. I trust him not. I just know by now there is no way back to what we once had, that special place of love we had shared only just last month was gone forever.

No matter what he does for me or how hard he tries to rectify the wrong he did, nothing helps. He offers me a new donkey, which I refuse, then he tries to get Gucci back but it is way too late as by now he has been sold on. He wants so much to make me happy, whole once more as I am in pieces; he tries to make us better again. But we are in fact broken beyond repair, just like Humpty Dumpty, because all the king's horses and all the king's men couldn't put Humpty together again or me or us. I just want to be with my little dogs, I am grateful they are my real soulmates, not Brad as I had once believed. I feel nothing for him. This time all his pish talk cannot replace the cold emptiness he has left inside me. I can't even stand the thought of him near me let alone sexually.

The weather is changing too, it is even getting as cold outside as I feel inside. I am in the garden in the storm as my little dogs sit watching me from in the dry doorway of the house, a lot wiser than me not to go out in this weather. Brad comes up the path, turning the corner of the house, he wanders over the garden to where I sit; sitting down beside me in the torrential rain, he hands me a small blue velvet box. I open it to find the most beautiful pair of gold- and diamond-set earrings shaped in the style of teardrops. The diamonds glisten more so as the rain enhances their sparkle.

"I'm so sorry for all the hurt I have caused you. On finding these in an old-fashioned jewellery shop window, they reminded me of every single teardrop you have ever cried, either over me or because of me. I realise, no Coco, I know I'm not worth it. Not worth a single tear. If you want me to go, then I will, Coco, because I feel I am losing you, I know that I have lost you now anyway actually. I am praying you stay with me and for you to please give me another chance. I'm so sorry about everything that happened and I miss you so much," he speaks in such a sad pathetic voice, which is probably heartfelt. I look at him, acknowledging our clothes were soaking wet, and I say nothing, not a fucking single word as we both sit crying in the pouring rain.

16th September

We leave to go on holiday to stay in a log cabin at for a week at Drumnadrochit. It is a luxury cabin just for two and is very exclusive, with Denbigh dishes and crystal glasses and a huge four-poster bed. How romantic, I think sarcastically. It sits right up very high on the top of a steep hill, and the views over the valley are stunning, especially when the sun is going down. There are red squirrels about, which are few and far between, they are taking hazelnuts off a tree outside the bedroom window. Brad also collects some nuts, as well as them he picks wild brambles and apples, which he then makes into a fruit butter crumble for me. It is delicious served warm with Channel Island thick cream. He is trying hard to heal the hurt of the last few weeks and I am grateful but feel just sort of lost, I guess.

17th September

Today we have another secret wedding, this time in an ancient church that sits by a loch between the cabin and

Drumnadrochit. The church is empty at six o' clock at night when we enter, Brad comments I looked stunning as I stand in a black silk totally backless dress. My hair, which is very dark, is up but has curls tumbling down, creating a soft messy look. My nails are painted black with Swarovski crystals and I wear black satin high heel shoes. My jewellery is simple with diamond earrings and slim diamond bracelets worn on each wrist, my fingers sit bare, waiting to wear that plain gold circle once again. Brad removed both our rings before we left the cabin, and they sit in his pocket in the little pouch which is very similar in shape to the small bag or sack a garden gnome has on a stick, carrying in it all his worldly belongings over his back.

We go to the altar, and Brad opens the handmade cloth and carefully lays down our gold wedding bands there on top of a gold and red velvet cloth. Brad takes my ring, putting it back on my finger as he makes vows and promises to me eternal love. I then place Brad's ring back on his finger as I do likewise. We then kiss and light candles. We sign a paper with both our signatures as a commitment to each other, with the date and time of our secret wedding. We leave the church and go to a very exclusive hotel at Loch Ness. We have our wedding supper with two bottles of the finest champagne and a red velvet wedding cake. Everything is perfect and the food is amazing. On leaving there the two of us go to Loch Ness, there on the banks by the loch we have a slow dance in the dark with music coming from the jeep, as we sway to the love song he holds me close whispering how much he loves me. Tears of happiness and of sadness run down my face as I think of my little dogs, the lies he told and what he did with my donkey, I don't forgive him and I shall never forget that, I think of all the fights as well as the love we share. My life, like tonight, is either total bliss filled with love and happiness beyond belief where deep down I am still tinted with a little hurt, or it is purgatory and the darkest place in the world to be.

We go back to the cabin and have strawberry wine with dark chocolate. I put on expensive pure white lace underwear and negligee set. Brad removes it gently as he makes love to me slowly on the four-poster bed, then carries me naked through to the huge red leather sofa, where he makes love to me again. The French doors are open so afterwards we stand naked on the balcony, kissing under the stars and drinking the sweet wine from the crystal glass while I show the surrounding woods how much I love him and whisper to the trees that tonight he is my hero but not always, definitely not always.

18th September

We both sleep late, I lie in bed a little longer while Brad makes breakfast, the smell of bacon and the noise of it sizzling in the pan is so tempting, I pull myself out of bed to have some. Just at that Brad appears at the room door with a tray. Breakfast in bed for me. I climb back under the duvet, enjoying the toasted rolls with the bacon smothered in maple syrup with milky coffee, now this is my kind of morning. Afterwards we make love, shower and get dressed. I sit and write my manuscript as Brad heads into the village for some food shopping. I like being alone in the cabin in the woods, I love the solitary feeling with the calm mood it creates. I put down my book and sit out on the balcony with coffee; I smile at the memory of last night, a good job it was jet black out here like being in a tomb of the dead because if anybody had seen us, well I guess we would have been charged with indecent whatever. I think of my mum and dad and daughter when we were here on holiday in April, not exactly here but we visited the village. I remember another balcony and how Brad pissed out over it early one morning as my father sat below, wondering where the water was coming from, how we laughed, another charge for Brad Blake, well he has already been charged by the police for pissing outside, he paid the fine but obviously never learned his lesson. I also think about and miss my son, my little dogs and still miss Gucci; I am feeling very nostalgic today for some reason. I feel a deep sense of sadness, just some sort of loss of the past and empty inside yet, I am not sure exactly why.

Brad returns with lots of treats and expensive foods to eat. He brings me some new night cream to try and Black Opium perfume, which I adore. The smell is so sweet and exotic; I discovered that men find it intoxicating on my skin as the comments made have been things like, "You, Coco, smell good enough to eat!" Brad has also bought me the most unusual gift of a voodoo wizard with a wand which has a jewel in the shape of a star at the end of it and he is wearing long purple robes. Its magic is to bring me absolute success in all I do, I am ecstatic with the wizard. Voodoo is black magic, is it not? I am a white witch; however, perhaps for now I should move to the dark side, I smile. Either way, however, I intend to use this little wizard and the spell he brings with him to get me to where exactly I want to be. Voodoo or not, this little wizard shall be casting spells with me very soon.

22nd September

It's Mabon, also known as Autumnal Equinox amongst many other names. The second festival to celebrate the harvest. Brad shares in this with me today. As in the first one, it is done with a lot of feeling of loss. As it reminds us that everything is temporary, no season lasts forever. Neither light nor dark ever overpowers the other for long. Then how come I ask The Horned God and The Goddess, *why do I feel so much in the dark all the time?* Last time I cast a spell to bring Gucci to me. This time after the other celebrations of the second harvest, I sat alone conjuring a spell, to please keep Gucci safe, warm, loved, healthy and happy. The music box once again plays in my head. My friends sing along, *"I love him? I hate him not? I hate him? I love him not?"*

End of September

With the holiday over, I return home with Brad and I still cry a lot of the time, finding only bleakness in everything. I write my manuscript non-stop but that is all I do, as I do not eat that much or hardly sleep, so consequently, I look awful plus lose a lot of weight. A stupid row between us comes out of nowhere over Christmas, Christmas of all the fucking things to argue about, more so especially this time of year. Brad raises his hands to me again, knocking me into the wall. A lot of things are said by both parties which should not have been said; therefore we just fuel each other's fire, making it all so much worse. I am so distraught I just walk upstairs to pack my clothes. "Don't go, Coco," he informs me, "I will." I start to unpack then just leave the room, while he packs his clothes I sit down in my lounge staring at the walls looking for the image of my wolf, without realising that I won't find him because it needs to be dark inside the room, with candles lit to create the shadow on the wall I am looking for – my wolf.

He packs up the car. I go upstairs and take off my wedding band and put on under wear. I stand in a pale blue lace bra, tiny pants with lace top stockings and suspenders in the same shade of blue. I hand Brad the wedding band and shake his hand goodbye. I do not intend to have sex with him before he leaves, I just think, well the voices tell me, my friends in my head, they think it would be a good idea to wear this outfit as it is very befitting of me and appropriate for our relationship, besides the colour reminds me of the lyrics of a country song that I once heard a long time ago. She sang blue was the colour of sadness as was the dress she wore when she told him goodbye. He tries to take my hand as I walk away, he asks me to put my ring back on, begging me to stay with him. I don't – I don't think I want to anymore. I just keep on walking away in the underwear as he stands desperately watching me. I go down the stairs, out the house, along the street and I walk half naked in the pretty lingerie into the woods. That cold September night I sit there for hours alone in the dark. I am freezing while he searches everywhere for me, and the friends in my head, my only true friends I feel I can trust apart from my little dogs, tell me to hide, so that is exactly what I do, I listen to them and I hide from him. For how long, I have no idea, as I have no conception of time; the only one thing I do realise but do not care about is how cold I truly am.

Eventually, dressed like a hooker, I walk back home as the cars on the road, pass me peeping their horns. That night I go to bed and sleep lightly. I dream I am in a world of pink bubbles filled with happiness. With fluffy clouds and bunny rabbits. All my little dogs are there and Gucci the donkey. Everyone whom I have lost, who are dead, are alive again as we dance in the soft wind, singing all day and night with the fairies and the good white witches.

In the morning I wake feeling worse than ever as I realise what I had dreamt about. The dream was teaching me a lesson on looking at my life. It was not going to be as I wished for, not fairy-tales for evermore. Now I have to face another horrible day in this world with the reality I am going off my fucking head and acknowledging so clearly this relationship is fucked on wakening from this fantasy slumber.

Chapter IX
Descent into Darkness

October 2013

The beginning of the month starts with me up unusually early on a frosty morning, with the sun looking weak in its warmth but bright enough high in the sky. I feel elated this morning as this is my favourite month of the year, whereupon I just like to think I own October. Miss Coco October, I call myself. My enthusiasm of giving myself the present of declaring the month to be mine does not last for long though, because just as I finish my coffee once again, I begin to feel dismal inside about the hopelessness of this love in my life. Shaking my head in the mirror, I stupidly try to put my thoughts aside for the present before deciding to go out for a walk. I wrap myself up from the cold by putting on warm clothes, and then pulled on my wellies. I leave the house with hope and anticipation of being in a much happier mood on my return. I don't take the little dogs with me as the chilled weather is not to their liking.

I ramble through the woods, then stroll past the river to find the water is making a lot more noise than usual, bubbling furiously as it rushes over rocky areas, causing little white waterfalls and almost bursting its banks in its haste to wherever it is rushing to. For a while I watch the twigs that had fallen into it being bobbed about as the water plays with them. Moving on I get annoyed at myself as the thoughts I want to bury for now come back with a vengeance.

Frustrated by this I suddenly stop walking, lying before me is a broken tree trunk, which must have been blown down by the storm last night. I find that a huge pile of leaves has gathered beside it, *sheltering from the wind,* I smile. Effortlessly, I kick them up in the air, and then I just stand staring at the rich fusion of the vivid colours of autumn tumbling round in the damp atmosphere before floating back down to the ground. As the delicate clothing of the trees have no choice but to accept their forfeit, I feel ashamed, upset even as they retreat slowly to where they lay once before in peace. Unpredictably, I start to make a wish upon each one of them as they land. Abruptly, I point over and begin poking at them, surprisingly but distinctively saying, "I make a wish on this one and now I make a wish on that one." *Wishes of what?* I ask myself, to which the answer being returned is a conclusion of I do not know what it is that I truly want. Perhaps I should ask the friends in my head for their opinion on which requests I should place in my pursuit? They sit in silence with no reply, I hear nothing. I must then assume that me disrupting the harmony of the woods, attacking the foliage for no reason, is in fact me only confirming to myself this is not a responsible way to behave, especially at my age. Neither is pretending that there are fairies that are sat nearby watching me, while I destroy the beautiful part of the landscape which was created by Mother Nature, whilst wondering why I am looking so sad on doing so. Maybe the real reason for the sadness they notice is that I am childishly just wishing my life away. A voice appears from one of those deceptive friends in my head, *"How ungrateful is that, Coco, to play with your life?"* It questions me unforcedly or is rather stating fact with a sarcastic note.

"Fuck up, you!" I answer back too loudly, my voice echoes through the calm stillness of the forest; I can only imagine that now on this occasion my invisible fairies are affronted with justification. I go over the bridge heading for home, while convincingly and agreeably I dictate to myself who cares what the fucking fairies think or mortals, for that matter? I am at this moment in time so lost in my own Coco world, crying all the time, feeling sorry for myself or maybe I am honestly just showing signs of deep depression. The last reason on my list of choices, which I had prepped for use in the making of a decision on my personal diagnosis on the state of my mind, is wrong.

Me doing this depression shit? I don't think so, me being diagnosed as suffering from a mental illness is a definition – that shall not in reality be the case. I hate the very thought of it. Worse still, I detest that you suffer day and night for months with an awful feeling of perception that there is a glass wall between you and the rest of the world. Now there in the statement lies the correct answer of my position, the one which I have to finally admit grudgingly yet arguably to my ego. I go home.

7th October

Another row starts with me suffering more mental torture from him. This is my world now; hurt, I sit angrily wondering what had happened to Brad, I had somehow lost the man I used to know. Perhaps it is me that has caused all this, maybe I deserve it, well that is what being in an abusive relationship is like, it makes you begin to blame yourself. His bullshit, however, is not going to wash with me anymore, certainly not tonight. I go for a bubble bath, planning to have a girlie night of pampering myself and casting candle spells while he sits downstairs sulking. And guess what? He can sit there until the fucking sun comes up, because I am done running after him. The evening passes tranquilly, I go to bed totally relaxed as still he sits in a moody silence exactly where I left him.

12th October

Today we go on holiday with my parents to a log cabin at Fort Augustus. (Brad and I had gone there before; we'd stayed in an exclusive hotel at the beginning of Loch Ness. We went on to Oban, where we stayed in another hotel for a few days. From there we drove to Loch Awe where sat an old church on the banks of the Loch. I lit candles inside and out the back of it, Brad went down on his knees, asking me yet again to one day marry him there just as a rainbow shone over the loch. I smiled answering, "Yes!" After that special loving holiday, yet again he returned home to his wife. Oh! He was always going on fishing trips, he told her, and actually he was always on holiday with me and not once was a fishing rod placed in the water, not ever.) On arriving the cabin is difficult to find as it sits right in the middle of thick woodland; quite quickly though we get our bearings, finding it sooner rather than later. On first impression of its appearance, my mother comments that the look on my face would have sunk a thousand ships. I stare in horror, thinking surely this cannot be the place we had booked to stay in. It looks from the outside in bad need of repair, resembling some sort of old hunting lodge.

Horrified, I get out of the jeep as my father entered the premises with Brad; I anxiously follow them inside, instantly stopping in my tracks. I am stunned, this clearly is not what I had expected to discover. It is amazing, the heating is on, making it very warm, along with being precisely tidy, and it is spotlessly clean inside. There is a basic welcome pack filled with all the necessities you needed to get started or in case you arrived late at night. This package is gratefully accepted as we all are desperate for a cup of coffee. The size of the interior is very deceiving on looking at the cabin from its exterior. It is so cosy in simple décor, with the lounge upstairs; in that room there are huge worn leather sofas situated around a real log-burning fire. Taking pride of place, there facing the front of the cabin, stands a wall made of large panes of glass overlooking the forest. These windows showed everything off to the extreme, and it is magical to be able take in the forest from this height.

Then later in the evening when it is dark out, you feel you can reach out and just touch all the stars that shimmer silver in the cloudless night sky. They shine like diamonds glittering in the pitch black; they remind me with fondness of an evening gown I once had, which was made of delicate black silk covered in tiny Swarovski crystals. I sparkled as I walked in that dress, creating attention beyond belief. It was so me. This night though, I am just dressed in my usual bedtime attire of pyjamas worn with Ugg boots, sitting on the porch drinking a glass of wine. It is so peaceful out, with only the quiet sounds of the tired forest whispering as some of the animals settle down to sleep for the night while others in their nocturnal ways of life stay awake hunting for food. I jump with fright as Brad appears from out of nowhere; sitting down beside me laughing, he takes me into his arms. I look up at him, first pretending to be annoyed but just playfully winking, he winks back. On turning my face away from him again, I smile secretly in the darkness at my erotic thoughts. My eyes search over the dark silhouette of the fir trees, as I remember a time not so long ago, when under the moon both of us were naked, making love out on the patio of another log cabin. The wooden structural design of the balustrade box was similar to this one. That night in particular, the love we shared between us I would have described as being infinitely unbelievable. Perhaps now tonight, though it is a different story, no perhaps about it, because I know it is just another tale to tell, as the love we shared back then is starting to leave us, maybe it had already gone in that short space of time, who knows? It seems to me that night had happened very long ago, which obviously was not the case. Everything just feels so distant, surreal even, as if it had only actually existed in my undisturbed dreams. I get up to go back inside, feeling the chill from mist falling in a blanket covering over the woods. As I stand up Brad pulls me backwards with the hem of my top, I lose my balance then clumsily stumble over his legs, nearly falling on my arse as he catches me in his arms, both of us burst out laughing. He kisses me again, whispering, "I love you, Coco!" I cuddle up into him for a moment longer than I should have done. Now in the warmth of the country-style kitchen whilst pouring more wine for us both, I acknowledge regretfully to myself that his statement has made me feel a little better inside but it is nothing to write home about. The friends in my head inform me perhaps I should write a 'Dear John' letter instead. I ignore them, gulping down my wine, and then pouring myself yet more.

15th October

Brad and I, along with my parents, have been getting up smart every morning to have an early breakfast, so we can leave the cabin at a reasonable time soon after. It gives us all day to visit the different tourist attractions in the surrounding area. Up here at Loch Ness the scenery is fantastically stunning. The loch itself is as fascinating and as mysterious to look at as the legend of the monster that is supposed to abide in its waters. Scotland really is one of the most beautiful countries in the world, holding its place with pride and rightly so.

This morning we stick to our schedule as usual, so mid-morning finds us at the top of Loch Ness, wandering through a small quaint village called Drumnadrochit. It is full of unusual shops selling all the Loch Ness Monster memorabilia and shows off with the wonderful Loch Ness Museum. It has a very highly recommended bar restaurant serving excellent food, besides that, it also accommodates lots of coffee shops to take a break in. I am totally at ease, walking slowly along the central street hand in hand with Brad. I love this place and the hotel sits at the top of the road, where we once had our wedding dinner after our secret marriage in the little church just along the way from there. Both of us look very happy together, strangers would easily assume, well mistake us, for any regular couple in love. In my own way, I guess I still do love him, besides deep down I hope he still loved me too. Well at times, we do still actually feel that way, I correct myself.

We have coffee in one of those exclusive little coffee shops, and then lunch in a hidden-away restaurant, which is so retro, with a superb choice of dishes on the menu. Brad today is seriously being so romantic, with or without my parents' presence. He makes me laugh, kisses me all the time in public, he keeps on buying me gifts and expensive Harris Tweed handbags, in fact he buys me anything I want regardless of the cost. He buys me a beautiful pair of crystal clear hand-blown glass teardrop-style earrings, second pair representing the tears I have cried over him. He hands them to me with trembling hands. *I am touched with the genuine look of love or is it regret that shows in his eyes?* His sense of humour is one of 'My Brad from the past'; he treats me like he used to when together we made an inseparable team. He momentarily makes me question yet again or rather change my perception of our future together. Maybe we would be okay after all, as today he really showed how much he loved me, with confirmation of that in the amount of money he spent on me alone. To whoever witnessed that it had made a statement that I truly was his spoiled 'Princess Coco'. One he was definitely buying.

Later that evening Brad comes up to me in the lounge whispering, he is informing me that we were going on a trip. I glance at the glass wall behind me, looking at the dark forest, I was thinking, *has he gone mad?* It is freezing cold outside, besides it is almost eleven-thirty p.m. I go down to the kitchen for more coffee, intending to ignore the stupidity of his idea. He follows me down as he whispers to me repeatedly that we are going out; while observing him more thoroughly, I realise he is serious in his intentions of following through with this incredible proposition. He orders me to go for my jacket, boots, scarf, with gloves and to be quick on doing as we don't really have much time. Half frightened, casually unsure, I hurriedly oblige him. I half run, half walk up the log cabin's open stairway to the lounge, off from there is a door leading into our bedroom, which is very large with an en-suite bathroom, much the same. On searching in the wardrobe for my outdoor jacket, I also pull out a pair of jeans with a thick jumper. I need warmer clothes on too as I only stand in my pyjama bottoms worn with a silk camisole top. Brad appears in the room behind me, he looks frustrated plus he is still ushering me on to rapidly get dressed.

"Move, Coco! Move! I don't want us to be late," he says very clearly but in a quiet voice.

"For what? Late for what? Why are you whispering?" I ask curiously, to which I receive no answer. He about turns, lifts his wallet with the car keys, and then flies out the room, running back down the wooden stairs. I follow shortly behind without the jeans and jumper on. My parents are in the kitchen making supper for us all, as is situ, when Brad informs them we would be out for a while; before they have time to absorb the news or even ask where or why, Brad grabs me by the hand rushing me out the door into the jeep, thus leaving my parents standing looking astonished at this new development in our plans so late at night.

Brad drives quickly through the night. I enquire again as to where we were heading, he acknowledges me this time but explains very little in his answer,

"I am taking you on magical mystery tour," he says secretly, smiling over at me. I laugh.

"Get out of here!" I respond loudly, laughing some more. He doesn't even smirk.

"No way!" I shout at him whilst continuing to laugh at the very thought.

"Yes way!" He returns with a look on his face of real seriousness in his statement. I stop laughing.

"Where have you planned to take me then? Am I going to Hogwarts? To Aldovia? (A land ruled by the Christmas Prince.) Or The Shire? Or Rivendell (*Lord of the Rings*)? Or maybe to a land made out of cake and sweets? Or am I going into the woods to see a real Big Foot MOOONNNSSSSTTTTEEERR?" I tease him and at the end of the sentence I raise the volume of my voice to create an effect as I pretend to look like a monster. Whatever that is.

He takes his eyes off the road for a second as he nods to me. "I don't know if we shall see the monster tonight, but we sure are going to look for it!" he says with confidence. Once more I stop playing around as I can see that he fucking means what he said.

The car comes to a halt and as I hadn't been paying attention, I have no idea where we were. Brad gets out of the car, I follow him. We are down at the Caledonian Canal in Fort Augustus, at the beginning of Loch Ness. He walks over towards the pier side, where a man is standing down the way; he is dressed in dark clothes, waving his hands in the air, trying to attract Brad's attention. Brad sees him, and then waves back.

"Hurry up, Coco, and be very careful," Brad says taking my hand; he pulls me behind him as he marches on ahead. Even more unsure now, I try to pull away from him, he resists my tugging to free myself by tightening his grip, and he just walks on even faster towards the man, ordering me to behave in the dim light. As we approach the man gets on a boat, one of the tourist ferries that go up and down Loch Ness. Brad halts and I bang into him from behind, then I stand staring at him, asking him unspoken questions with my eyes. He speaks first, actually. "Would you please get on the boat, Coco?" I think I hear him say to me; I am stricken, totally shocked. He knows I hate boats. I fucking hate deep water. I am frantic, I panic big time, wondering if he honestly meant what he said, it was a joke, right? Trembling, I feel my legs wouldn't hold me; I am so light-headed that I get the impression I am going to pass out with fear. I start breathing steadily, trying to think about this rationally, I began to debate whether we should be going out on that loch or not, especially at the time of night. I decide it is crazy, even more so because I assumed that nobody but us knew we were going out there or was even aware of the fact that the boat was being used. Everything seemed to be so secretive.

"NO!" I tell Brad. "Fucking no chance and that is it!" I reinstate quite clearly.

The man comes over to the side of the boat.

"OH! C'mon now, Coco, I'm Jerry, yer all right to be sure, tis safe as houses. Now would I be going mesel if it weren't?" he says jokingly.

Brad is already on the boat, and I am numb with disbelief, wondering how he can do this to me.

"NO! NO! AND NO!" I shout even louder at them both this time.

"Coco, get on the boat please, darling, this has cost me a small fortune tonight," Brad pleads.

"'Tis to be sure!" Jerry interrupts.

"You will love this, trust me," Brad informs me smiling, also holding out his hand to me as Jerry, with both of his hands grasping the edge of the boat, stands squinting his eyes watching us.

"For a while thee night, Coco, well ye see to tell ye, Brad has hired mesel 'n' this boat! Now Mhuirnin that cost few pennies, but ye don't want to come, well then it makes no difference to me, a still get me money. Worked these boats for many a year 'n' niver got a request to take a lady up the loch at midnight or someone paying into the bargain fir my whole vessel fir jist one, Coco!" he says in an Irish accent.

"Now c'mon, Coco, get on the bloody thing, yer all right, yer jist acting daft, now c'mon Mhuirnin be optimistic lass," he coaxes me.

"Coco, baby, come on! You will love it, I know you will darling!" Brad begs me.

This is my worst fucking nightmare!

Shaking I get on the boat, basically I feel that I have no choice but to do so. As the boat starts up and turns to go up the loch, I am shaken, both angry with Brad yet terrified of the depth of the water at the same time. Brad takes me down below the deck, underneath there is a sitting area, it is unexpectedly cosy, with a nice atmosphere. Behind a bar in the corner there is a young man working away, he looks up over at us then smiles warmly,

"Well, hello there! Welcome, Coco, I'm Jake, so ye came on all right, ye came out on our boat after all, did ye?" he says in the same accent as Jerry.

"Yes," I smile slowly. He comes towards us carrying a silver tray on which sits a bottle of champagne with two crystal champagne glasses and a single white rose.

"Well, yer man here, to be sure, has ordered two of the best bottles in the house tonight!"

He sits the glasses down, pops the cork, and then pours out the champagne, and then he gives Brad the rose, which he then hands to me. The petals are so delicate with its scent so light.

Brad and Jerry are looking at me, I smile, saying "Thank you" to them both.

"Cheers to ye both 'n a hope to be sure the lord gives ye a lot of happiness," Jake says, walking away, as he goes he is singing the lyrics of an old Irish song. Story of a woman whose eyes sparkled like diamonds and she wore her hair tied up in a band made of black velvet. It is a very beautiful song and his voice is incredible.

"I love you, Coco," Brad says, kissing me. We hold our glasses up in a toast to us before we drink the champagne. It is lovely; in fact, it is up there with the best I have had, but then again mostly you only get what you pay for. After we finish the bottle I begin to relax, I forget how initially scared I was as bravely yet quite happily enough I go back up the stairs, out on to the open air top deck with Brad. The night is so untouchably beautiful, the stars in their presence shine as proud as ever, it is so peaceful out on the calm water of the loch. The boat suddenly stops and all the lights immediately and inexplicably go out. It is pitch black on the loch but before I get time to panic further asking why, Brad quickly explains, then to confirm his story he reassuringly hands me a packet of chocolate chip cookies. He tells me that I have to fling them out on the loch at midnight for Nessie, she really likes them, he confides in me, continuing to say that not a lot of people knew that. He says Jerry and Jake had told him this, it is their secret and they often come out here to this very same spot just to feed them to her. Whereupon sometimes Nessie comes up to the surface to eat them, but only sometimes. Only on the very odd occasion does she ever come right up out of the water, showing herself unreservedly just to say, "Hello and thank you!" I smile at him. That is such a wonderful fantasy story. It is so sweet and heart rendering that he makes me completely forget my fears of the deep water.

"Well, maybe she will come up tonight," I whisper back. "So I better feed her these cookies just in case," I reply excitedly. I fling the large whole chocolate chunk cookies into the water one by one. The boat stays put as Jerry and Jake come sneaking up onto the deck. There we all stand so quietly as we wait for Nessie to appear in the dark and claim her cookies. She doesn't come. Jake sings a song to tempt Nessie up to the surface of the water. It is another old Irish song as he sings about getting older and how wishes take place of your dreams. As his clear soulful voice echoes hauntingly through the night way out across the loch to the bay, I drink my second bottle of champagne. He sings on just for her, "If wishes were fishes he knows where he would be. Casting out those nets into a dark sea and if the net was empty, when he hauled it ashore, then nets would be thrown away as he would not go fishing anymore." The sorrowful song filled with woe he sings on but still she doesn't come up.

As Jerry with Jake goes back below deck Brad holds my hand. As the lights come on, slowly the boat starts to move away, sadly I whisper "So long" to Nessie. Brad puts a little silver Celtic band on my finger; it only cost three pounds but it is stunning in design. He had bought it at a little shop at Fort Augustus just at the beginning of the loch, where once a long time ago he got me a teddy bear wearing blue tartan, it matched the other one he bought me way before then dressed in a chocolate tartan kilt. I looked down at the ring, smiling both at it and subtle memory of the bears. He promises he would take the ring into the goldsmiths' shop when we get home and get a replica of it handmade in twenty-two carat gold. He probably would, I think as the boat comes into dock. I am so glad to get my feet back on dry land; it is not until I have done so that the fear of the deep water hits me all over again. I shake Jerry then Jake's hands in farewell. As we walk back to the car, Jake is singing in the distance, as he ties up their boat for another while, I can hear the words of Danny Boy coming home when summer was in the meadows as I close the jeep door. As I look over at Brad, I am shaking, I can never do that again, never go out on that loch again, not for a million pounds. But do you know what? I never saw the monster but I will never forget that night for the rest of my life.

Brad starts the car engine whilst I glance back at the loch; the stillness of it makes me shiver again. On leaving the boat behind, I am delighted on heading back to our log cabin; I am so distracted in thought as Brad pulls in at the side of the road, stopping the jeep, he gets out. I follow him curiously in the dark but I don't question him as he goes down the rugged embankment, roughly edging his way through the trees to the border of the water. At the bottom of a steep hill he'd reaches what looks like a little shore made of pebbles with sand; quietly we both just sit down on it, this time waiting in anticipation at the side of Loch Ness for Nessie to appear. Although, of course, we both see movement with ripples in the water it isn't her, it makes the loch look so eerie but strangely magical under the moonlight as a while longer we sit but still Nessie never comes. Brad pushes me backwards to lay me down on the uneven sand, I feel the rocks jagging into my back as he kisses me before climbing on top of me; thus now with his added weight, it pushes my back even deeper into the stones, further hurting me. I can't be fucked with this, especially not right now anyway, feeling him growing harder as he starts to pull at the top of my PJs' trousers so he can put his hand in to play with me, I abruptly push him half off as I try to sit up, "There she is!" I shout, "She is over there, IN THE WATER, BRAD!" I scream pointing at the loch over the top of his head. Brad in shock gets up as if struck by lightning as he gets off me quicker than he got on; he stands up hurriedly, pulling his trousers back up whilst staring out over the loch. With as much speed, possibly faster than him, I get off my arse, running as fast as I can back up through the trees towards the jeep. Brad follows, running behind me laughing, still with half an erection in his trousers, he is shouting obscenities as he chases me, knowing he's been had.

We sneak easily enough back into our abode, we go creeping to start with, bringing no bother, but on the way to our bedroom, the noise we made banging about and giggling is awful, surprisingly enough though my parents stay asleep or pretend to be. I am very happy as while kissing we strip each other, both of us naked tumble onto the bed, and then we snuggle in together. I touch my finger in the dark, smiling secretly, declaring to myself that I am more than contented with him in a strange way tonight. I feel the ring on my finger just as plainly, as for the second time tonight; I feel Brad's hard cock on my leg, this time it is throbbing against my bare skin.

19th October

We have all got up very early as usual, sadly yet quickly packing up our belongings. This morning we are leaving the log cabin, heading for home nostalgically as our holiday is over. It has been quite romantic holiday for Brad and me, considering everything else that appeared to be underlying in our relationship. Perhaps it was because my parents were here with us, who knows really? Just Brad, I guess, maybe because inside our head we tell ourselves lies, I suppose, other stories we all make up, wishing to believe and to pass as the truth.

The journey home passes just inconclusively, suddenly we are there, then on entering the cold, dark place, I, like it, just feel empty inside, but not for long though as I soon realise that all the ghosts of the past few months have also returned to the house along with me.

22nd October

It is exactly two years that have since passed by, that on this date I started to write my diary for my manuscript, lying sprawled along my lounge floor. Brad came in unexpectedly that day, I gave him oral sex in my bedroom, then afterwards whilst downstairs making me some coffee, and he informed me that he had told his wife he was leaving her in the morning. I still feel as anxious right now as I did back then. I just close my eyes and I am right back there in that night, feeling so distinctly every single raw emotion all over again as if it was only yesterday.

23rd October

So now it is exactly two years to date today since Brad left his wife, just as he promised that he would. He had left her in in his hometown as we left Ayr; we went to York to Megan's house. It is a strange atmosphere in my world today as I remember that time hour by hour, remembering every fucking single detail just like I did yesterday too, feeling the sharp hurt slicing through memories like a knife going through butter, as I take myself back in time. I rush upstairs to be physically sick, I feel awful as sour stomach contents spurts out of my mouth, landing all over the bathroom floor. I clean up the stinking mess, realising that now I am as nervous at the thought of having sex with him tonight as I was back then, if not more so. I feel hopeless, lost and not sure of anything anymore. Brad takes the little Celtic band off my finger today. It is taken into the goldsmiths' shop to be used as a mould to have another one made for me in 22ct gold. , .

25th October

We have a special night out tonight with old friends of Brad. My outfit is very expensive as is my appearance fool proof, which had to be it for him. The hotel, the wine with the food is excellent; consequently, we have a nice evening, but only up until the journey back home in his friends' car. Then, fuelled by alcohol, Brad begins to start another one of his fucking arguments with me, it is about nothing in particularly yet still he goes on showing off. Whereupon reaching the house we both get out of the car, Brad continues his nonsense, wanting to argue more with me. I answer him back with some home truths, which he finds hard to swallow; on losing his stance by getting beaten verbally in front of this guy, his answer is to just hit me in the street. He takes his hand off my face so hard that he knocks me backwards on to the road. This is the second time he has hit me in public; I am shocked, tears stream down my face with the force he hit me, I can't believe what had just happened. He gets back in the car, as it is heading back to his hometown he goes with it. I go inside, locking the front door behind me, he can stay out all fucking night if he wanted. I have a bath and remove my make-up gently; my face and eye are red and stinging with the heat of the slap. We have no Chinese food for supper; we share no bottles of our wine as planned. He goes back drinking in a bar in his hometown, stupidly I sit alone, wondering where and when this so-called relationship had gone so wrong. The fucking answer is simple really – it had never been fucking right to start with – I think on looking down at my little dog called Versace, who is sitting happily beside me. I lift him up as he tries to comfort me by licking me and snuggling into me with his soft fur-covered body, which is so warm, he smells like a brand new pure wool carpet. This tiny dog is real love; my other little dogs come over to join us as we all sit in the darkness waiting for Brad. Waiting for what? Why are we all sitting waiting for him? I realise that in my life these three little boys are my real soulmates, these are my little heroes, not that clown Brad Blake. Tears run down my sore face as I hold my little Chihuahuas. I sadly smile thinking of our trip up Loch Ness, which was just a few nights back; it seems to me now that our love was just a dream, one from so long ago.

Maybe I should have fucking flung Brad in the water for Nessie to eat and ate the fucking chocolate cookies myself. No. I change my mind, if she ate him then she would surely die of food poisoning, I smirk in the dark, pleased with myself at my own analysis of that hypothetical situation.

I take my little dogs to the kitchen with me as I make coffee, they have some hot milk, and then between us all we eat the large bag of chocolate buttons before going to bed. Let Brad Blake come rolling in drunk, let him arrive home bringing the cows in for milking with him or better still, perhaps, is to hope that the cows come in for milking alone and Brad Blake doesn't come back home at all.

26th October

He gets up late this morning, coming down the stairs wearing an angelic expression as if to say chocolate wouldn't melt in his hands. I stand in front of him, with so much venom in my voice, I inform that if he ever raises his hands to me again, I promise to do away with him. Brad Blake is then instructed that better still, I don't need to do it, as I can quite easily have him done away with. Guess what? He says fucking nothing. He knows for a fact that is exactly the kind of power I have, because of the friends and the connections I still hold to this day from my past.

I leave him sitting thinking about this, as I go off to write my manuscript. My tears fall once more, while Versace just sits yet again listening to me as I promise myself out loud, "If Blake shows any more violence towards me ever again, Versace, I intend to leave him for ever." The little dog just looks up at me with big brown eyes; I wonder how much he really understands as he lies down beside me, whilst determinedly wiping away my tears from my puffy eyes and inflamed face, I start to type my manuscript.

30th October

Brad and I celebrate the anniversary of our first secret wedding in the woods tonight. It is supposed to be special as we share a bath together in candlelight, just as we did way back then after taking those fateful vows in my bare feet and cream

199

coloured silk underwear. Sitting in a bath with bubbles scented with champagne and strawberries, it feels so romantic. Brad then pours in real champagne then actually drops some of the fresh strawberries into the water. Both of us sit amidst it, holding a crystal glass each with contents of the same in them, champagne with soft sweet red fruits. I smile at the extravagance of it as he pours even more of the bubbly champagne on top of my body watching it run into the soft fragmented soapy liquid bubbles, the sweet even more expensive wine begins to burst the bubbles, so Brad reaches over for the rest of the liquid left in the expensive bottle before spilling it all into the water to make some more. How the other half live, I lie back contemplating, then I think of the changes in our life since that wedding night; if I had known then what I know now, would I still have gone through with it all? Probably not, hindsight is a wonderful thing but a little too late in showing its true colours. We get up out of the water; however, I feel I would like to stay but I would have dissolved if I had sat in there much longer. Or maybe it is our love that is dissolving, I acknowledge, realising it is a real possibility. Brad smiles, complaining he is all wrinkled. I giggle cheekily, "You always were, Blake." He lifts me up into the air before plonking me wrapped in my warm dry fluffy towel back into the bath of cooling champagne water. I scream in temper with fright, he leaves the bathroom laughing at me while I sit mortified at the situation I am now in; raging, I yell "You stupid bastard!" after him. Splashing angrily with the towel soaking wet, with water going everywhere, I get out of the bath once again. Stomping for another dry towel, I leave wet prints all over the place. I am cold now, wrapping another towel round me I think of him, *fucking idiot.*

Upon going down the stairs, I find that Brad has all the lights out with just lit candles glowing in the darkness of the lounge. The log fire is still burning, making the place look subtly cosier. I am still annoyed with him as I begin to search quizzically for the images of my wolf in the shadows, but it is not to be found there at all tonight; I cannot find his shape anywhere on the ceiling or the walls made by the flickering, dancing flames. I sit down beside Brad on the rug in front of the fire, feeling the soft thick wool tickle the skin of my bare legs. As Brad lays me down naked onto my back, I sink into the soft sheepskin fur, enjoying the sensation of it on my bare body as he licks me gently between my legs. He flickers his tongue over my clitoris until I come time after time. I float in another world as I raise my hips to his mouth, grabbing his curly hair; I pull his face into me, greedily demanding more. After I am spent, he turns me round, putting me up onto my knees. He enters me from behind, pushing his cock into me fast and hard before emptying himself right up me. Contented, I roll back over onto my back once more as the smouldering wood on the fire projects a soft heat that caresses my nakedness. Brad then takes my hand, kissing it before putting the little gold Celtic ring back on my finger, promising to love me forever and then some.

Brad then gets up leaving me where I lie; holding my hand up into the air, I smirk at the gold ring sparkling in the firelight whilst stretching my body out, this time on the rug like the white on rice. Brad goes into the kitchen fridge for more champagne, I hear the fridge door open then close again with a quiet thump. The noise of the champagne cork comes out with a pop, which echoes loudly, before Brad fills the glasses with the golden liquid, which sounds like water running. On lifting them, they make a tinkling sound as they clink together; next his footsteps are heard as he makes his way back; while lying listening to every single sound of him, I raise my eyes looking upwards at my ceiling. There, consequently, so clearly right above my head in those shifting shadows is an image, it's showing the dark picture of my wolf. My wolf has a name, it told me its name, but I can't remember what it is called tonight. Perhaps it will tell me again tomorrow.

31st October

I take Brad to hell and back tonight. It happens after we celebrated Samhain, the Witches' Sabbat for Halloween, after we had celebrated the traditional Sabbat of Samhain, which is the Druid New Year. It is a sacred festival and the most important one of all the four Sabbats. It marks the end of the goddess-ruled summer and welcomes in the beginning of the god-ruled winter. Samhain Eve is the night when spirits of friends and dead loved ones are believed to return to rejoice, albeit very briefly, with the living. It is also time in the witches' calendar to give thanks for the year's harvest and celebrate the gathering of the crops. The carving of pumpkins or jack-o-lanterns, as sometimes they are referred to, is an ancient custom belonging to and dating all the way back to the ancient druids. It is believed their eerie grotesque faces lit up from inside with candles possess the power to scare away malevolent spirits of the bad witches who return, haunting the living on the night of Samhain. The drink I serve tonight on Samhain is homemade Samhain cider; we drink it accompanied by warm home-baked wild berry bread. There are other traditional foods used to celebrate Samhain but this is all I made for us tonight.

At the end of the Samhain rituals, I run upstairs to change the robes I donned into another set of black ones. I wear a black lace bra underneath the flowing gowns but have no pants on. I just put in a tampon as I am bleeding, quite heavily actually. Having my period appear uncalculated was more than suitable, Mother Nature being in perfect timing for what I had planned on ahead for this evening. Smirking at myself in the mirror, I feel like the Wicked Queen looking at the reflective glass in the story of Snow White, as just like her, I am also plotting an evil plan. Not with a Huntsman but with my wolf in my head, who is instructing me in the nicest but most sick evil terms what I must do at midnight. I am a white witch. I am also a black witch, as I practise both white and black magic now. White witches do not worship or sell their souls to Satan as they don't believe in the existence of the devil. They never have! Wiccan believe that everything that exists in the universe is divided into male and female, also darkness and light, death and life, positive and negative, bringing in the balance of nature. I however perform both sides of magic now and that is entirely up to me. I am also protestant of the Christian faith; therefore, I believe in God and in Satan, as you cannot believe in one without the other. I am also a confirmed member of the Catholic Church studying the Catholic Religion, so I am very aware of good from bad, right from wrong; still I make my own choices. My wolf in the shadows is fast becoming my friend. The wolf in my head is perhaps my very own devil, my ruler occasionally, so at justified times I shall follow its instructions. Or is this just an excuse to do exactly as I please? I choose to worship both religions as I choose to worship both forms of magic. You see, this gives me a lot more scope to do just that; exactly as I please. Whenever I want, I change my beliefs, then my tactics to be whoever and whatever I want to be. As a solitary witch, I make my own rules! What we think we become, what we feel we attract, what we imagine we create. As above. So below.

"You are clever that way, don't you think, Coco?" asks my wolf in my head. *"Yes, I am, very clever, Mr Wolf!"* I answer silently but very pleased with his conformation on this matter.

Brad sits downstairs waiting in the lounge while upstairs I clarified my position with myself and my new best friend, the wolf as I swap my clothes to go out with Brad. He just did not know what I'd changed into or where we were going in a while, besides it was very wintry out with drizzling rain. Good enough, no perfect for me, I agree with my reflection, as still I stand approving myself in the mirror. There, for definite, would not be a lot of people about tonight albeit Halloween, especially now, not out in this weather, besides it is very late. Blowing myself a kiss in the mirror after admiring myself a little longer, I turn then walk away. The mirror never lies, just a few moments before it had told me that I looked very good tonight, I think sure, yes, the statement it had concluded really is absolutely right. *"Confidence with vanity tonight, Coco, dangerous mixture of the allure,"* whispered the wolf sarcastically. *"Fuck off!"* I reply, then I ignore the wolf; I've listened to it enough for one night.

Going downstairs I whisper into Brad's ear, "Let's go." He gets up quickly, lifting the car keys, he opens the car doors then as he stays behind to lock up the house, I run to the jeep. Glad to be inside the car, at least it is dry in here but also bitterly cold. Brad jumps into the driving, seat slamming the door on the now pouring down rain. He starts shaking himself like a dog to dry off a bit, thus causing all the rain droplets from him to sprinkle the wet all over the car, also onto me. "Brad!" I say no more than his name because he sure is going to be a whole lot more than a little wet where he is going.

He drives under my instructions to a place called The Auld Kirk that sits out in Alloway. (Scottish phrase auld means old, Kirk is a church. The place is historically famous especially for being brought to life in one of the most famous Scottish poems called 'Tam o' Shanter', which is known worldwide, written by the famous Scottish poet Robert Burns.)

As we arrive at the Auld Kirk, we both get out of the car. In the dark of the night the wind is howling, with heavy rain still falling, it soaks right through all my robes before I even reach the middle of the ancient graveyard. Brad is holding my hand as struggling against the elements I plough on. I am used to this by now as I am always out making my spells in all kinds of weather; this is a regular thing for me to be soaked and chilled to the bone. *Need to find a spell to control the weather or wear waterproof gowns,* I stupidly decide. Brad's voice breaks my thoughts, I am aware of him shouting at me from behind, "COCO!" then, "COCO, WHERE THE FUCK ARE WE GOING? WHAT ARE WE DOING IN HERE?" I just keep on moving, stepping over the hundreds of years old tombstones, searching desperately for a suitable place to cast my spell.

Brad is following me to start with but then backtracks, hoping to shelter some from the storm up against the side of the old church wall. I change my mind. I won't cast my satanic spell here after all. I have too much respect for this graveyard. I know of another old abandoned graveyard it is not far from here, that would do just the same. I run back to the kirk wall, taking his hand, I shout above the storm, "Let's go!" Brad is so pleased he runs like fuck out of the place to the car.

We drive out to the other old graveyard and after finding an appropriate place to cast my circle, I approach Brad suddenly and unexpectedly I kiss him roughly on the mouth. I hold him in place by the hair; I tease him by gently flickering my tongue in and out of his mouth. Upon distracting him now I can lift up my robes, searching with my free hand between my legs, my fingers search for the string hanging from the tampon I wear, on finding it, I gently pull on it as I removed the Tampax from my bleeding vagina. I smirk happily whilst now licking his neck, before dropping the tampon at his feet on the ground a sacrificial offering of my blood to Satan. *"Queen of the witches, Coco!"* shouts the wolf. I accept congratulations with glee, as the wolf continues, *"Just dance to Satan playing the fiddle, dance round and round all the tombstones in the middle!"* Abruptly, I move away from Brad, running through the pouring rain around all the graveyard while screaming and screaming. Then I stop yelling, stare at him coldly and begin to sing instead, holding my face and arms up towards the sky, holding my athame I cast my magic circle back to front. Then I dance, I dance for my wolf, I dance for Satan but not for Brad Blake. Spinning around and around, jumping and twirling in a large circle time after time, I begin screeching in a high-pitch voice, chanting my spell in unknown tongue as in a language of old, I invite the Devil to my party, and I beg him to accept my invitation as my words fly into the wind and torrential rain. I now draw in from the east the Witches' Circle drawing the pentagram upside down as Brad stands a few feet away watching me; he must be fucking terrified then horrified on thinking I am possessed. I am now singing out my chant, my chant I wrote especially for tonight. I sing in our own language, so Brad along with the Devil can hear exactly what I say,

"The hurt you brought down on me
May it be returned times three
Head to toe, hair, heart, skin and nerve
I cast upon you what you deserve

OH! High Priestess I call on you
Hear me now as you always do
I shall cast a spell on him, damning him to me forever
Date on witches' calendar is until the end of never
Spirits of Water, Fire, Earth and Air come as one
I cast this curse never to come undone
My vows of his ream are broken
As thou shalt harm none
This shall now return to me times three
So Be It! and So M It Be!!!
I walk now in the darkness of the witching hour
Goddess leave me now or enhance my power

I conjure thee, O Circle of the dark I entrance
Come join me Satan bring your fiddle to the dance
I close the circle now turning from the light
I offered my soul to the Devil tonight
In return, I damned Brad Blake to me
It was worth it don't you see? Don't you see?
Don't you see? Don't you see? Don't you see?"

Dancing further away from him, I hear my music box playing the notes as I sing out loud, *"He loves me? He loves me not? He loves me? He loves me not? Oh! He loves me now, until time has been forgot!"* Brad is still shouting: "COCO, COCO, STOP THIS NOW!" then, "COCO, COCO, ARE YOU GOING FUCKING NUTS?" I walk slowly over to him, my eyes scanning the horror and panic showing on his face, I cannot only see it in his eyes; in fact, my wolf can even smell the fear in his breath. "COOOCOO, LET'S GO, COCO, NOW!"

I secretly smile, staring back at him, and then rolling my eyes I say out loud in a very deep voice: "NO! NO! LET'S JUST STAY!" Brad just about shit himself. I dance around singing, "By the pentacle that I wear, Water, Fire, Earth and Air ruled by spirit for all to see, as I speak so mote it be." Then squeal even louder to the dark side, "Come to me Brad, you I enthral. Come dance with me and Satan at my ball!"

I take Brad by the hand into the middle of the circle. I take my mouth to his, biting down extremely hard on his lips to make sure this time I draw blood. "OUCH! FUCK, COCO!" he roars, putting his hand to his sore mouth. I remove his hand, which is all covered in blood. I do not answer but on kissing him, I spread into both our mouths his fresh red blood. Then I put my fingers between my legs and taking blood from me, I smear it across his lips as I kiss him harder, as we taste our blood mixing together, I feel him grow hard. I take the robe off my shoulders, unclip my bra and on removing it, fling it over a tombstone. Laughing sickly at that, wondering what my priest Father Peter would say, but not giving a fuck, not anymore. I run away from him and sit down resting my back on a tombstone, throwing my head backwards I take my athame to my neck, I cut my neck deeply, making it bleed badly. I sit on the grass bleeding, pulling the petals off a black silk rose, I brought with me. I pull at the petals of the rose saying, *"He loves me? He loves me not?"* I stab at the rose petals, *He loves me? He loves me not?* I stab my knife into the wet ground keeping in time with the notes as the music box plays in my head, *He loves me? He loves me not?* now I hear deep witch chanting music as a high-pitched voice echoes through the dark raining night, squealing an enchanting sound. Then a heavenly voice singing,

"He loves me? He loves me not?"

I get back up off the ground, walking over to him soaking with blood and the rain. He holds me tight into him as he kisses my neck, which is now very sticky, covered in blood along with the pouring rain. His head lowers further still as he kisses my hard nipples, they are rigid with the cold, and they are also covered in small droplets of the running blood. I lie down, opening my legs wide on the wet hard ground; then as the wind howls and the thunder rolls with the lightening flashing above us, I demand Brad Blake to enter me, I order him to fuck me hard at midnight in a haunted graveyard, then as he comes to me, shaking, he tries to put his cock into my already sticky pussy, he can't manage but still I cover his cock in my thick red blood, laughing out loud, I scream into the night. I shout out loud, chanting in the darkness; I cast a spell that will bind us together, either in hatred or love but forever, until the end of time, bonding us with our fresh blood, while the Devil along with the dead and my wolf are my witnesses. As Brad stands up, he is trembling as he helps me up on to my feet. We are freezing cold and soaking wet. Shivering as he pulls up his pants, Brad begins to panic as he just realises that not only does he smell blood, he can taste it too before he sees t everywhere.

"COCO, WHAT THE FUCK IS THIS? EVERYTHING IS COVERED IN BLOOD! I AM COVERED IN BLOOD, OH! HELP ME! COCO, COCO YOU'RE, YOU'RE COVERED IN BLOOD!?" The fear in his voice pleases me.

I whisper, "EXACTLY!" Then I kiss him. He is so bewildered looking as I then take his hand and leave the graveyard. He follows but says nothing. My wolf whispers, *"Good girl!"*

He wants to go home. I don't. We walk back to the jeep hand in hand and I feel Brad is trembling. I am shaking too but not with fear. I decide I want to spend the night in the very famous hotel near the Auld Kirk. I have stayed there before, on my own, room one, I smile at the memory. For some reason I want to go back and stay there tonight. We drive back and stop at The Brig O Doon. I get out the car soaking wet, covered in blood. He wants to go home. I still don't. This bridge is just as every bit as famous as the Auld Kirk, if not more. Brad keeps talking nervously, rubbish I am not interested in. Something is pulling me here tonight. I wish he would just shut the fuck up. He keeps talking as he explains he had fishing rights of the waters under here many moons ago. He tells me it was very expensive way back then but even more extortionate today. I walk to the bridge with Brad, listening but still not interested in what he had to say. I have managed to stem the flow of blood from my neck for now. There is a lot of atmosphere here, one of a kind of magic of people from long ago, with ghosts from yesteryears, yet as much as it feels ancient and eerie, it holds something very romantic about it too, I guess. But me, I don't like it here, not particularly. Apart from the fact, as you already know, I don't like deep water; I certainly won't go near it or cross the bridge when wearing my witch's robes. Just like in the poem, by Scottish poet Robert Burns, the witch called Nannie in the famous poem, she won't cross the water either; she only goes so far whilst chasing Tam o' Shanter on his horse called Meg towards the brig, Tam just gets away and Meg is left with no tail as nannie pulls it off, all this happens just because he shouted, "Well done, Cutty Sark!" at her as he watched her dance to the Devil Auld Nick playing the pipes while the all the other witches and warlords did the same in a reel of the dance in the that Auld Kirk Graveyard where I had wanted to cast my spell. I had wanted to dance there too, so my wolf could shout out at me "Well done Coco!" just as was shouted at that witch in that poem long, long ago. I pull Brad backwards with the arm, now it is my turn to say, "Let's go!" We walk away from the bridge. I hold Brad's hand as we both hurry back to the jeep, very cold, very wet, covered in blood. I really wanted to spend the night in the hotel, I feel I belong in that place, like I am coming home. *Look at the state I am in, how can I walk over to the hotel reception to book a room? Besides it so late.* I walk back over to the Auld Kirk and just walk about the graveyard on my own thinking of the past. I think I have been here in a past life. As a child, I once took part in a film being made out here. As I wander wondering in witches' gowns, contemplating if I could have possibly been here in a previous life, Brad stays in the car. Eventually with a bewildering peace within I go back to the jeep. As I sit down on the car seat, I remember that I have no pants on or the black lace bra as it had been left behind in the old graveyard on the old tombstone, with the tampon still lying where it was flung on the ground as a gift for St Lucifer himself.

Later back home, I perform more sex rituals. I tie him tightly, blindfolded; I just like the fact that his world is in total darkness, I guess. I feel power over him now because that is what he does to me on so many occasions, puts my world into darkness, now ditto – his fucking turn. I feed him horrible foods, unusual foods which he had to guess the flavour of, which he can't because he has never eaten them before. He won't recognise the taste, flavour or texture or smell.

So just like the sex game we play with the jellybeans and other pleasant foods, i.e. melting chocolate, whipped cream, if he loses on answering the wrong flavour or food, he has to perform a sexual forfeit of my choice. On playing this game, particularly tonight, he is losing each round, giving a wrong answer every time as he tries to guess what each piece of food is; my plan is working to my advantage as I had predicted, fuck him. His forfeit is – I command him to lick me, demand him to give me oral sex whilst I am bleeding, disgusting as it is. I don't care, he will take his punishment or he can stay fucking tied up all night – because believe me, he will pay back. I shall leave him there bound in the cold dark room for hours without a second thought. After the game, this is exactly what I do, walk away leaving him tied up whilst still blindfolded in the dark for almost four hours. I go downstairs not giving a toss and sit drinking homemade witches' wine. My rituals and sexual routines are becoming more and more extreme, I realise, I have cursed him in White Magic binding him to love me, also again in a candle spell cast in the woods just to make him want me and only me, then cast a spell on him, too far it came about that he misses me and feels that he can never be without me. All of it worked on him. Since then though I have cursed him twice also in Black Magic. What the fuck is it I want? Seriously! I just don't know as further and further I spiral downwards, my wolf is becoming such an important part of me as quickly as my descent into darkness.

Chapter X
You Left Me Behind

1st November

The month arrives with the weather as bleak as my mood. I hate everything. I hate everybody on thinking back to Halloween I can't believe what I almost did on heritage ground at the Auld Kirk. I mean no disrespect to the people of Scotland or to the memory of the famous poet Robert burns. I silently apologise to all. I guess it is just another part of my chosen decline towards the darkness. I can pretend it is not, but I am only hiding from myself. I am just numb with shame at the thought of my performance on considering it, yet I nearly did go through with the satanic ritual there all the same. I hate myself. I hate the world. I don't have time for anything or anybody. I only want to be with my little dogs; I wish the rest of the world would just disappear. I feel shivery ill after being so cold and getting soaking wet by the rain last night. The paper stiches on the wound on my neck are annoying me. It had to be cleaned then dressed in the early hours of the morning as on this occasion it would not stop bleeding. I had very little sleep, which is making my foul temper worse. My head hurts and I just want to curl up in bed, you know in a *Fuck off all of you day.* I want to be left home alone.

6th November

By this first week in November, the fights between us had stopped again, *but for how long?* I ask myself. No more sex had taken place since the night at the graveyard; I don't want him near me. I think he feels very much the same way about me after all that blood. He says he was really scared of me when I was behaving like that. Fuck him! Still he was meant to be scared, otherwise what would have been the point of it all? The spell was important, yes. The spell using blood was the essence of the night. It had been used to bind us together; of course, with the hot sex including the pleasure I sickly took out of his fear added bonuses, it worked well enough, for me anyway. I had achieved the result that I had strived for, so why should I care about what Brad Blake had thought? Nobody really would care, certainly not me. Fuck me paying homage to him. I am getting stronger each day. I am a witch, don't push me. Knocking me down is the easy part but keeping me there, trust me, it will take more than you Blake. Especially now as I prepare another spell, perfect for matting. As you think, so shall you become. So mote be it!

7ᵗʰ November

The wolf in my head talks to me too much today. I try to shut him out by going to sleep for a while. It doesn't work though, because as I close my eyes in the silence of my bedroom, it still goes on and on. I could scream for the want of peace. Then the voices of my other friends in my head join in, talking to me along with and over him. Non-stop chitter chatter goes on all day long. I wish they would all just fuck up, even just for one hour, but it is so obvious to me that they won't. I reach for some Diazepam as it might help me to relax a little for now anyway. I undo the top of a spare bottle that I had hidden away in case of emergencies like today. I put four of them in my mouth, flinging in another two for luck before swallowing them, then I spit them back just as I did once before. This time though, I really do want to take them, besides that reason the wolf is also clarifying to me that I really do need them; in fact, tonight he orders me to take them. I defy him. I don't mostly because for some reason yet again I just can't seem to get them over my throat.

The consequences which follow that action of not taking them is well, just as the wolf had predicted, I don't get any sleep at all, with my mood blackening even further. I try to write my book, being honest and truthful in its contents, but it is hopeless today, I am not concentrating at all as too much noise is going on inside my head. I shut the manuscript for now, thinking that in total reality of our everyday lives, we all hide a lot from the outside world, hide the truth about our relationships as well as about ourselves; we find it easier that way, don't you think? Like

I do with that bastard Blake. I don't trust his words, I even question most of his actions, but I never ever doubt his patterns. Nobody knows you like you know you! That is the last memory of today I have, which is asking myself questions to which every time I have a different answer. I look at me, trying to see myself as others would see me; then again everybody would have a different answer.

9th November

This morning VERSACE died.
Love is composed of a single soul inhabiting two bodies,
Be it mankind or animal form.
Aristotle.

Four am I wake up feeling cold. I go downstairs to put the heating on; glancing towards the window on the way; I noticed it is all icy; it must be starting to freeze outside. On checking my little dogs, I find them all sleeping together happily in the basket, snuggled nice and cosy under their blankets. Tired and cold, I run back up to my bed, knowing the house would now heat up quickly, yet hoping the frost would last – it makes everything sparkle as if covered in glitter. Makes a grey day look pretty.

Eight am I wake up again, my instincts are telling me that something wasn't right. I get up out of bed, immediately heading straight down the stairs, stopping in my tracks as I hear an unusual noise. Looking downwards towards my feet, I find little Versace lying out of the basket on the hall carpet and he is not breathing properly. His little chest cavity is going in and out very deeply, with his breathing heavily laboured. I gently lift him up, taking him outside for some fresh air. He is very weak with his little legs giving way under him as I hold him up, and there is no way he can possibly stand up on his own on the grass. I know instantly that my worst fears have been confirmed. I know that I needed to get Versace to a vet immediately as he is showing signs of going into heart failure. I speak to a vet on call, who informs me of the expense of the treatment. I don't care about the financial cost, I tell her, emphasising that I would bring Versace there to her as soon as possible as she couldn't come to me as she was the only vet there. *Fuck sake!* The vet also advises me that if I don't, then potentially Versace can die at home, suffering. I know this that is why I was pleading her to come, send somebody, another vet. That is horrific and I would never have allowed that to happen, under no circumstances. I put Versace back down beside his little friends as I run up and down the stairs whilst trying to pull on clothes, check on Versace at the same time try phoning Brad on his mobile. Eventually, I get through to Brad, who at this point is in the supermarket after a night shift buying Versace his favourite chicken for dinner. My heart is breaking. I tell Brad that he should leave the chicken and come here straightaway as Versace is seriously ill. I stay calm. Did I fuck! This is fucking surreal and I just can't believe this is happening. I can't accept it; I am so scared yet so focused on getting Versace to the vet. I am terrified that I would run out of time as he is already struggling. I am not that much aware of myself; I feel I am out of my own body, like I am just watching all this going on in my surroundings from a distance but it is not really happening to me. I am trying to focus through the mist in my head as I keep on repeating myself, saying one word over and over: *VERSACE!VERSACE! VERSACE!* Whilst begging with The Horned God, to please not let him die.

Brad enters the house through the back door as I come out of my lounge holding the soft fleece cream and fawn blanket that Brad had bought me a long time ago. This is (my comfort blanket, I call it my sooky blanket) I took it everywhere with me when Brad left me to go to Canada. This is the same blanket Versace, along with my other little dogs, sat on with me for hours upon hours, their company comforting me as I cried for days on end, cuddling the blanket along with them. I wrap Versace up in the blanket. His little head is peeking out of the end of it as he looks down at Rio and Solo while they look up at him. It is so sad; I feel they know that something is terribly wrong. Only for a split second I consider kneeling down to them, to the level of the basket so little Versace can say his goodbyes. I don't. Unknown to me then, I make the wrong decision, holding so much regret, which I would have to learn to live with for the rest of my life. Hurriedly, I just turn away with Versace leaving the hall, walking towards the door, saying to Rio and Solo, "Mummy won't be long!" as they sit quietly watching us from behind.

Brad is still in the kitchen, it is then that I notice that Brad had left a bag on the kitchen table, it held the dinner that he had already bought for Versace, the chicken that the wee soul would never eat, and I am broken inside at the thought. I watch Brad looking at the bag, perhaps thinking the same as he picks up his car keys then just stands staring at Versace in the blanket as he plays nervously with the car keys as I walk out the door. Brad follows me.

I know deep down as I carry him out of his home that this is the very last time he would be here with me alive, I know that I am losing him fast. Going on through his garden, I realise with a deep sadness that he would never play there again, running through the trees. I carry him on out of the gate, knowing he wouldn't be coming back home through it with me not today, not ever. My heart is breaking; I am like a zombie as I get in the jeep. I note, angry with myself, that Versace had never been in this fucking new jeep and now that he is, I think ashamed; it is because he is dying. I cuddle him to me, holding him tight in the blanket as I rub his little back; he relaxes enjoying the attention, it is calming him down as he listens to my voice while I talk away. I tell him I love him so much and I thank him indefinitely for all the love he has ever given me. He looks up at me with big sad eyes as I wonder how much he really does understand. He is so weak now and frustratingly I am so desperate to get him help. We get lost as roads are all closed. *FUCK!* The Sat Nav is taking us in circles due to road works; I am so stressed out, screaming at the workmen and at the stupid bitches' voice on the Sat Nav. I begin to panic as the realisation of what is happening started seeping through the numbness I am feeling. I need to get to the vet urgently. I am screaming, crying out the jeep window and begging people on the street for directions to the veterinary practise.

We eventually reach the place; my tears are flowing down my face as Brad hurriedly parks up then gets out the car. I talked on to Versace as Brad comes around to my side of the jeep to open the door for me. I whisper to Versace, "Mummy loves you so much, you're Mummy's world, baby; I am so sorry, Versace. I will miss and love you still every single day, thank you so much for showing me, for teaching me what love really is. Goodnight and goodbye, Versace darling, you will always, always be Mummy's wee boy." I get out of the car carrying Versace so delicately in his blanket; I can hardly walk up the steps at the front of the building. The vet and her nurse greet me; they are waiting at the door for Versace. The vet takes Versace as my legs give way. On entering a room little Versace is put on a table in his blanket. The vet touches my arm with sad eyes as Brad stands behind me crying; I bend down to kiss Versace's little head, gently rubbing his tummy as the vet goes to get the injections. On her returning, I bend down again, this time kissing his little face, his breathing now I hear is a lot worse, I kiss his little mouth goodbye, whispering, "I love you." He tiredly lifts up his little head as with his little hot tongue he licks me weakly for the very last time; I feel his little soft laboured warm breath on my face as he tries so hard to kiss his mummy goodbye.

I leave the room, going to sit nearby the door on cold hard stone steps. I cannot stay with Versace, cannot watch the vet put my baby to sleep forever. Holding my tummy, I lean forward on those concrete stairs towards the floor as I scream and scream out in pain, I am so distraught, making the most horrible noises that are coming from deep down within my throat, which echo hauntingly all through the old, cold grey building. Afterwards, after Versace is put to sleep in his little blanket, I go back in to see him. He is lying peacefully now, just as he always did when he was sleeping. I look directly at the vet then at the veterinary nurse (who knew Versace as a puppy, which I am glad of under the circumstances), I ask them to keep Versace in his little blanket because it had my smell on it, and we share it for a while now. I am stating clearly that it is very important to me for him to be kept wrapped in that blanket until his little body gets picked up by the pet crematorium. I hold him, cuddling him I gently kiss his wee head once more for the last time ever before I leave.

Brad tells me he was fighting the injections, he tells me that they could hear me screaming and that he feels Versace was fighting it to get to Mummy, fighting to stay with me. I feel I am going to collapse, Brad is trying to help me and he has just actually made it a million times worse on me. Versace always ran to me when I was crying, always first to be with me when I was upset. Now he is gone. He even tried to get to me when his little life was at an end. I am dead inside. I just can't believe that I am going home without him. He hated to be cold and he didn't like to be left alone and as I leave him lying there in that soft blanket he is alone, will be cold, I feel that I have let him down.

I want to wake him up. I just want him back. I cannot understand why after all these years with me he is gone. Just gone.

At night when Brad goes to work (I want him to go to get him out of the house, so I can pretend Versace is still here with me.), I wander the house for hours calling his name. I keep going out into the garden all night long in the pouring rain, shouting out his name and searching under all the trees, expecting to find him back there. He isn't and no matter how much I call his name, he never comes. I keep looking for him as I just can't accept his death that he is no longer here with me because I can still see his little ghost everywhere about the house, about the garden and when I hold him in my arms.

I crawl about the carpet collecting loose hairs that had fallen from his little coat. I can smell him, feel him, hear him and see him, so why isn't he here? How can Versace be dead? My son, River, is panicking as I walk about with my nightdress on back to front and inside out, he sadly watches me holding an imaginary dog, which I call Versace. He tells me to stay inside as I am soaking wet with the rain and Versace is in heaven now, not behind the hut or under the trees in the garden. I say nothing. This is one of the saddest days of my life; my life would never ever be the same again. Versace had gone and left me behind. River goes to his bedroom with tears in his eyes. I look down and pretend he is still with me, I can see him; I hold Versace and I show him to Solo and Rio, of course he is still here. Then I put Versace to bed like I do every night. Next, I take Diazepam and this time with no problem at all, I swallow the whole fucking lot.

15th November

Brad had stayed with Versace as he was put to sleep. The events surrounding Versace's death had prompted me to forgive Brad for every single wrongdoing that he had ever done to me. Firstly, because of Brad coming and taking Versace immediately to the vet meant he never suffered needlessly. Secondly, Brad stayed holding him until the end, when I just could not. I would be eternally grateful to him for all this as wee Versace knew and loved him as Daddy. A 'daddy's boy' he was too and for that I was indebted to Brad infinitely.

I am totally devastated and destroyed on losing Versace. I tell Brad that I forgive him for everything he had done to me in the past with a calmness that is frightening. Versace is coming back home today. His little ashes are returned to me in a little dark wooden box with a little brass plaque, which is engraved with a loving inscription of

WEE VERSACE

"Our wee boy"

Love you.

He was 'our wee boy'. He is missed more than words could say. I am lost. Brad is lost. Rio and Solo are lost.

I cry and cry, shaking and confused as I carry that little box about with me all over the house. It is like holding a tiny coffin, with a tiny wreath of dark purple flowers on top. The dark purple flowers are very appropriate, it is the exact colour of the costume I used to wear when dancing in the purple rain to the song called 'Purple Rain' by Prince. The little casket came from the pet crematorium with those little purple flowers; they are for me, from Versace. A small card accompanying them read, 'For Mummy'. I also receive from the vet a beautiful card with a sachet of forget-me-not seeds to plant, which in spring would grow into flowers. My world is empty. My boy is home. I tell myself Versace is back where he belonged with his mummy and that nobody could ever take him away from me, not ever again. The friends in my head are back and this time just like Versace, but unknown to me, they are also back to stay for good. That night the blackness enveloped me. I start to decline into the darkness of hell. I have no reason to fight it anymore; I want to go now to the Rainbow Bridge. The place above the clouds where you meet your little dogs again. Versace and Cece (who was my other little dog that died some time ago) would be there waiting for me, and we would all cross over the bridge together to go through the gates of heaven. I want to go there tonight, go to the best little friends I ever had.

"Solo and Rio are going to die too, Coco, leaving you alone behind in an empty world." The evil voices whisper in my head, *"So, Coco! Well, Coco! Don't stay here then!"* I speak back to them, shouting out loud: "I will not be alone, I have Brad Blake." I try to otherwise convince myself. *"He is not your hero. He will let you down. You know this, Coco! All your real little heroes will be dead; that is also where you truly belong, you should be dead too, so in death you can be with them again forever."*

217

Tonight, I agree with the friends in my head, tonight I know they are speaking the truth to me as I start to yet again sink, sink and keep sinking into the deep darkness of my other world.

30th November

A world of nothingness for two weeks, I must just have functioned. I was only interested in Solo and Rio and of course, Versace. I had no idea where Brad was most of the time and I didn't care. I was aware of the fact though that, he was not around because he never slept here, except for maybe one night and that was on the sofa. In a mist of time River would come and go. It suited me to wander in my fantasy world with nobody around as the little wooden box containing Versace's ashes became Versace once again. As I told you all once before a long time ago, my way of coping with reality is to go into unreality so that is exactly what I did, I stayed there for two weeks, pretending Versace wasn't dead. I wanted to stay like that in my pretence world longer, but life would not allow me too.

"Versace, little Versace," I whisper, "Why did you have to go and leave me? Can you hear me? I just want all of us to go with you!" I just lie staring at the ceiling as my mouth moves, my lips speak, forming all these weird silent words as the flickering candle's flames make picture on the walls. I don't see my wolf tonight amidst the shadows, I see formed on the wall an outline of little Versace's face, no more quiet words as I scream piercingly up at the moon...

"VERSACE! VERSACE! VERSACE! YOU LEFT ME BEHIND! YOOUUU LLEEFFTT MMMEEE BBBEEEHHHINNNDDDDD! You left me behind!"

Chapter XI
Living Without the Enemy

1st December

Daylight was inevitable. I sat on the sofa in the lounge, hoping the sun wouldn't come up. I wanted the world, well Coco's world, to stay in darkness. I had been up all night sitting in the grimness of the Egyptian blackness while Solo, Rio and Versace in his little casket, all lay sleeping beside me. I don't know where the hours (or days) went as the time to me seemed to have passed so quickly. An orange, but not blood red dawn arrives. A fact I hate this morning, along everything else about my day ahead, including the obvious that I am still breathing. I prayed so hard last night none of us would wake up but then again I never slept. I cramp, stretching out my arms, I decide I had better get up, let the little dogs out and make some coffee. I am debating with myself; knowing deep down today is the day I have to stop carrying the little box out to the garden, stop putting Versace down on the grass to pee.

Just at that my fucking waking nightmare just gets even worse, the door opens and in walks Brad Blake, who starts on me immediately for standing holding the little wooden box. The little purple flowers lie on the lounge table in front of me.

"Are you going fucking nuts, Coco?" he asks me. "I honestly think that you're going off your head! I swear to fuck I have looked after people in psychiatric units who are less crazy than you are. First the blood dancing for Satan, sex in the graveyard, then this behaviour after Versace's death. You don't even care about us, you're in another world, you haven't even noticed that I wasn't around!" he speaks to me like I am four years old.

"Oh! I did notice you haven't been around, which was brilliant, because I didn't want you here anyway!" I speak in a deep voice full of hatred. "Now fuck off back out to wherever it is you have been staying!" I finish quietly. He stands looking at me without uttering a word back. I march past him still carrying the box and shout for Rio and Solo, who follow behind. Brad follows me too, then he stops suddenly at the doorway, he stands stock-still staring in disbelief as when the dogs go out to the garden for the toilet, I now follow them, placing the little box gently down on the grass, saying to it, "Do a wee pee for Mummy, Versace!" He says nothing. He stands continuing to stare before he eventually comes down the steps, walks right past me, heading straight out of the gate. I hear him start up the car to leave. I pick up the little box, whilst holding it tight into me, holding little Versace, I watch his car until the tail lights disappear out the street, out of sight, just as I had always done once upon a time.

5ᵗʰ December

I have more time than I thought to live in my world where I keep Versace still alive as Brad stays away a while longer than I had expected. *Thank Fuck!* Yet speak of the devil, then he is sure to appear, rightly so. He just walks in. Brad Blake is fucking back. Before Brad can say anything to me, I speak first, I ask him to leave again. I tell him to remove all his belongings that are left here as I have no more storage space. He asks me to sit down to talk about all this, explaining he still loves me and he always would. We are a team, if only I would let him help me, then I would be okay. *Fucking class!*

"HELP ME, YOU, YOU HELP ME!" I scream at him, "I don't need any help. What part of all this do you not fucking get? I don't want you anymore; I don't want to be with you anymore!" I stand in front of him a few feet away, looking straight into his eyes as I speak to him, using such a serious tone of voice that I can see in his eyes and on his face what can only be described as a look of devastation.

"Tell me you don't love me anymore, Coco. I promise you I will go, I promise to never come back!" he says.

I attempt to walk away from him but he grabs me unexpectedly by my arm, turning me around to face him, "COCO!" he says again, now he has raised his voice louder than mine. I stare at him with tears streaming down my face,

"JUST GO, BRAD!" is all I say. I have no idea if I still love him or not. I take his hand, gently removing it from me. I pick up the little box, beckoning Rio and Solo, I go upstairs to my bedroom. I get into my bed; I cuddle them all under the quilt with me as Brad packs up the rest of his belongings. He leaves.

Darkness has fallen by the time I get up. I attend to my little dogs. I shower, take Diazepam, spat them out, and then drank wine, before going back to bed feeling legless and light like I am floating on a magic carpet. *Maybe I would see Aladdin in my travels!* I laugh sarcastically at me. I am aware of my actions that have taken place today but truthfully, not fully understanding the consequences of the events that followed them, which now confirmed Brad has gone forever.

6th December

I expect him to return. Of course he would. Fucking magician he is, disappearing then re-appearing. I wait and wait for Brad today but still he does not come back.

7th December

I stop waiting. I damned him to me. He will return. I am not sure now if I want that. Besides I knew that it would come back to me times three. *Then remove the Curse Coco. Remove it and be done with him, you stupid, stupid, stupid coward of a witch!* Remove the curse. My friends in my head advise. Remove the fucking curse. Perhaps.

15th December

Brad has been gone for ten days now, which for me during most of that time has been almost hell. But not at eventide, when night time fell, I sort of felt my spirits come alive in some sort of caliginosity kind of happiness. The house was kept immaculate in the hours of daylight along with my hair, the shallowness and vanity of my flawless tan with impeccable polished nails. I programmed myself to be perfection beyond compare, to keep it unblemished I thought of nothing but to remain matchless and blameless of anything. Look at my pretence, I believed if he made love to me in the snow, as he once did, it wouldn't melt. I pretended I was like a gallery full of expensive art, just the bastard couldn't see it, could he? So during the brightness of noon everything shone gloriously. In the evening though, I made a mess of the place, a fucking tornado hit type of mess. I pull all the cushions down and scatter them all over the ground, in addition to turning up the rug and putting ornaments upside down on shelves, I broke things he bought me, flung gifts of clothes and stuff from him all over the wooden floor. I chanted spells; I danced around naked, lighting candles and drinking witches' homemade wine. I baked witches' cakes, locked River out of the house, as I remained exemplary in my terrene, I tell myself I am unmarred and unequalled in everything I do. I am sickly happy in dead of the night besides I slept very well in the inferior house. It was just that during the daylight hours, when I missed him the most, I kept everything untainted and untarnished so it was only my soul that you could see was broken. I lay Versace to rest with all the love in the world. I questioned my life.

I asked myself, is the enemy that I live with in human form or does the enemy lie within me? Am I my own worst enemy? Is Brad my husband in my world? Or is Brad really someone else's husband playing in my world? Will my future be with Brad Blake? Does he love me or only think he does? Do I still love him? At the start of this book, at the beginning of our relationship, he was my hero, I worshipped beyond human form. Where does he sit on the scale of admiration now? My wolf knows. *"OH, right off that fucking pedestal!"* I have no answer to any of these questions.

Will my life ever be the same again without Versace? No.

Will Versace's unconditional love always remain with me in memory? Yes.

These are the only two definite facts I know tonight.

16th December

I lay sleeping when Brad Blake returned. I must have been, because I wake up early and confused to find him lying naked in bed beside me. I look at him sleeping, then go down under the quilt and suck him awake. He holds my hair, moaning my name. I think that I had wanted him to fuck me, but I didn't, I felt nothing. He comes in my mouth, I spit it back out onto him. I feel dirty, it is dirty. *Black dirt!* Then I gently bite his penis, well actually, I bite it quite hard intentionally. He jumps surprised, gasping at the pain. *Fuck him!*

"You hurt me, Coco!" he moans, holding himself with both hands I hope he is bleeding. I get out of the bed smirking, I walk, leaving the strong smell, disgusting rank mess of his sperm behind me like a tub of out of date cottage cheese spilled all over him.

"Oh! I am so sorry, Brad," I sneer with a smug look on my face on leaving the room. *How dare the bastard just come back into my bed and assume it is all right? Just expect everything go back to the way it was. I am, unfortunately for him, not that fucking desperate or easy for that matter.* I still feel indebted to him for staying with Versace, however though I am struggling to honour that debt.

Later in the day, he takes me to lunch and buys me some chocolates and very expensive perfume, not that it is working but better than appearing in my bed. Brad is kind, funny and very loving; he is sleek, I will give him that, because I am starting to fall for him all over again. NOT! When we go to bed at night, with my permission he makes love to me so slowly, until I come time and time again. He kisses me with so much passion afterwards, yet still I feel myself pulling away; I am scared that is it, I am so scared of how he is making me feel about him yet again. He makes me feel both brumous and peiskos at the same time, but evidently my metanoia for eleutheromania right now is stronger than feelings for him. Facing our demons and challenges is what makes our life interesting and overcoming them is what makes it all worthwhile I acknowledge.

17ᵗʰ December

I wake up and go downstairs to find the house as usual left in a mess, but different kind of mess this morning, the atmosphere is soulless. The house empty, Brad has gone yet again. This time he has left his house keys on top of the kitchen table. After we had made love last night, he asked me if I wanted him to come back home to stay. I had pretended not to hear him, so I didn't have to be the one making that decision. Guess he has made it for me now.

Where is home for him anyway? With her? In the land that time forgot perhaps? Here with me? I am so glad he has gone.

The day passes as I wander the house along with the silence. Nobody speaks to me at all day, not a phone call, not even my friends in my head. I do not clean the house today, my jet-black hair is so knotted, and it can easily have been mistaken for a raven in its nest. I sit poised in old Ugg boots worn with crushed silk pyjamas, underneath which my body is still all covered in his sperm from last night. I had only cleansed my face, so in comparison I believed that I look like I was related to a rag-n-bone man wearing expensive Christian Dior face cream. You can take the girl out the gypsies' camp but you can't take the gypsy out of the girl. It is late in the evening when I realise that I have had nothing to eat or drink since the coffee I had made this morning, which still sat half drunk, freezing cold in a mug on the lounge table. On removing it, I decide to go and make another cup.

Fuck the coffee! I open a bottle of wine instead, and then reach up to take a tall black glass out of the kitchen cupboard. "This wine is better for me, it's better than him, better than chocolate, better than anything just now!" I speak out loud to my witch's broom. I laugh as it answers me, *"Yea Coco, you drink the wine, cheers, farewell and so long to Brad Blake!"* I laugh again, raising my glass to the broom. This is me; this is me back in my own world of fantasy, with the deep darkness still to come.

I go out into the garden to sit in the pouring rain, just as I always did, then I change my mind. I come back indoors, going straight upstairs soaking wet to change into my black robes, I had decided out of the blue just to practice some witchcraft instead. I sit wearing my robes in the shadows of my lounge, sit staring at the dancing flames of the fire as my wolf sits patiently behind me, watching from his position on the wall. I look round at all the candles I'd lit to complete my spells with, then with a feeling of hopelessness washing over me, I sigh in sadness. I just get up numb and open another bottle of wine, deciding instead that all the candles are lit for Versace. I lift my glass towards the candles in a toast, I declare, "To you, little Versace! For all the love that you gave me, if you can see me now, then know how much I miss you as you left me behind."

I just continue to sit on the sofa drinking the wine lost in thought. Soon it would be Christmas. A black Christmas for me. All the Christmas tree fairy lights will twinkle all over the world but where is my light in the eclipse? What will the sparkling lights of Christmas hold for me? Then there will be the New Year bells to come, bringing in with them hundreds of women in new affairs with married men and vice versa. *Fuck me, God love them all and let the devil take care of his own!* Maybe in the coming New Year my manuscript will be published, as without hope of the book, what else is there left for me.

"*What about Brad Blake? What do you think the future holds for you and him, Coco?*" I don't think there is one. Do you follow your heart or your head or your instincts? I still question this, making no sense of the conclusion I reach each time, which is that I still don't make the right choice. I still don't know the answer. I do know this though that in this life there two things you can be certain of. One which is death, it must come to us all. The other is to love. To love is to hurt. To love is to suffer loss. A world with no love would be no world at all. A life with no love would be no life at all. A life in which we suffer loss we must learn to survive. I must know how to survive. *Do you, Mr Wolf?* I wonder. I consider writing the last chapter of my book, knowing that will be another sad part of my life closed. I wonder if my book would go to print and if people read my story, who would they claim my enemy to be?

Every single day now I feel ugly, deformed and incomplete. Brad has told me so many times now that I am not a real woman. I believe him. Was it him that really made me feel this way, or was it me that put that in my head, I wonder for the umpteenth time. I am ashamed of my legs and my breasts now, but why? Is that a woman thing? I just don't feel good enough anymore as a woman or a person for that matter. I hang my head in public; I hardly smile, or sing and dance; besides I can't remember the last time I really laughed. The world is once my playground yet now I hide away, my confidence has just slowly disappeared. I lived with, in the end, his constant abuse most days. He called me names, kept shouting and swearing, then ultimately hitting me. He continued to threaten me with her. Threaten to leave me for good to go back to her. Eventually, unknown to him, in the end it was no longer a threat to me as deep down I silently fucking begged God that he would. She could have him back.

The voicemails he leaves me now are soul-destroying. The abuse continues. It breaks my heart. No matter what I did or how hard I tried, nothing seemed to be good enough for him in the end. This mental torture I had suffered daily, did I really do this to myself, and am I really mentally ill? Perhaps! It can make you feel that way, all the abuse, make you blame yourself. No perhaps about it, that is exactly how it works. Illogically, you question you.

I just wanted to be in a relationship, what with a husband of my own or someone else's husband? Fuck knows. I chose to have an affair with someone else's husband so I guess the latter. The love, all that love shit with him was not supposed to be part of the deal. I want it now. I want to be loved. Sometimes I still want him, I want to be pretty and just perfect for him; I'm not asking for a lot, then again perhaps I am. Maybe someday I can have it all though, everything I ever wanted, but for the present I shall just exist. I live my life the only way I know how. I PRETEND. I sure am one helluva actress and if nothing else, I am a survivor. I smile sadly in the dark at the fond memories of Versace, as I feel the loss of his presence, tears stream down my face. I look down at the other little dogs beside me, it's comforting to feel the heat coming from their bodies against my leg, and I must have been sitting there for a while in an alcohol mist dreaming, as the second wine bottle is empty. The little dogs look up at me with all their adoration for me showing in their eyes; I realise I am rich in love; the little dogs' love is unconditional. *FUCK BRAD BLAKE!*

I will manage without him, although I am almost penniless, I shall have peace at last. If tears were pennies, I would be a millionaire. Brad's love once upon a time made me feel like a billionaire. Once he made me feel like the most precious thing in the world. Once I was that happy, lucky, confident, classed as a beautiful woman. THE COCO! is what they used to call me. It seems to me that had happened a very long time ago now. Tonight, I am only a shadow of the person I was a way back then. Well, why is that now? Was that all his fault or was it mine?

I go to the kitchen for more wine. As I lift down another bottle, I notice that I am staggering. "Fuck me!" I say to the broom, as clumsily I try to put the unopened bottle back into the wine rack above my head. No more alcohol tonight. I have lost Versace. I have lost his love; along with him, I also lost love in the name of Brad Blake. It's very sad but I have always lost everything I've ever really loved in this world. I looked down at Rio and Solo, wishing I could keep them for the rest of my life but thinking, knowing nothing lasts forever.

I sit down on the cold floor crying, back to where I began, back to where I have been many times before. I better get myself up, perhaps go to bed. As I leave the kitchen I order my witches' broom, "Clean the fucking house for me and brush every bit of hurt out my life!" The fire and the candles will burn themselves out just like me. Yule, Winter Solstice will be here soon. No doubt I won't celebrate it. I lost a lot of my white witchcraft along the way. I have lost a lot of things, some I will never replace. I hardly do my spells anymore, I have lost part of my soul on losing my witchcraft. I climb the stairs, thinking I need to go now to face my enemies. The facts of your life that you fight with in your head. The thoughts, the voices, the memories of the past that all come back to haunt you as you lie alone awake from dusk to dawn in awareness, just listening to that fucking music box playing over and over, hearing that beautiful haunting voice singing to the notes, *He loves me? He loves me not?!* wishing for amnesia, sometimes alcohol stupor will hold blankness, not for me in the dead of this night!

"Face your enemies as I go to do now, I also tell you, to keep the wind on your back and to always remember that I told you so!"

Maybe tomorrow Brad will come back. Maybe tomorrow he will love me like he used to do. Tomorrow never comes. I wonder where he sleeps tonight. I wonder what he thinks about, who wakens him, arousing him sexually, from that land of untold dreams. It wouldn't be me. Maybe it was love we shared or maybe it was just sex. You need to be prepared to let something or someone you love go free, if it belonged to you, then it would come back, and if it didn't, it was never meant to be. I let Bradford Riley Blake go free. I climb into the cold bed as I go now to try to sleep alone. I think I hear the back door open and close again. I left the door unlocked in case Brad returns. I am sure I can hear soft yet heavy footprints on the carpet coming up the stairs. Was it my imagination; was it River or him? Tears are running down my face in the witching hour of this lacklustre night, my bedroom door creaks slowly open as I wonder what or who is moving in the shadows. The wolf in my head distracts me, interrupting my thoughts as he confirms to me, "*It was love, Coco! Maybe conceivably it was love; perhaps though it was sex living with the enemy! Or simply just sex under purple sheet!*"

The end perhaps!